The Career of Andrew Schulze

1924–1968

The Career of Andrew Schulze,

1924–1968

LUTHERANS AND RACE IN THE

CIVIL RIGHTS ERA

Kathryn M. Galchutt

Kathryn M. Galchutt

MERCER UNIVERSITY PRESS
MACON, GEORGIA

ISBN 0-86554-946-X
MUP/P296

© 2005 Mercer University Press
1400 Coleman Avenue
Macon, Georgia 31207
All rights reserved

First Edition.

☐The paper used in this publication meets the minimum requirements of American National Standard for Information Sciences—Permanence of Paper for Printed Library Materials, ANSI Z39.48-1992.

Library of Congress Cataloging-in-Publication Data

CIP data are available from the Library of Congress

Contents

Acknowledgments   ix

Foreword by Milton C. Sernett   xi

Introduction   1

Chapter 1 Early Years, 1896–1920   9

Chapter 2 Springfield Years, 1920–1928   31

Chapter 3 St. Louis Years, 1928–1947   58

Chapter 4 Chicago Years, 1947–1954   117

Chapter 5 Valparaiso Years, 1954–1968   146

Chapter 6 Later Years, 1968–1982   222

Bibliography   239

Index   261

*This publication has been made possible
due to the support of the
Lutheran Human Relations Association.*

Acknowledgments

First and foremost, I wish to thank my family, my parents, my sister, and my brothers for all their love and assistance through this endeavor and many others. I have also enjoyed the support of Andrew Schulze's family through his three sons, Paul, Herb, and Ray. They have been tremendously helpful to my understanding of Andrew Schulze and his life's work. In addition, I am thankful for former friends and colleagues of Andrew Schulze, who have shared their memories, insights, and enthusiasm for my research. Pastors of Andrew Schulze's former congregations—John Brazeal, Thomas Clay, and Robert Jensen—gave me a picture of the living legacy of Andrew Schulze. And I am grateful to one of Andrew Schulze's parishioners, the late Enid Yancey of Milwaukee's Trinity Lutheran Church, who first told me about her pastor.

As an Arthur J. Schmitt research fellow, I was able to spend much of the 1999–2000 academic year on the road, traveling to the places where Andrew Schulze lived and worked. Local historical societies, in particular the Cincinnati Historical Society, the Lincoln Library in Springfield, Illinois, the Missouri Historical Society, and the Chicago Historical Society, guided my research and helped to provide "a sense of place." I was grateful to have numerous people who provided me with hospitality and housing during my research travels: Fred and Elaine Boettcher, Martin and Judy Henrichs, Ray and Margaret Schulze, Ed and Lois Staubitz, and Rodger and Pat Venzke.

I have enjoyed meeting many of the historians associated with the Lutheran Historical Conference, who have been an important resource for my understanding of Lutheranism. Other scholars have also welcomed me to the profession. Martin Marty was especially generous in sharing his thoughts and his time. John McGreevey was also a gracious host, and his excellent work on the history of Catholic integration has been inspirational to my work. Several archivists aided me in my research: Marvin Huggins and Robert Shreckrise at the Concordia Historical Institute, Elizabeth Wittman and Joel Thoreson at the Evangelical Lutheran Church in America (ELCA) Archives, and Mel Doering at the Valparaiso University Archives.

My undergraduate experiences at Concordia, St. Paul prepared me in many ways for what I am doing today. Professors Fred Bartling, Don Epps, Bob Kolb, Nan Hackett, and John Solensten provided the foundations and the encouragement for graduate study. Bob Holst has been a constant supporter every step of the way. Peter Wiesensal of Macalester College provided me with good advice about graduate school and warned me of the occupational hazards of academia. Overseas experiences allowed me to get to know Alan Storkey and Jim Dimitroff, both models of the humble scholar. Friends from my two years in Russia—Melissa and Bill Oberdeck, Jean and Morris Olson, Tom Sluberski, and Luda Ignativa—have enriched and encouraged my work in many ways.

At Marquette, I enjoyed the company of a good group of fellow graduate students. In particular, Jennifer Speed and Tim Wood provided friendship and much needed relief from studies. Professors Phillip Naylor and Julius Ruff gave me encouragement and words of wisdom along the way. New colleagues at Concordia, New York have also provided support, especially Karen Bucher, Kristen Koenig, and Merlin Rehm.

Back when I was an undergraduate at Concordia, St. Paul, Bob Kolb was the first person to suggest that I specialize in the history of Lutherans in America. Even though I originally dismissed the suggestion, he has taken an active interest in my academic pursuits ever since. Finally, it was Steven Avella who really stimulated my interest in American religious history and convinced me to study Lutheran history. He has been both a patient and persistent guide throughout my studies. He has also served by example, being both a dedicated teacher and a dedicated scholar.

Foreword

The Reverend Andrew Schulze retired in the summer of 1968, the year I graduated from Concordia Theological Seminary, St. Louis, Missouri. When this Lutheran seminary awarded Schulze an honorary doctor of divinity in December 1966, I was away from campus serving a vicarage at a Lutheran congregation in Milwaukee, Wisconsin, where the headlines told of the crusade of the Reverend James Groppi, a white Catholic clergyman active, on behalf of African Americans concentrated in Milwaukee's segregated and inferior housing. I remember telling fellow Lutherans at the time that our fellowship of Christians could be proud of our own Father Groppi. I doubt now that my analogy was a good one, for the two men, both champions of racial justice, were quite different in style. While Groppi was confrontational and attuned to the more combative political spirit of the late 1960s, Andrew Schulze was disarmingly pastoral (He might have said "evangelical.") in both method and message. In the wake of the assassination of Dr. Martin Luther King, Jr., the eruption of violence on the streets in many of our nation's larger cities, and the rallying cry of "Black Power," Schulze's gentle spirit seemed to have been smothered by louder and more rancorous voices. To borrow from the title of his autobiography, Andrew Schulze had raced "against time," but now the times themselves had changed and there was the danger that a record of his good work would be relegated to a footnote in the writing of someone else's story.

Thankfully, Kathryn Galchutt has not let this happen. This book is both tribute and testament. It gives witness to the faith-filled life of a Lutheran pastor who went against the grain in a highly ethnicized, theologically conservative, predominantly white and Midwestern denomination when it was neither popular or politically expedient to challenge the notion that African Americans were the "other"—potential mission converts but never "neighbors," to use Schulze's term. Galchutt's book is also a tribute to Schulze, for in its retelling of his self-sacrificial ministry and his bold and prophetic voicing of the gospel mandate to love above all else, the author has enabled Schulze to be heard once again. This honors the man himself, though Schulze characteristically deflected self-praise.

Were Schulze still with us, we could counter his protests at having his life written up by a trained historian with the argument that this book is not, by the strictest of definitions, a biography, certainly not a work of hagiography. There is much of the personal and private left out. I suspect that Schulze would have wanted it this way, for it was the message and not the man that defined his ministry. In the process of tracking out decade by decade how Andrew Schulze, the son of German-speaking parents of modest means who was born in Cincinnati near the close of the 19th-century, became the leading Lutheran spokesman for breaking down the racial caste system in American Lutheranism as well as in society as a whole, Professor Galchutt also has much to say about the contexts in which this pioneer, who did not like being called a pioneer, lived and worked. There are circles within circles to explore. Readers will learn about the urban contexts where the Reverend Schulze, his beloved wife Margaret, and their three sons lived. We follow Schulze from his student days at Concordia Theological Seminary, the "practical" Seminary in Springfield, Illinois, where I once taught, to parish and community in St. Louis and Chicago. As we do, we learn too of his friends and allies in the cause, black and white, as well as of his critics, especially in the hierarchy of the Lutheran Church—Missouri Synod, to which Schulze was loyally devoted, despite being viewed as a "thorn in the flesh."

In 1954 the Schulzes moved to Valparaiso, Indiana, where with the blessing and encouragement of Valparaiso University's president, O. P. Kretzmann, the Reverend Andrew Schulze set in motion what would become the Lutheran Human Relations Association. Schulze ably served the LHRAA until his retirement from leadership positions in 1968. Many people, myself included, once thought that the LHRAA was Andrew Schulze, a one-man "race relations" dynamo who traveled about the land speaking truth to power not unlike the peripatetic prophets of the Old Testament. The Reverend Karl Lutze, Schulze's aid-de-camp who served as executive secretary of the LHRAA until 1979, disabused me of this idea long ago. Kathryn Galchutt likewise shows that Schulze did not march alone in the "race relations," later "human relations," campaign. She does a particularly fine job in calling to mind many in the first rank of ordained black clergy in Lutheran circles, individuals truly deserving of the accolade "pioneer." I think here of the Reverend Dr. Marmaduke Carter, whom my mother once head preach in German; of the Reverend Clemonce Sabourin, anchoring Lutheranism in Harlem; and of the Reverend Samuel Hoard, whom Schulze supported in his efforts to get a theological education on an equal footing (in the classroom and in housing arrangements) with white seminarians. There are others of note, of course. Readers should pay special attention to their stories as Galchutt interweaves them into the larger tapestry she has created.

The LHRAA got caught up in the theological and political controversies that wracked and eventually rent the Lutheran denomination. Schulze had been ordained in after the election of J. A. O. Preus to the presidency of the Lutheran Church—Missouri Synod in 1969. It was difficult for Lutheran Christians to keep their "eyes on the prize" while their professional careers were being threatened. Perhaps is was for the better that Andrew Schulze had accepted retirement as the gift it is by the time that the institutional body of Christ was at war with itself. Schulze's personal views on such contested issues as biblical inerrancy and the application of the Lutheran confessional documents to contemporary issues had evolved from the fundamentalism of his professors at the Springfield seminary, largely due to his exposure to the views of colleagues at Valparaiso University, but he was certainly no gospel-reductionist, as the ultra-conservatives in Missouri Synod circles characterized the moderates. When called upon to voice where his allegiances lay in the denominational struggle that eventually resulted in schism and the birth of Evangelical Lutherans in Mission and later the Association of Evangelical Lutheran Churches, Andrew Schulze, though sympathetic with the moderates, especially as they were more likely also supporters of the LHRAA, generally echoed the pastoral and evangelical core message which his life and ministry embodied.

I regret that I did not have the opportunity to meet Andrew Schulze in person. I was too young and too inexperienced in matters of substance, both in the church and in the circles Schulze moved in, to have the good sense to make the effort to seek him out and hear his story from his own lips. I did see him once, but then at a distance and only as a face in a crowd. But talk of him circulated in student company, and some of us thought of him as a Lutheran saint—something quite paradoxical given our Reformation-based bias against the making of "saints" in the church. Schulze, as Galchutt reminds us time and again, would have been embarrassed by hearing such talk. I do remember that Schulze, then in his seventies, appeared to me appropriately thin and gaunt, with a face that looked as if it had known many a sorrow and many a tear, as I imagined a saint ought to appear. His physical self had become husk-like, as if so many years of racing against time had simply worn him out.

It is good, therefore, that we have this book-length study of Andrew Schulze's most important contributions to church and society. Galchutt's portrait of Schulze is not that of a saint who has withdrawn into contemplation as the great mystics did, ignoring the weal and the woe of the world about them, nor does it show us a political firebrand for whom the end justifies the means. Instead, we have a balanced and fair appraisal of the life work of a Christian pastor whose neighborhood was both inclusive and gospel filled.

Dr. Milton C. Sernett
Professor of African American Studies and History
Adjunct Professor of Religion
Syracuse University

Introduction

This is the story of Andrew Schulze (1896–1982), Lutheran pastor and civil rights pioneer, who dedicated his life and ministry to improved race relations in both church and society. Andrew Schulze was a white pastor of the Lutheran Church—Missouri Synod who spent his early ministry serving black Lutheran mission congregations in Springfield, Illinois (1924–1928); St. Louis, Missouri (1928–1947); and Chicago, Illinois (1947–1954). Over the course of his career in the Lutheran Church, Schulze eventually became committed to ending segregation in both church and society. Schulze presented his case for integration in the church in his first book, *My Neighbor of Another Color*, published in 1941. Over the next three decades, Schulze fought continual battles against social customs and a resistant church hierarchy. Schulze was behind the development of the Lutheran Human Relations Association of America (LHRAA), an organization officially begun in 1953, which grew to have over fifty local chapters throughout the nation. While the number of active LHRAA supporters only consisted of a few thousand of the nine million Lutherans in America, they were a particularly influential group in the area of Lutheran race relations. From the 1950s to the 1970s, the Lutheran Human Relations Association of America was based at Valparaiso University, in Valparaiso, Indiana. Schulze ended his career at Valparaiso University, serving as head of the LHRAA and as a part-time professor of theology.

However, this narrative is more than just the story of Andrew Schulze; it is also the story of how Lutherans encountered the issues of race relations and social justice in twentieth-century American society. The Lutheran Church in America originated as an immigrant church, made up primarily of German and Scandinavian immigrants. For much of the colonial period of American history and through much of the nineteenth century, Lutherans were set apart by their immigrant subculture. But then in the twentieth century, "the powerful forces unleashed by the depression and the two world wars brought Lutheranism into the 'mainstream of American life.'"[1] As Lutheran churches and communities Americanized, they increasingly interacted with people from different racial and ethnic backgrounds. While Lutheran theology has emphasized the evangelical tradition of Christianity, Lutheranism has, at times, had difficulties moving outside its traditional ethnic boundaries. As Lutherans placed a greater effort toward reaching out to American blacks and other minorities during the twentieth century, they increasingly came into conflicts with their own ethnocentrism.

Lutherans were also challenged by the great social issues of the twentieth century.[2] It was the Lutheran tradition that began the Protestant Reformation of the sixteenth century. Unlike Catholicism, which stressed the corporate community of faith, Protestantism has been known for its emphasis on the individual. Lutheranism was concerned with developing an individual's relationship with God and with developing a sense of personal piety. This focus on individualism has sometimes made Lutherans unmindful of larger societal problems. Additionally, the Lutheran emphasis on salvation by faith alone, at times, has meant that there has not been an emphasis on works of faith. Lutheran theology does not promote works, but rather "fruits" of faith, which develop naturally from one's life of faith. In comparison to other Christian traditions, Lutherans have not been known for having a very activist heritage.[3] But the religious and moral demands of

---

[1] E. Clifford Nelson, ed., *The Lutherans in North America*, rev. ed. (Philadelphia: Fortress Press, 1980) ix.

[2] E. Clifford Nelson raised the following questions about Lutheranism in the late twentieth century, "In the face of the so-called great issues of the last third of the twentieth century was there anything unique, and therefore worthy of preservation, about Lutheranism? Did the staggering problems of racial crisis, the Vietnam War, poverty, the Third World, political scandals, and the world energy crisis demand a 'secular ecumenism' which minimized Lutheran particularity? Or could Lutherans under the lordship of Christ practice a fruitful coexistence and collaboration with others in the amelioration of the massive social, political, and economic problems while remaining unabashedly and unapologetically 'particular' and 'confessional?'" (*The Lutherans in North America*, ix).

[3] It could be argued that there is a positive social aspect to this Lutheran emphasis on faith alone. "As Mark Noll has pointed out in *One Nation Under God?*, American Lutherans have a potential contribution in their theology of government, since they do not expect social reform to be salvific and therefore may be less

the civil rights movement brought new levels of social consciousness and social activism among some Lutherans in America.

Andrew Schulze was a leader among those Lutherans who became involved with the issues of racial relations in twentieth-century America. Schulze played a unique role in the history of American Lutheranism. As Richard Luecke concluded in his study of Lutheran urban ministry, "The story of interracial change and urban mission in this church body cannot be told apart from that of a soft-spoken, lifelong reformer, Andrew Schulze."[4] Yet this is a story that has not been fully told. Schulze did leave his memoirs, *Race against Time: A History of Race Relations in the Lutheran Church—Missouri Synod from the Perspective of the Author's Involvement, 1920–1970*. However, there is no scholarly biography on Schulze, and his work is only briefly covered in Richard Luecke's "Themes of Lutheran Urban Ministry, 1945–85" and Jeff Johnson's *Black Christians: The Untold Lutheran Story*.

This biography of Andrew Schulze provides a concentrated view of American race relations in both its Lutheran and local dimensions. It provides an important perspective on the history of American Lutheranism and on the history of the American Midwest. In addition, it contributes to the growing body of scholarship on the history of the civil rights movement, one of the most dramatic and influential social movements in American history.

Within the field of American religious history, there is a need for greater attention to Lutheran history. As Mark Granquist explained, "When it comes to monographs or articles, Lutherans again are conspicuously missing from the national scene. Another American historian has observed that every year numerous works appear on the Shakers, a virtually extinct group that probably numbered no more than six thousand members at its height, while works on the nine million American Lutherans remain

---

tempted to pursue social reform to the extremes that confuse the work of God with human efforts" (Christa R. Klein, "Denominational History as Public History: The Lutheran Case" in *Reimagining Denominationalism: Interpretive Essays*, ed. Robert Bruce Mullin and Russell E. Richey [New York: Oxford University Press, 1994] 315).

[4] Richard Luecke, "Themes of Lutheran Urban Ministry, 1945–85." *Churches, Cities, and Human Community: Urban Ministry in the United States, 1945–1985*, ed. Clifford J. Green (Grand Rapids: Wm. B. Eerdmans Publishing Co., 1996) 139.

scarce."[5] Much of Lutheran history has been written primarily from a narrow denominational perspective. Instead, this work describes Andrew Schulze in his wider social and cultural context. As L. Deane Lagerquist noted in *The Lutherans*, social and cultural approaches to history have only recently made an impact on Lutheran historiography.[6]

Much of the previous historiography on Lutheranism in America has focused on Lutherans during the colonial period of American history or during nineteenth-century American history. Lutheran historiography has also been concerned with the Lutheran influence on German and Scandinavian immigrants or on rural communities throughout the United States. The story of Andrew Schulze's life and work is different in that it focuses on both black and white Lutherans in twentieth-century urban America. Another mark of traditional Lutheran historiography is that it has primarily focused on the internal dynamics of Lutheran development, with relatively little attempt to relate Lutheranism to the wider spectrum of American religious history. A study of Andrew Schulze's ministry involves paying attention to the relationship between Lutherans and other American religious denominations as well as the interaction between religious institutions and society in general.

Despite the nationalizing and homogenizing trends of twentieth-century America, recent historical scholars have stressed the continuing significance and persistence of American regionalism. The religious geography of America has been one factor that has developed and deepened the regional variety of the United States.[7] While significant historical attention has been devoted to the northeastern and southern regions of the United States, more research is needed on the history of the American Midwest.[8] Lutheran history can contribute to this area as Lutherans have

---

[5] Mark Granquist, "Five American Lutheran Histories," *The Lutheran Quarterly* 12/2 (Summer 1998): 197.

[6] L. Deane Lagerquist, *The Lutherans* (Westport CT: Praeger, 1999) 163. A helpful "Bibliographic Essay" on the history of American Lutheranism is included in Lagerquist's study.

[7] See Samuel S. Hill, "Religion and Region in America," in *Protestantism and Regionalism*, ed. Martin Marty (New York: K. G. Saur, 1992).

[8] In their history of the nineteenth-century Midwest, Andrew R. L. Cayton and Peter S. Onuf wanted to "encourage historians to think about the region in more

made a mark on the social and cultural fabric of the American Midwest. Many of the original German and Scandinavian Lutherans who migrated to the United States settled in the Midwest. Even today, Lutherans continue to be more highly concentrated in the Midwest than any other region of the country.

It has been said that "all race relations are local." While the civil rights movement was a struggle that achieved national prominence, it was a struggle primarily based at the local level, as community after community fought local battles for racial justice. Much of the history of the civil rights movement has concentrated on the dramatic racial conflicts that took place in the Deep South. But the civil rights movement had national implications and had a profound impact even on the largely white population of the Midwest.

Both the East Coast and the West Coast of the United States have been known for being more racially progressive than the Midwest. A study of churches in mid-twentieth century America showed that after the South, the Midwest was the region of the country with the fewest racially inclusive congregations.[9] During the last half of the twentieth century, the Midwest was the most residentially segregated region of the country.[10] Relatively little attention has been devoted to the impact of the civil rights movement in the Midwest. Schulze's story is based in the Midwest and provides valuable glimpses of race relations in major Midwestern cities. This narrative shows that Lutherans were both shaped by the racial climate of the Midwest and also were a force in shaping the racial climate of the Midwest.

---

systematic ways than they have in the past few decades. Many historians of the South have made it their business to demonstrate that nineteenth-century America was not New England writ large…[the Midwest] was also a place with a distinctive character of its own" (*The Midwest and The Nation: Rethinking the History of an American Region* [Bloomington: Indiana University Press, 1990] xii). Also see Edward L. Ayers, Patricia Nelson Limerick, Stephen Nissenbaum, and Peter S. Onuf, *All over the Map: Rethinking American Regions* (Baltimore: The Johns Hopkins University Press, 1996).

[9] David Reimers, *White Protestantism and the Negro* (New York: Oxford University Press, 1965) 174.

[10] Jon Teaford, *Cities of the Heartland: The Rise and Fall of the Industrial Midwest* (Bloomington: Indiana University Press, 1993) 235.

This narrative also adds to the growing body of scholarship on the history of the civil rights movement. While the historiography of the civil rights movement has noted the remarkable role of black churches in the struggle for racial justice, only recently have scholars given significant attention to the response of predominantly white churches to the civil rights movement.[11] By highlighting the contributions of Andrew Schulze, this work brings attention to a somewhat unknown and under-appreciated hero of the civil rights movement.

The first histories of the civil rights movement in the late 1960s and 1970s studied the movement from a national perspective, concentrating on its leadership and its political accomplishments. The second generation of scholarship in the late 1970s and 1980s approached the movement from a local perspective, stressing the grassroots character of the movement and its ordinary participants and its social accomplishments. The present historiography attempts to bring together the local and national, the ordinary participants and the leaders, the political and social achievements. Though this is currently a flourishing area of scholarship, there has been little overall synthesis in the history of the civil rights movement. As Steven Lawson concluded, "Differences of interpretation are as evident among civil rights scholars as they were among civil rights activists. In part, this explains why interest in civil rights history show little sign of abating."[12]

The history of Andrew Schulze's life and work corresponds to some of the larger currents of civil rights historiography. The historiography of the

---

[11] Some of the noted works on the response of white churches to the civil rights movement include James Findlay, *Church People in the Struggle: The National Council of Churches and the Black Freedom Movement, 1950–1970* (New York: Oxford University Press, 1993); John T. McGreevy, *Parish Boundaries: The Catholic Encounter with Race in the Twentieth Century Urban North* (Chicago: University of Chicago Press, 1996); and Andrew Michael Manis, *Southern Civil Religions in Conflict: Black and White Baptists and Civil Rights* (Athens: University of Georgia Press, 1987). Another important study on the white religious response to the civil rights movement is Michael B. Friedland, *Lift up Your Voice Like a Trumpet: White Clergy and the Civil Rights and Antiwar Movements, 1954–1973* (Chapel Hill: The University of North Carolina Press, 1998).

[12] Steven F. Lawson, "Freedom Then, Freedom Now: The Historiography of the Civil Rights Movement," *American Historical Review* 96 (Spring 1991): 471.

civil rights movement involves differing emphases on change and continuity within the dynamics of American race relations. Some of the early historical scholarship on the civil rights movement focused on the seemingly sudden and dramatic change in race relations in the 1950s and the 1960s. However, recent historical scholarship has stressed the earlier antecedents for racial change that were evident in the 1930s and 1940s. Andrew Schulze's relatively early "conversion" to the cause of improved race relations shows that there were advocates of racial justice who were active decades before the movement began.

The historiography of the civil rights movement also includes a significant debate over the place of leaders in this mass movement for racial equality. The new social history that emerged in the 1960s and 1970s, inspired, in part, by the civil rights movement, emphasized the historical experiences of ordinary people. Traditional political history, which often focused on the life and deeds of the "great men" of history, became a style of the past. In some scholarly circles, biography became seen as a passé subject, but biography has continued to persist, not only as popular history, but also as scholarly history. Some individuals do stand out in history as being particularly noteworthy or particularly influential. However, even individual leaders should not be seen apart from their larger social context. One can conclude that "leaders do make history, but never by themselves."[13] While Andrew Schulze took some early and lonely stands for the cause of racial justice, his career witnessed a growing network of supporters who shared his commitment.

Lutherans remain a predominately white denomination; less than 2 percent of Lutherans in America are other than European descent. One could suggest then that Andrew Schulze did little to change the culture of American Lutheranism. But one could make a similar argument with regard to the legacy of Martin Luther King, Jr. Since America remains a *de facto* segregated society, a case could also be made that King did little to change the culture of American society. Yet Martin Luther King, Jr. is remembered for his contributions in creating a vision and laying the foundations for a more inclusive society. In the same way, Andrew Schulze can also be

---

[13] Manning Marable, *Black Leadership* (New York: Columbia University Press, 1998) xvi.

recognized for his role in promoting the theology and practices of a more inclusive church. As parish pastor, author, college professor, organizer, and activist, Andrew Schulze made a broad and lasting mark on the history of American Lutheranism.

Chapter 1

Early Years, 1896–1919

Andrew Schulze was born on 8 March 1896, in Cincinnati, Ohio, the fifth child of John and Katie Schulze. A little over two months later, on 18 May 1896, the United States Supreme Court handed down its decision in the case of *Plessy v. Ferguson*, declaring that public accommodations for black and white Americans could be "separate but equal." The Supreme Court ruling gave federal sanction to the pattern of segregation that had become more and more formalized in the decades following the Civil War and Reconstruction.[1] The practice of segregation was pervasive, affecting all American institutions, including its churches. The black intellectual and activist, W. E. B. DuBois, predicted in his most famous work, *The Souls of Black Folk*, first published in 1903, that the problem of the twentieth century would be the color line.[2] As Andrew Schulze grew older, he dedicated his career to ending the color line in both church and society.

Andrew Schulze came to believe that segregation was the primary social and theological challenge for the church in the twentieth century. Over the course of his career in the ministry, Andrew Schulze became one of the great champions of integration among Lutherans in America. But there was little in Schulze's early years that distinguished him from other Lutherans who shared similar immigrant roots. Schulze grew up in a typical

---

[1] As Edward Ayers pointed out, many late-nineteenth-century Americans saw segregation in an amoral light: "Segregation was not a throwback to old-fashioned racism; indeed, segregation became to whites, a badge of sophisticated, modern, managed race relations" (Edward Ayers, *The Promise of the New South: Life after Reconstruction* [New York: Oxford University Press, 1992] 145).

[2] W. E. B. DuBois, *The Souls of Black Folk*, with a foreword by Henry L. Gates (New York: Bantam Doubleday, 1989) 1.

German-American Lutheran community that had a distinct subculture of its own. Yet Andrew Schulze emerged as a leader in prodding and inspiring Lutherans to reach out beyond their ethnic backgrounds.

More German-speaking people immigrated to the United States in the nineteenth century than any other ethnic group. Most German immigrants came to America for social and economic reasons related to the slow process of industrialization in Germany.[3] However, a few of the German Lutherans who immigrated to America were unique in that they came primarily for religious reasons. Some German Lutherans in the early part of the nineteenth century chose to immigrate rather than compromise their religious beliefs to accommodate the theology and practices of the official state church in different parts of Germany.[4] The Schulze family had strong roots in the Lutheran Church, but it seems that their primary motivation for migration was for new social and economic opportunities in the New World.

German migration to America began from the southwestern German states in the early nineteenth century and then spread to the central and northern German states in the middle and latter parts of the nineteenth century.[5] Andrew Schulze's family was part of this larger pattern of immigration. The Schulze lineage can be traced back to the northern

---

[3] Kathleen Neils Conzen, "The Germans," in *Harvard Encyclopedia of American Ethnic Groups*, ed. Stephen Thernstorm et al. (Cambridge: Harvard University Press, 1980) 406, 410.

[4] "The Old Lutherans' trek in the late 1830s was partially in protest against Prussia's forced unification of the Lutheran and Reformed churches in 1837; Saxon followers of Martin Stephan came in 1839 to distance themselves from the wickedness of the Old World" (Conzen, "The Germans," 410). For a brief history of the Old Lutheran immigration to America, see Ralph Dornfield Owen, "The Old Lutherans Come," *Concordia Historical Institute Quarterly* 20 (April 1947): 3–56.

[5] Germany did not become a unified country until 1871. "The emigration of the Old Lutherans, which began in 1836 and was much publicized, helped implant the idea of Auswanderung in the East." One of the first groups of Old Lutherans immigrated to Australia (Mack Walker, *Germany and the Emigration, 1816–1885* [Cambridge: Harvard University Press, 1964] 78).

German city of Osnabruck in Niedersachsen and Schulze's paternal grandparents came to America in the middle part of the nineteenth century.[6]

Many German immigrants settled in the German-American cities of Cincinnati, St. Louis, and Milwaukee, or in the area known as the "German Triangle," located between these three cities.[7] Andrew Schulze's grandparents settled in Cincinnati during its heyday, when Cincinnati was known as "the Queen City of the West." Prior to the Civil War, Cincinnati attracted many immigrants as the commercial and cultural hub of the Middle West.[8] After the Civil War, in the great age of the railroads, Chicago, with its position along the Great Lakes, came to dominate the Middle West. But during the first half of the nineteenth century, in the era of the steamboat, Cincinnati, with its strategic location on the Ohio River, was "Queen."[9]

Already in the early nineteenth century, Cincinnati became a favorite place for German immigrants. The beautiful contours of the Ohio River Valley reminded Germans of their own Rhine River Valley.[10] The Germans immigrants in Cincinnati even named their section of the city, Over-the-

---

[6] Mrs. Andrew Schulze to Mrs. George Reinhart, 10 October 1973 (copy), Schulze family papers, in the possession of Raymond Schulze.

[7] Don Heinrich Tolzmann, *Cincinnati's German Heritage* (Bowie MD: Heritage Books, 1994) part 3, p. 1.

[8] The Saxon immigrants who came to America in 1839 and formed the nucleus for the Lutheran Church—Missouri Synod debated traveling through New York to Cincinnati, but instead it was decided to travel through New Orleans to St. Louis (Carl S. Mundinger, *Government in the Missouri Synod: The Genesis of Decentralized Government in the Missouri Synod* [St. Louis: Concordia Publishing House, 1947] 70).

[9] "In the first half of the 19th century, the heavily German and Irish makeup of Cincinnati's immigrant population was fairly typical. In the last half of the 19th century, the origins of the bulk of European immigration shifted from northwestern sections of Europe. Rapidly growing cities such as Cleveland and Chicago attracted a great number of immigrants, and a majority of them came from central, southern and eastern Europe. Cincinnati grew much more slowly in this period.... As a result, Cincinnati retained its strong German identity" (Cincinnati Historical Society, *Cincinnati: The Queen City*, 3rd ed. [Cincinnati: Cincinnati Historical Society, 1996] 104). For an excellent history of the urban Midwest, see Jon C. Teaford, *Cities of the Heartland: The Rise and Fall of the Industrial Midwest* (Bloomington: Indiana University Press, 1993).

[10] Tolzmann, *Cincinnati's German Heritage*, part 3, p. 2–3.

Rhine. The Cincinnati Germans developed a rich community life in Over-the-Rhine. As described in *Cincinnati: The Queen City*, German immigrants "founded organizations and institutions which helped cushion the impact of the American environment for themselves and others from the 'Fatherland' while making lasting contributions to the quality of life in Cincinnati. Churches, schools, breweries, and beer gardens sprang up throughout the area."[11] By the end of the nineteenth century, German Americans were geographically dispersed throughout the city, but Over-the-Rhine still served as a cultural center for Cincinnati's German Americans.[12] The German-American community thrived in Cincinnati from the early part of the nineteenth century until World War I.

There is no record of why Andrew Schulze's grandparents chose to settle near Cincinnati, but their choice of the urban setting was probably related to the fact that they chose to be involved with businesses rather than farming. Both sets of Schulze's grandparents became involved with small business ventures in the suburban villages just to the west of Cincinnati. Henry and Henrietta Schulze ran a grocery store and Andrew and Mary Mandery ran a dairy. Though they lived and worked on the outskirts of Cincinnati, the Schulzes and the Manderys remained connected to the city center. Both the Schulzes and the Manderys were active members of Trinity Lutheran Church in Over-the-Rhine.[13]

Andrew Schulze's parents, John and Katie, were both born in the Cincinnati area in the 1860s. In his teens, John Schulze went off to Concordia College in Fort Wayne, Indiana, to study for ministry as a Lutheran pastor. But John was diagnosed with tuberculosis, and it was suggested that he get a job where he could work outside in the dry night air. John returned to Cincinnati and took a job driving a bread wagon for Muth's Bakery. In 1888 John Schulze married Katie Mandery, and the couple was blessed with six children: John Jr., Mathilda, Carl, Catherine,

---

[11] Cincinnati Historical Society, *Cincinnati: The Queen City*, 45.

[12] G. A. Dobbert, "The Cincinnati Germans, 1870–1920: Disintegration of an Immigrant Community," *Bulletin of the Historical and Philosophical Society of Ohio* 23 (October 1965): 231.

[13] Andrew Schulze to his mother, 27 September 1956 (copy), Schulze family papers, in the possession of Raymond Schulze.

Andrew, and Louis. Andrew was named after his maternal grandfather, Andrew Mandery.[14]

The Manderys gave John and Katie land next to their dairy where the young couple built a house at 2051 Harrison Pike. It was here that Andrew Schulze was born and lived for the first sixteen years of his life. In 1913 Schulze's oldest brother and his wife took over the house on Harrison, and the rest of the Schulze family moved to a house on nearby Boudinot Avenue. Andrew Schulze lived in this home until he enlisted in the United States Navy in 1917.[15] The Schulze homes were located in an area of residential communities, known as the Western Hills, located to the west of the industrial Mill Creek Valley.

The area where the Schulzes lived was annexed by the city of Cincinnati around the turn-of-the-century. Cincinnati developed in a basin with the Ohio River to its south, surrounded by an amphitheater of hills to its north, east, and west. The original "walking city" of Cincinnati was confined by these topographical limits; thus Cincinnati developed as one of the most densely populated cities in America. In the late nineteenth century, with advances in transportation such as the incline and the trolley, those who could afford to began a "scramble up the hills," expanding the hilltop communities that surrounded the city center.[16] The Western Hills and other outlying areas of the city became home to a variety of people from different ethnic and religious backgrounds.[17] Living in an outlying area of Cincinnati, the Schulzes were not part of a particularly German-American neighborhood.

---

[14] Ibid. Mrs. Andrew Schulze to Mrs. George Reinhart, 10 October 1973 (copy), family photo album, Schulze family papers, in the possession of Raymond Schulze.

[15] *Cincinnati City Directories* (Cincinnati: Williams Directory Company, 1896–1917).

[16] Cincinnati Historical Society, *Cincinnati: The Queen City*, chapter 3 ("Scramble Up the Hills, 1870–1914").

[17] Zane L. Miller, *Boss Cox's Cincinnati: Urban Politics in the Progressive Era* (Chicago: University of Chicago Press, 1968) 55. The famous political boss, George B. Cox, operated out of Wilert's Café and Beer Garden on Vine Street, located just a couple blocks away from Schulze's home congregation, Trinity Lutheran Church on Race Street. Cox's political machine, which dominated Cincinnati from 1891 to 1916, was heavily dependent on the German vote.

Because of the urban setting, Andrew Schulze's upbringing was different from that of the majority of Lutherans in early twentieth-century America. Until the middle decades of the twentieth century, Lutherans had a slower rate of urbanization than the American population as a whole.[18] Growing up in Cincinnati, Andrew Schulze experienced the jumble of American urban life. He had frequent opportunities to travel into the city center. The Schulze home on Harrison was situated right along one of Cincinnati's major streetcar lines. The Harrison Avenue streetcar line provided a direct route into Over-the-Rhine, where Trinity Lutheran Church was located.[19] In an article, written years later, describing his home congregation, Andrew Schulze explained that "since the turn of the century, many of the congregation's members commuted to church from outlying areas, first by horse and buggy, then by street car, and now by bus and automobile."[20] Schulze's description was a record of the changes in transportation that he witnessed growing up in Cincinnati.

When Andrew Schulze was a young boy around the turn-of-the-century, over half of Cincinnati's population was of German descent.[21] The Cincinnati Germans were a diverse lot. As Kathleen Conzen explained, "Because of their numbers and diverse backgrounds, Germans transferred to America much of Old World urban life, including its divisions. In the cities of the New World, Catholics rubbed shoulders with Lutherans and atheists, Bavarians with Prussians, university graduates with peasants. No single set of associations and institutions could embrace such diversity."[22] Joseph Michael White's study of religion and community among the Germans of Cincinnati concluded that "personal identification as German was simply too vague a concept to have meaning for ordinary Germans. Being a

---

[18] Fred W. Meuser, "Facing the Twentieth Century, 1900–1930," in *The Lutherans in North America*. rev. ed., ed. E. Clifford Nelson (Philadelphia: Fortress Press, 1980) 421–22.

[19] Cincinnati City Maps, Cincinnati Historical Society Library, Cincinnati OH.

[20] Andrew Schulze, "That the Church May Lead," *The Vanguard* 10 (July 1963): 2.

[21] "A high point in the German immigration was reached in the 1880s so that by 1890 the German stock reached its zenith with 57.4 percent of a total population of 296,908" (Tolzmann, *Cincinnati's German Heritage*, part 1, p. 47).

[22] Conzen, "The Germans," 416.

German meant being a German Protestant, German Catholic, or a German Lutheran. Only through identification with and participation in the life of a particular religious subculture could Germans belong to a community."[23]

Andrew Schulze's family, along with Trinity Lutheran Church, provided the formative influences of Schulze's life. Shortly after Andrew Schulze was born, he was baptized into the Christian faith on 22 March 1896 at Trinity Lutheran Church. Schulze grew up in a very committed and devout Lutheran family. In a letter written later in life, Schulze described his mother as "God-fearing" and "virtuous." He said that his father's "pious example and Christian counsel helped to guide the six children into the way of truth and to consider the Sunday worship a most important part of their lives."[24]

Schulze's home congregation had its origins in Zion Evangelical Church on Bremen Street. A pastoral candidate from Berlin, Germany, the Rev. Theodore Wichmann, was sent to Cincinnati in 1848. Wichmann agreed to serve Zion "with the proviso of filling his office in conformity with the confessions of the Lutheran Church."[25] However, controversy arose as the majority of Zion's members were of a Reformed background and objected to the idea that their new church building be declared a "Lutheran" church. So after serving Zion for about a year and a half, Wichmann resigned his position. Nineteen other members joined him in leaving Zion. On 21 November 1849 this small group organized Trinity Evangelical Lutheran Church of the Unaltered Augsburg Confession. Trinity's first church building, located on Race Street in Over-the-Rhine, was dedicated in 1850.[26]

In 1851 Trinity joined a new church body, the recently formed German Evangelical Lutheran Synod of Missouri, Ohio, and Other States.

---

[23] Joseph Michael White, "Religion and Community: Cincinnati Germans, 1814–1870" (Ph.D. diss., University of Notre Dame, 1980) 363–64.

[24] Andrew Schulze to his mother, 27 September 1956 (copy), Schulze family papers.

[25] "Brief History of Trinity Lutheran Church of Cincinnati Ohio, From Its Organization in 1849 to Its 75th Anniversary November 16th, 1924," Church files, Concordia Historical Institute (CHI), St. Louis MO, 13.

[26] Ibid, 13–14. According to legend, Race Street was named for the races that used to take place up and down this street during Cincinnati's early years.

Under the leadership of the Rev. Dr. Carl F. W. Walther in St. Louis, this church body, later known as the Lutheran Church—Missouri Synod, emerged as the largest and most influential group of Old Lutherans. "Old Lutherans" was a common name used for those who wished to cling to the old Lutheran faith of the Reformation. Old Lutherans strictly adhered to the Lutheran confessional documents of the sixteenth-century Reformation such as the Augsburg Confession (1530) and the Formula of Concord (1580). They opposed the rationalizing and liberalizing trends of the Enlightenment that took the miraculous out of the accounts of the Bible. The Old Lutherans also opposed unionism, the joining of churches despite doctrinal disagreements. The strong stance of the Old Lutherans on church doctrine and fellowship was meant to preserve, without compromise, their understanding of God's Word and Sacraments.

Andrew Schulze was influenced by a religious ethos that heavily depended on German language and culture. While Schulze's immediate family used English, the services and business of Trinity Lutheran Church were primarily conducted in German.[27] To conservative German-American Lutherans, the German language was part of their theological as well as their cultural heritage. Not only were the Lutheran confessions originally written in Latin and German, most Lutheran theological writings were written in German. Many German-American Lutherans were deeply concerned that switching to English would impair the purity of the church's theology.[28]

It has been suggested that "the history of Lutherans in Ohio is a reflection on a smaller scale of Lutheran history in America."[29] Lutherans in

---

[27] Ibid. 17.

[28] See Everette Meier and Herbert Mayer, ed., "The Process of Americanization," in *Moving Frontiers: Readings in the History of the Lutheran Church—Missouri Synod*, ed. Carl S. Meyer (St. Louis: Concordia Publishing House, 1964) 344–85. Up to World War I, the continuous flow of German immigrants as well as the synod's system of parochial schools enabled Missouri to develop and maintain a distinct subculture despite the forces of American assimilation.

[29] Willard Dow Allbeck, *A Century of Lutherans in Ohio* (Yellow Springs OH: Antioch, 1966) 4. Ohio has been considered the most typically American state, with characteristics from all regions of America, North, South, East, and West. This explained Ohio's supremacy in national politics. "Not since the Virginia dynasty

the East, organized by the Rev. Henry Melchior Muhlenberg during the colonial period, were much more assimilated to the American environment than later Lutheran immigrants. In the nineteenth century, Lutherans debated to what degree they should adapt to their American environment.[30] As William Kinnison explained, "Much of that debate centered in Ohio and along the Ohio River Valley from the Muhlenberg tradition in Pennsylvania to the Missouri Synod Lutherans with their Zion on the Mississippi in St. Louis."[31] Trinity Lutheran Church developed in the midst of these theological and cultural controversies and took the traditional, conservative side. Josepth White noted that for many years "Trinity Lutheran Church enjoyed a monopoly on Lutheran orthodoxy as the only Cincinnati congregation emphasizing the traditional Lutheran confession and practice."[32] Just a few blocks from Trinity, also on Race Street, stood the more liberal and accommodating First English Lutheran Church.

The tensions between liberal and conservative Lutherans in Cincinnati were compounded by the city's diverse religious environment. Lutherans made up only a small part of Cincinnati's religious mosaic. Cincinnati was not chosen as a particular site of settlement for Lutheran immigrant

---

dominated national government during the early years of the Republic had a state made such a mark on national affairs. Between the Civil War and 1920, seven Ohioans were elected to the presidency.... Ohio's politicians addressed constituencies at home that generally were the same as those across the nation" (R. Douglas Hurt, "Ohio: Gateway to the Midwest" in *Heartland: Comparative Histories of the Midwestern States*, ed. James H. Madison [Bloomington: Indiana University Press, 1988] 216–17).

[30] See David A. Gustafson, *Lutherans in Crisis: The Question of Identity in the American Republic* (Minneapolis: Fortress Press, 1993).

[31] William A. Kinnison, "German Lutherans in the Ohio Valley," *Queen City Heritage* 42 (Fall 1984): 3. For a history of Missouri Synod's beginnings, see Walter O. Forster, *Zion on the Mississippi: The Settlement of the Saxon Lutherans in Missouri, 1839–1841* (St. Louis: Concordia Publishing House, 1953).

[32] White, "Religion and Community," 97. For example, Trinity Lutheran Church did not consider the baptism of the union churches of Cincinnati as valid. Conservative Lutherans opposed cooperation with Reformed churches as Reformed churches did not keep any sacraments. While Roman Catholics believed in seven sacraments, Lutherans believed in two sacraments. Lutherans regarded baptism and holy communion as precious sacraments, or instruments of God's grace.

groups.[33] Additionally, many German Lutherans chose other denominations once they settled in the United States.[34] Through the first decades of the twentieth century, there was only a handful of Lutheran churches in Cincinnati. German Catholics were much more numerous as Cincinnati attracted many immigrants from the southern and Catholic regions of Germany. Cincinnati was one of the most important centers of German Catholicism in the Midwest.[35] Cincinnati was home to a significant number of Jewish residents and was a major center for Reform Judaism under the Rabbi Issac M. Wise.[36]

Cincinnati was a popular site for émigrés of the failed European revolutions of 1848. The German Forty-eighters promoted secular

---

[33] The Missouri Synod originated with groups of Lutherans who came to America as intact religious communities. Many of these Old Lutherans settled in rural areas such as Perry County, Missouri, and Freistadt, Wisconsin. "The Synod's geographical strength lay roughly in a triangle including Wisconsin's Prussians, Michigan's Bavarians, and Missouri's Saxons" (Dean Wayne Kohlhoff, "Missouri Synod Lutherans and the Image of Germany, 1914–1945" [Ph.D. diss., University of Chicago, 1973] 7).

[34] "If the descendants of all the German Lutherans who immigrated here were still Lutheran, the Church would at minimum be two or three times its present size. Rather than nine million Lutherans, there would be some twenty million. As it was, thousands left the Lutheran Church for a variety of reasons. Thus, while it is instructive to trace the development of the German Lutherans in America, perhaps it would be an even more fascinating study to follow those hundreds of thousands of German Lutherans who, for one reason or another, abandoned the faith of their fathers in the New World to adhere to other denominations" (Kinnison, "German Lutherans in the Ohio Valley," 5).

[35] Philip Gleason, *The Conservative Reformers: German-American Catholics and The Social Order* (Notre Dame: University of Notre Dame Press, 1968) 4. The German-American Catholic experience was in many ways parallel to the German-American Lutheran experience. German-American Catholics were also on the side of the conservatives in the debates over Americanization in the Roman Catholic Church. They wished to preserve their linguistic and cultural heritage, with the understanding that "Language Saves Faith" (Gleason, *The Conservative Reformers*, 29–39.

[36] For more on Cincinnati's religious and ethnic diversity, see Henry D. Shapiro and Jonathan D. Sarna, ed., *Ethnic Diversity and Civic Identity: Patterns of Conflict and Cohesion in Cincinnati Since 1820* (Urbana: University of Illinois Press, 1992).

humanist values through their Turner societies. The Cincinnati Forty-eighters were the first émigrés who established a Turnhalle, a recreation center for the development of mind and body. The Turner movement soon spread to other German-American communities. The Forty-eighters were small in number but had an influence disproportionate to their numbers. Cincinnati became known as a center of rationalist and anti-religious attitudes. Trinity Lutheran Church, in particular, was attacked by the secular press as well as by German Methodists for its traditional, conservative beliefs.[37] Cincinnati's German Lutherans felt themselves under attack and "felt that they were being stabbed in the back by English Lutherans who weakened the old doctrinal loyalties."[38]

Trinity was not only pressured by outside theological controversies, but also by internal tensions. In 1871 Trinity dedicated its new, stately Gothic church building, which still stands today on Race Street. But with this new building came new burdens, and Trinity struggled for a time with difficulties incurred by the church's financial debts. In 1891 Trinity purchased a building on York Street for its parochial school, which had outgrown its space on Race Street. Around the turn-of-the-century, controversies arose related to Trinity's parochial school, which had been a part of the congregation since its inception.[39]

At the turn-of-the-century, Trinity was a fairly large church, made up of over eight hundred communicant members, along with their children. But because of internal dissensions, over the school and other issues, several groups broke away from Trinity to form their own congregations. Our Savior, Emmaus, and Cross Lutheran churches, all had their beginnings in the first decade of the twentieth century as groups which broke away from Trinity.[40] The stormy nature of Trinity during Andrew Schulze's early years

---

[37] Tolzmann, *Cincinnati's German Heritage*, part 1, p. 57.

[38] Allbeck, *A Century of Lutherans in Ohio*, 108.

[39] "Brief History of Trinity Lutheran Church of Cincinnati Ohio," 15–17.

[40] Ibid., 15–17. Religious controversies have always been a significant part of Lutheran history. But such discord has also been considered a German trait. "An unfriendly critic writing from Gottingen once remarked that wherever three Germans congregated in the United States, one opened a saloon so that the other two might have a place for their quarrels" (Carl Wittke, "Ohio Germans, 1840–1875," *The Ohio Historical Quarterly* 66 [October 1957]: 345). However, such

may have prepared him in some way for the controversies that would be so much a part of his career in the church.

In 1911, the Rev. Theodore Moellering took over as pastor of Trinity and served the congregation until his death in 1927. Moellering restored a sense of peace and stability to the congregation and also served the interests of other Missouri Synod congregations in Cincinnati. Under Moellering's pastorate, Trinity was behind the formation of the Federation of Lutheran Churches of the Missouri Synod in Cincinnati, the organization that was responsible for mission outreach in the city.[41] After his death, Trinity was reconciled with the break away congregation of Emmaus, in part due to a prior arrangement made by Moellering and another pastor. In 1927 the two congregations merged and took the name Concordia, the Latin word for harmony.[42] Schulze's experiences at Trinity provided him with a solidly conservative theological outlook, but also instilled in him an evangelical spirit.

Andrew Schulze celebrated his confirmation on Palm Sunday in 1910. Although Lutherans did not consider confirmation to be a sacrament, the rite of confirmation was an important ritual. Confirmation marked "a festive and solemn entry into mature membership."[43] After years of religious instruction at Trinity Lutheran Church and School, Schulze confirmed the faith in which he had grown since baptism. Soon after, Andrew Schulze was considered an adult, taking on full-time work outside the home.

Schulze had not even completed two full years of high school. He was different from his siblings in that he very much enjoyed learning and wanted to continue his studies. He expressed an interest in becoming a pastor, but this idea met with resistance from his family. It is somewhat odd that

---

conflict was not a characteristic limited to German Lutherans. "The massive, beautifully constructed churches of the first generation which still dot the urban landscape were often troubled places.... No institution in immigrant America exhibited more discord and division than the church" (John Bodnar, *The Transplanted: A History of Immigrants in Urban America* [Bloomington: Indiana University Press, 1985] 144, 166).

[41] "Brief History of Trinity Lutheran Church of Cincinnati Ohio," 16–17.

[42] "A Century of Grace, 1849–1949: Concordia Lutheran Church, Cincinnati, Ohio," Church files, CHI, St. Louis MO.

[43] L. DeAne Lagerquist, *The Lutherans* (Westport CT: Praeger, 1999) 146–47.

Schulze was not supported in his wish to be a minister as his father once had the same desire. But his father had since worked in a very practical occupation and knew the financial demands of supporting a large family. Schulze's family encouraged him to take up more practical work.[44] Schulze worked downtown, first with the John Shillito Company, a large dry goods store. Later, Schulze worked for Muth's Bakery, where his father was employed.[45] In 1917, with America's involvement in World War I, Schulze enlisted in the United States Navy, in part because he was not satisfied with the jobs that he worked in Cincinnati.

World War I was a transforming event in the life of Andrew Schulze. It not only changed him, but also had significant repercussions for the German-American culture in which he was born. Andrew Schulze's interests did conform with the immigration historian Marcus Lee Hansen's law, "What the son wishes to forget the grandson wishes to remember." Schulze did have the "third generation interest" in his own cultural heritage, but it was somewhat submerged for a time after World War I.[46] After Schulze retired in 1968, he and his wife, Margaret, spent almost a year in northern Germany, researching their family history and reconnecting with their cultural heritage. In their later years, Andrew and Margaret used German in their daily devotions.[47] But in the middle decades of his life, Schulze connected with a people and a culture that were not originally his own.

Andrew Schulze first became involved with the African-American community in an intentional and active way as a young seminary student in Springfield, Illinois. However, his first contacts and interactions with black

---

[44] Raymond Schulze, interview by author, 10 July 1999.

[45] *Cincinnati City Directories* (Cincinnati: Williams Directory Company, 1914–1917).

[46] Marcus Lee Hansen was "a great pioneering figure in the study of immigration to the United States, who encapsulated what he called 'the principle of third generation interest' in these memorable words—'what the son wishes to forget the grandson wishes to remember.' This striking formulation has been known as Hansen's law since Will Herberg called it that in his influential study of the postwar revival of religion, *Protestant-Catholic-Jew* (1955)" (Philip Gleason, *Speaking of Diversity: Language and Ethnicity in Twentieth-Century America* [Baltimore: Johns Hopkins Press, 1992] 231).

[47] Raymond Schulze, interview by author, 10 July 1999.

Americans began in Cincinnati. Situated across the Ohio River from Kentucky, Cincinnati was a place of symbolic significance in African-American history. Cincinnati was the first city in the Old Northwest Territory to develop a significant African-American community. As Henry Lewis Taylor, Jr. explained, "Located on the fringe of slavery, Black Cincinnati, because of the critical role it played in the underground railroad and the abolitionist movement, became one of the most important antebellum black communities in the country."[48] Harriet Beecher Stowe wrote *Uncle Tom's Cabin* based on her experiences in Cincinnati. In a famous scene of this anti-slavery novel, one of the main characters, Eliza, with her baby, fled across the frozen Ohio River to freedom.

But even though Cincinnati was a major center for the abolition of slavery in the early nineteenth century, it also had a history of racial unrest. Cincinnati was a part of the borderland; it was both a Northern and a Southern city.[49] Race relations deteriorated in Cincinnati in the late nineteenth century as they did throughout the United States.[50] Joe William Trotter, Jr.'s *River Jordan* quoted Cincinnati's *Commercial Gazette* in 1889, confirming "a regional and national trend when it declared, 'The color line is everywhere.'"[51] In a study of Cincinnati around the turn-of-the-century, a doctoral student, Frank U. Quillan, found a city full of prejudice. Quillan

---

[48] Henry Louis Taylor, Jr., "On Slavery's Fringe: City-Building and Black Community Development in Cincinnati, 1800–1850," *Ohio History* 9 5 (Winter/Spring): 8. Additionally, "Ohio had one of the largest black populations in the North throughout the nineteenth century" (David A. Gerber, *Black Ohio and the Color Line, 1860–1915* [Urbana: University of Illinois Press, 1976] x).

[49] Henry Louis Taylor, Jr., ed., *Race and the City: Work, Community, and Protest in Cincinnati, 1820–1970* (Urbana: University of Illinois Press, 1993) xiii–xiv. Cincinnati was home to many white Southerners who moved north. For a brief description of this white Southern migration, see John D. Barnhart, "Sources of Southern Migration into the Old Northwest," *Mississippi Valley Historical Review* 22 (June 1935): 49–62.

[50] See C. Vann Woodward, *The Strange Career of Jim Crow*, 3rd. rev. ed. (New York: Oxford University Press, 1974) and Joel Williamson, *The Crucible of Race: Black-White Relations in the American South Since Emancipation* (New York: Oxford University Press, 1984).

[51] Joe William Trotter Jr., *River Jordan: African American Urban Life in the Ohio Valley* (Lexington: University Press of Kentucky, 1998) 73.

thought the prejudice in Cincinnati was related to the city's close connection with the South, both in terms of trade and migration from the South.[52]

German-American attitudes on race were not clearly distinguishable from Anglo-American attitudes. Some have claimed that German Americans had a better record on race as Germany did not have connections to New World slavery like other European powers. Additionally, comparatively few German Americans were slaveholders.[53] Some have also claimed that the German vote was critical in the election of President Lincoln, but historians have shown that the German vote was only decisive in the state of Illinois. German Americans did generally oppose slavery, but mainly for economic, not moral reasons. German Americans "harbored many of the same racial prejudices that blinded other white Americans."[54]

Lutherans in America did not have a history of taking strong positions on racial issues. As Milton Sernett concluded, "With the possible exception of the Episcopalians, no other major American denomination exhibited as much benign neglect or demurred so long in addressing the moral and

---

[52] Miller, *Boss Cox's Cincinnati*, 31.

[53] In their study of Perry County, where the Missouri Synod Lutherans originally settled, Stafford Poole and Douglas J. Slawson found that "although Missouri Synod Lutherans eventually found biblical justification for owning slaves, few if any of their number in Perry County ever became slaveholders. They were too poor and too shocked by the peculiar institution" (Stafford Poole and Douglas J. Slawson, *Church and Slave in Perry County, Missouri, 1818–1865* [Lewiston NY: Edwin Mellen Press, 1986] 20).

[54] Randall M. Miller, introduction to *States of Progress: Germans and Blacks in America over 300 Years*, ed. Randall M. Miller (Philadelphia: The German Society of Pennsylvania, 1989) 13. Certain groups of Germans such as Quakers and Forty-eighters did have better records on racial issues. However, "it is not possible to discover any single body of beliefs and social habits that has governed the behavior of Germans toward blacks, and vice versa.... Where German culture has been most pronounced, blacks have historically been few in number. By the time significant numbers of blacks did move to areas where many Germans resided, German ethnicity had eroded or disappeared altogether. As blacks became more visible, Germans became less so...Little direct evidence of German-black perceptions and interactions survives" (Miller, *States of Progress*, 2).

political crisis occasioned by the enslavement of African peoples."[55] A small Lutheran group of abolitionists known as the Franckean Synod was the noted exception to this generalization.[56] Among Lutherans, the German Evangelical Lutheran Synod of Missouri, Ohio, and Other States, headquartered in the border state of Missouri, held some of the most pro-Southern sympathies. It attempted to stake out a position of theological neutrality, emphasizing the separation of church and state. However, Missouri's C. F. W. Walther also made clear that he found biblical justification for the existence of slavery.[57] Nonetheless, in 1877 the German Evangelical Lutheran Synod of Missouri, Ohio, and Other States, along with other conservative Lutherans, began mission work among African Americans in the South.

Andrew Schulze remembered positive impressions of black Americans based on his experiences in Cincinnati. A little more than 5 percent of Cincinnati's population was black American when Andrew was growing up in Cincinnati.[58] The majority of Cincinnati's black citizens lived in areas of the city such as "Bucktown" and "Little Africa." But there were also clusters of black residences located throughout the city. In an article Schulze wrote for *The Walther League Messenger* in 1939, he described his memories of the African-American community in Cincinnati. As Andrew Schulze recalled:

> Near my childhood home there was a little cluster of Negro cottages. Though some few of them were of better construction, the majority were made of the boards of dry-goods boxes and of

---

[55] Milton Sernett, "Lutheran Abolitionism in New York State: A Problem in Historical Explication," *Essays and Reports of the Lutheran Historical Conference* 10 (1984): 16.

[56] In addition to Milton Sernett's article, see Douglas C. Stange, *Radicalism for Humanity: A Study of Lutheran Abolitionism* (St. Louis: Oliver Slave, Ltd., 1970) and Paul P. Kuenning, *The Rise and Fall of American Lutheran Pietism: The Rejection of an Activist Heritage* (Macon GA: Mercer University Press, 1988).

[57] Robert Fortenbaugh, "American Lutheran Synods and Slavery, 1830–60," *Journal of Religion* 13 (January 1933): 72–92.

[58] From 1880 to 1910, Cincinnati's black population rose from about 8,200 to 19,650, rising from about 2.3 percent of the population to about 5.3 percent of the total population (Trotter, *River Jordan*, 64–65).

other cast-off lumber that could be had for the taking. These hovels—for most of them were just that—were built on the side of a beautiful hill…. Few days would pass in the summertime but that my bare feet would carry me over the hillside to sit there sometimes for hours, to see the clouds and the sunshine on the valley and on the hill beyond, but more than all this, to watch from my place of vantage the Negro cottages and the Negroes…. I cannot say with any degree of certainty, after thirty years, whether it was the contrast between the beauties of that countryside and the jumble of Negro huts, or whether there was something in the life and manner of those Negroes that drew me; but I think it was the latter. It seems to me there was a joy in their lives unknown among my Caucasian friends and neighbors.[59]

Schulze also recalled his meetings with black Americans on streetcars and when he served as a water boy for a crew of workmen. Schulze's uncle employed a black worker in his dairy.[60] Perhaps most significantly, when Schulze reached the upper grades, he attended an integrated public school.[61] Cincinnati's pattern of segregation was uneven and Cincinnati continued to have a more mixed racial environment until about 1920.[62]

---

[59] Andrew Schulze, "A People You Can Love," *Walther League Messenger*, foreign ed. 48 (December 1939): 200.

[60] Andrew Schulze, *My Neighbor of Another Color* (St. Louis MO: Andrew Schulze, 1941) 36.

[61] Andrew Schulze, "A People You Can Love," 200. "Elements of racial progress also mingled with ones of prejudice and discrimination in defining the new black school situation. This situation was a product of local responses to the 1887 school desegregation law in southern and central Ohio" (Gerber, *Black Ohio and the Color Line*, 263). The downside to the integration of schools was that black teachers often lost jobs (Gerber, *Black Ohio and the Color Line*, 264).

[62] Henry Louis Taylor, Jr., "City Building, Public Policy, the Rise of the Industrial City, and the Black Ghetto-Slum Formation in Cincinnati, 1850–1940," in *Race and the City: Work, Community, and Protest in Cincinnati, 1820–1970*, ed. Henry Louis Taylor, Jr. (Urbana: University of Illinois Press, 1993) 178. Taylor demonstrated that residential segregation was reinforced by the emergence of the industrial city. "The city-building process played a prominent role in the ghetto-slum formation" (Taylor, "City Building," 178).

However, none of Schulze's experiences with black Americans occurred within the context of his involvement with Trinity Lutheran Church. After Andrew Schulze left Cincinnati, Trinity did become more connected with Cincinnati's African-American community. As a part of the Federation of Lutheran Churches of the Missouri Synod in Cincinnati, Trinity supported Immanuel Lutheran Church, a black Lutheran mission, begun in 1926.[63] Trinity took the name Concordia in 1927 when it merged with another congregation. Concordia's Over-the-Rhine neighborhood began to change in the 1930s. Appalachian whites first moved into the area, followed by black Americans in later decades.[64] For a time, Concordia served effectively as an inner-city congregation.[65] But in 1969 Concordia chose to re-locate on Central Parkway, on the western edge of Cincinnati. Concordia's Over-the-Rhine sanctuary became the site of another mission congregation, Prince of Peace Lutheran, which still operates in Over-the-Rhine today.

Prior to World War I, Schulze's home congregation had little contact with those outside its own ethnic group. With the onset of World War I, German Lutherans not only became more exposed to the outside world, they also experienced a brief, but intense period of ethnic persecution. While there was an active nativist sentiment and a desire for Anglo-conformity in late nineteenth-century America, German immigrants tended to be more accepted by Anglo-Americans than other immigrant groups.[66] But with the war against Germany, German Americans became the targets of anti-German hostility. Frederick Luebke concluded that "the crisis of war did not by itself create conflicts between the native-born and the German

---

[63] "Brief History of Trinity Lutheran Church of Cincinnati Ohio" 17.

[64] "Over-the-Rhine: A Description and History" (Cincinnati: Historic Conservation Office, 1995). For a history of Over-the-Rhine in recent times, see Zane L. Miller and Bruce Tucker, *Changing Plans for America's Inner Cities: Cincinnati's Over-the-Rhine and Twentieth-Century Urbanism* (Columbus: Ohio State University Press, 1998).

[65] Andrew Schulze featured his home congregation in his column, "That the Church May Lead." *The Vanguard* 10 (July 1963): 2, 4. At the time that Schulze wrote the article, his son, Herb Schulze served as Concordia's Assistant Pastor.

[66] See John Higham, *Strangers in the Land: Patterns of American Nativism, 1860–1925*, 2nd ed. (New Brunswick NJ: Rutgers University Press, 1992).

Americans. Rather, war was the occasion that converted latent tensions into manifest hostility."[67]

German-American communities across America came under tremendous pressure to prove their loyalty. German Americans were harassed with acts of violence and vandalism, but much of the pressure was psychological. Family, business, and street names became anglicized. In Cincinnati, German Street became English Street and Berlin became Woodrow. German-language papers were censored and German-language instruction was eliminated from the public schools. German books and music were now considered suspect. A "Germania" statue in Over-the-Rhine was quickly renamed "Columbia."[68]

Among German Americans, it was those with church affiliations, particularly the Mennonites, Lutherans, and Catholics, who experienced the most difficulties. Luebke found that "in few German-American churches was the identification with the German government so weak and the retention of German language and culture so strong as in the Lutheran Church—Missouri Synod."[69] The Missouri Synod, in particular, was singled out for criticism. As Carol Coburn explained, "The Lutheran Church—Missouri Synod's exclusive use of the German language, its pro-German stance before 1917, its rigid definition of the separation of church and state, and its aversion to ecumenical fellowship with other Protestant groups made it an obvious target for charges of un-Americanism."[70]

At the time of World War I, the Missouri Synod was still known as the German Evangelical Lutheran Synod of Missouri, Ohio, and Other States.

---

[67] Frederick C. Luebke, *Bonds of Loyalty: German-Americans and World War I* (De Kalb: Northern Illinois University Press, 1974) xiii.

[68] Cincinnati Historical Society, *Cincinnati: The Queen City*, 105–107.

[69] Luebke, *Bonds of Loyalty*, 311, 102.

[70] Carol Coburn, *Life at Four Corners: Religion, Gender, and Education in a German-Lutheran Community, 1868–1945* (Lawrence: University of Kansas Press, 1992). In her study of the rural community in Block, Kansas, Coburn found that "the generation of age just before World War I provided the pivotal point for change. The availability of birth control, increased economic options, military service, advances in transportation, and outside secular contacts served to change this generation's perceptions of themselves and their community" (Coburn, *Life at Four Corners*, 4).

Missouri quickly dropped "German" from its name. The war also expanded the use of English within the synod. Before the United States entered the war, approximately one-sixth of the congregations in the Lutheran Church—Missouri Synod had begun holding at least one English-language service per month. By the end of the war, nearly three-fourths of Missouri Synod congregations were making the transition to English.[71]

World War I somewhat dampened the 400th anniversary celebration of Lutheranism, dated from Martin Luther's presentation of his Ninety-five Theses in 1517. However, the war also hastened the assimilation process that had become more and more necessary for the Missouri Synod. German immigration had slowed by the time of the First World War and immigration was restricted in the aftermath of the war. Alan Graebner concluded, "Traumatic as it sometimes was, the war occurred at probably the most opportune time in the history of the Missouri Synod."[72]

German Americans were assimilating to American culture, but the war quickened and intensified the process. Further anti-German measures such as Prohibition and immigration restriction followed the war.[73] German-American culture lost its visibility and furthered declined with the rise of Hitler and the Second World War.[74] Yet even today, traits such as an emphasis on family, religiosity, and social and political conservatism remain attributable to German ethnicity.[75]

One of the most important ways in which German Lutherans proved their loyalty during the crisis of the First World War was through military

---

[71] Luebke, *Bonds of Loyalty*, 287.

[72] Alan Niehaus Graebner, "The Acculturation of an Immigrant Lutheran Church: The Lutheran Church—Missouri Synod, 1917–1929" (Ph.D. diss., Columbia University, 1965) 92.

[73] "By the 1890s prohibition had become the dominant political manifestation of cultural conflict...Prohibition was more than a mere issue to most German-born voters. It was the political symbol of a general clash of cultures which confronted many immigrants as they adjusted to American society" (Luebke, *Bonds of Loyalty*, 61, 99).

[74] "It seems unlikely that any other nationality group of equal numerical strength has ever before been so completely and so quickly absorbed in any country on the globe" (La Vern J. Rippley, *The German-Americans* [Boston: Twayne Publishers, 1976] 128).

[75] Conzen, "The Germans," 415.

service. A significant number of Missouri Synod Lutherans served in the army and the navy.[76] Twenty-one members of Trinity Lutheran Church in Cincinnati participated in the American war effort, including Andrew Schulze.[77] Schulze joined the United States Navy in 1917 and served on the *S. S. Conyngham*, a torpedo boat destroyer. Schulze not only experienced life in the military, he also got to see a bit of Europe.[78] Wartime service undoubtedly gave Schulze some perspective on what was important in life. Navy service broadened Schulze's horizons and gave him a measure of independence. When Andrew came home, he was determined to become a pastor.

Though his family was hesitant about a career in ministry, Schulze began a course of study at Concordia Seminary in Springfield, Illinois, shortly after he returned to the United States. Schulze demonstrated a certain stubborn independence that also served him later in life.[79] Friends and acquaintances remembered Schulze as being stubborn. However, Schulze turned this fault into a virtue as he applied it to the cause of improving race relations in the church. Later in life, he summed up his humble family background and the path that led him to be a part of the twentieth-century struggle for racial equality:

> My grandfather was an unlettered dairyman and my father spent almost all of his adult life driving a wagon, selling bread wholesale to groceries, restaurants, and saloons. My secondary education was cut short before I had finished my sophomore year. My alma mater, our Springfield seminary, accepted me in the fall of 1919 after I had finished a tour of nineteen months in the U.S. Navy during World War I. I was admitted into the then existing pro-seminary, where in one year I was able to make up for all my

---

[76] Frederick Nohl, "The Lutheran Church—Missouri Synod Reacts to United States Anti-Germanism during World War I," *Concordia Historical Institute Quarterly* 35 (July 1962): 63.

[77] "Brief History of Trinity Lutheran Church of Cincinnati Ohio," 19.

[78] Family photo album, Schulze family papers, in the possession of Raymond Schulze. There is a picture of Andrew with a group of navy men on horseback in Killarney, Ireland.

[79] Raymond Schulze, interview by author, 10 July 1999.

academic deficiencies so that I could in the fall of 1920 start my seminary work. But before my seminary work was completed, the Lord of the Church had already thrown me, as ill-prepared as I seem to have been, into the maelstrom of what was to be the most controversial issues of the 20th century, the race issue.[80]

Schulze was ill-prepared in numerous ways for the challenges that faced him. However, the early years of his life had also unknowingly prepared Andrew Schulze for the calling that he received.

---

[80] Andrew Schulze to Erich Heintzen, 3 September 1971 (copy), Andrew Schulze Papers, CHI, St. Louis MO.

Chapter 2

Springfield, 1919–1928

Just after Andrew Schulze arrived in Springfield, Illinois, in 1919, he experienced the encounter that changed the rest of his life. It occurred on the streetcar that Schulze rode when he first arrived in town. As he described it in his memoirs:

> It was a typical early September afternoon when I arrived in the city made famous, not by the seminary that I was to attend, but by the fact that here the great emancipator, Abraham Lincoln, lived, practiced law, and is buried…. I had learned through a number of unpleasant experiences when I was in the U.S. Navy during World War I, when on shore leave, always to inquire, at least once, where to get off a train, a bus, or a streetcar. A Negro gentleman, who no doubt had heard my inquiry, stopped in front of me as he was about to alight, to give me further information about getting to the seminary; and, pointing to a small frame church nearby, he added, 'Come and worship with us some time.' That was the beginning, that invitation, no doubt under the providential guidance of the Spirit of God, started me on a path of life on which I have traveled until this day.[1]

---

[1] Andrew Schulze, *Race against Time: A History of the Race Relations in The Lutheran Church—Missouri Synod from the Perspective of the Author's Involvement, 1920–1970* (Valparaiso IN: The Lutheran Human Relations Association of America, 1972) 5.

Schulze attended Holy Trinity Lutheran Church the next Sunday and soon became involved with Springfield's black Lutheran congregation as a young seminary student.

Once Andrew Schulze decided to become a pastor, the choice of seminary was easy. There have traditionally been two seminaries of the Lutheran Church—Missouri Synod. When Schulze went to seminary in 1919, the Missouri Synod operated Concordia Seminary in St. Louis, Missouri, and Concordia Theological Seminary in Springfield, Illinois. Since Schulze did not complete high school, he needed to attend the pro-seminary at Springfield to prepare him for seminary studies. If he had wanted to attend seminary in St. Louis, additional years of pre-seminary study at another institution would have been necessary. Springfield's Concordia Theological Seminary had fewer academic requirements: "In contrast to its sister seminary in St. Louis, which viewed itself as a 'learned' seminary aspiring to the pinnacle of German scholarship, the Springfield institution saw itself as a 'pastoral' and 'missionary' seminary."[2] In Missouri Synod circles, Concordia, St. Louis was known as the "academic" seminary and Concordia, Springfield was known as the "practical" seminary.

Concordia Theological Seminary was moved to Springfield in the 1870s, but had its beginnings elsewhere. Its history was connected with some of the early supporters of the Missouri Synod. The Rev. Wilhelm Loehe of Neuendettelsau, Bavaria, was influential in sending young men interested in the ministry to the American mission field during the 1840s. At the time, there was a great need for Lutheran pastors among the growing German-American community in America. Friedrich C. D. Wyneken began training many of these ministerial candidates in 1846 in Fort Wayne, Indiana. The progress of a couple early students suggested that even with only minimal training, some pastors could be quickly put into service and

---

[2] Erich H. Heintzen, *Prairie School of the Prophets: The Anatomy of a Seminary, 1846–1976* (St. Louis: Concordia Publishing House, 1989) 113. "Incredible as it may seem, it had been possible for many years for a student to enter the seminary, specifically the proseminary division, without an eighth grade education. Finally, in 1920 the synodical convention, acting on recommendations of a special survey committee, made completion of the eighth grade mandatory for entrance to the seminary" (Heintzen, *Prairie School of the Prophets*, 121).

still be effective.³ This was the start of the Missouri Synod's second seminary. F. August Craemer provided much of the leadership for the seminary from 1850 to 1891. Craemer was one of the pastors sent to America by Wilhelm Loehe. During his first five years in America, he served in a unique capacity as pastor of a mission colony aimed to convert the Chippewa Indians of Frankenmuth, Michigan.⁴ His outlook and experience contributed to the mission emphasis at Concordia, Springfield.

For a time, in the 1860s and 1870s, the Missouri Synod consolidated all of its seminary training at the seminary in St. Louis, which soon became overcrowded. In the mid-1870s Concordia Theological Seminary moved to Springfield where it remained until the 1970s when it once again became based in Fort Wayne, Indiana. In 1873 the oldest and largest Missouri Synod congregation in Springfield, Trinity Lutheran, purchased the campus of the former Illinois State University.⁵ The congregation then donated the campus to the Missouri Synod to provide for a synodical institution of

---

³ Heintzen, *Prairie School of the Prophets*, 23.

⁴ "The coming of August Craemer to the seminary ushered in an era that spanned 41 years in the history of the practical seminary. During this time the influence of this one man chiefly determined the character of the institution, molded a large segment of the clergy, and consequently affected the shape of the synod itself...work that has yet to adequately be assessed" (ibid., 41). For more on Craemer and the mission community in Frankenmuth, Michigan, see August R. Suelflow, ed., "The Beginnings of 'Missouri, Ohio, and Other States' in America," in *Moving Frontiers: Readings in the History of the Lutheran Church—Missouri Synod*, ed. Carl S. Meyer (St. Louis: Concordia Publishing House, 1964) 105–109, 118–22 and F. Dean Lueking, *Mission in the Making: The Missionary Enterprise among Missouri Synod Lutherans, 1846–1963* (St. Louis: Concordia Publishing House, 1964) 25–50.

⁵ Though it had a secular name, Illinois State University was associated with another Lutheran synod. Robert T. Lincoln attended the school and his father, Abraham Lincoln, gave a dedication speech for the campus in 1854. Carthage College in Kenosha, Wisconsin, and Augustana College in Rock Island, Illinois, trace their roots to this school (Heintzen, *Prairie School of the Prophets*, 80). The campus was briefly used as a Lutheran orphanage before becoming Concordia Theological Seminary (Copy of newspaper article "Concordia Not Forerunner of the University of Illinois," Concordia Seminary files, Sangamon Valley Collection, Lincoln Library, Springfield IL. Copy of newspaper article "Concordia in City Since '52; Growth Told," Concordia Seminary files, Sangamon Valley Collection, Lincoln Library, Springfield IL).

higher education. Soon after, the practical seminary separated from the St. Louis campus and relocated to Springfield in 1875.

Springfield was home to a fairly diverse mix of people. Northern Illinois was primarily settled by people coming from the northeastern United States, while southern Illinois was primarily settled by people mainly from the southeastern United States. These northern and southern cultures often met and clashed in Springfield's Sangamon County, located in the center of the state.[6] Beginning in the mid-nineteenth century, Springfield, along with much of the Midwest, attracted a large number of German and Irish immigrants. Corn fields and coal mines were a significant part of Springfield's attraction. In the years following the Civil War, a number of black residents also settled in Springfield. It gained a larger percentage of black residents than most cities in Illinois. However, the black community still only made up about 5 percent of Springfield's population.[7] German Americans tended to settle on the north side of the city, Irish Americans on the far east side, and African Americans on the near east side.[8]

Springfield was in many ways an average Midwestern city, yet it was distinguished by the presence of the state government, extensive railroad service, and many coal mines.[9] Springfield also played a unique role in the history and politics of the state and the nation. Since 1837, Springfield had been the site of the state capitol. Springfield was where Abraham Lincoln had made his home and his career. Upon leaving for the presidency, Lincoln made his farewell to Springfield, and following his assassination, his body

---

[6] Edward J. Russo, *Prairie of Promise: Springfield and Sangamon County* (Woodlands CA: Windsor Publications, 1983) 15.

[7] Roberta Senechal, *The Sociogenesis of a Race Riot: Springfield, Illinois in 1908* (Urbana: University of Illinois Press, 1990) 62. In 1920 Springfield was a town of about 60,000. There were 2,769 black citizens, about 4.7 percent of the population (Senechal, *The Sociogenesis of a Race Riot*, 60).

[8] Russo, *Prairie of Promise*, 36.

[9] Senechal, *The Sociogenesis of a Race Riot*, 55. "Springfield may hardly be regarded as a city of many extremes; it is rather a city of many averages. Located about midway between the northern and southern states and near the center of population of the country, it has shared in the cross-currents of political, social, and economic forces of the East and the West, the North and the South" (*The Springfield Survey: A Study of Social Conditions in an American City*, dir. Shelby M. Harrison [New York: Russell Sage Foundation, 1920] 3:30).

was buried in Oak Ridge Cemetery, just north of the city. In the decades that followed the Civil War, Lincoln's memory loomed large all over the nation but especially in Springfield.[10]

Though the Lincoln legacy brought the city pride, Springfield also became infamous in the first decade of the twentieth century for its race riot of 1908. With the deterioration of race relations around the turn-of-the-century, there had been several other race riots, such as those in Wilmington, North Carolina, in 1898 and Atlanta, Georgia, in 1906, but the riot in downtown Springfield was especially shocking. David Levering Lewis concluded, "The riot that devastated Springfield, Illinois, on the night of August 14, 1908, signaled that the race problem was no longer regional—a raw and bloody drama played out behind a magnolia curtain—but national."[11] As Roberta Senechal explained:

> Not since New York's draft riot of 1863 had the white public been so forcibly reminded of the vehemence of anti-black hostility in the North. The historical irony was too great to overlook: Springfield was Abraham Lincoln's hometown. Its riot presented the northern public with the startling spectacle of whites lynching blacks and burning their houses within a half mile of the Great Emancipator's homestead.... Even the timing of the riot seemed outrageous: in several months the nation would observe the centennial of Lincoln's birth.[12]

Springfield's riot was the motivation for a group of concerned citizens to meet in New York City in 1909. This meeting led to the formation of the National Association for the Advancement of Colored Peoples (NAACP). The NAACP was the first of the great civil rights organizations of the twentieth century. It achieved its greatest success through the use of

---

[10] See Merrill D. Peterson, *Lincoln in American Memory* (New York: Oxford University Press, 1994).

[11] David Levering Lewis, *W. E. B. DuBois: Biography of Race, 1868–1919* (New York: Henry Holt and Company, 1993) 387.

[12] Senechal, *The Sociogenesis of a Race Riot*, 2. Also see James Krohe, Jr., *Summer of Rage: The Springfield Race Riot of 1908* (Springfield: Sangamon County Historical Society, 1974).

litigation. The legal victories of the NAACP in the first half of the twentieth century paved the way for the civil rights movement of the 1950s and 1960s.[13]

These developments seemed far away from Concordia Theological Seminary.[14] Concordia was at Twelfth and Matheny Streets, located in the northeastern part of Springfield, in a more remote section of the city. To the north of the seminary was the Illinois Steel Works and to the west was the Wabash Railroad. To the south of the seminary was an area often referred to as the "Badlands," which included the huts where many of Spingfield's black residents lived. As Erich Heintzen described Concordia, "The German character and theological conservatism of the seminary, perhaps also its location in the northeast corner of town, fostered an insular outlook for many years with respect to the neighboring civil and religious communities."[15] Nonetheless, the seminary did support outreach into the community.

Based on a request from members of Springfield's black community, one of the professors of Concordia Theological Seminary, Henry Wyneken, began a study group for "colored" citizens of Springfield in 1882.[16] Henry Wyneken was the son of Friedrich C. D. Wyneken, the pastor who had first conducted seminary training at Fort Wayne and later became the second president of the Missouri Synod. The study group met in the home of one of its members on Twelfth and Reynolds, located just to the south of the

---

[13] For more on the NAACP, see Charles Flint Kellogg, *NAACP: A History of The National Association for the Advancement of Colored People* (Baltimore: Johns Hopkins Press, 1967) and Gilbert Jonas, *Freedom's Sword: The NAACP and the Struggle Against Racism in America, 1909–1969* (London: Routledge, 2004).

[14] According to Schulze's memoirs, Concordia Theological Seminary "housed and protected scores of Negroes until the riot had been quelled" (*Race against Time*, 20). In her study of the 1908 riot, Senechal found that German Americans were under-represented among the rioters and Irish Americans were the most prone to riot (*The Sociogenesis of a Race Riot*, 107). "German immigrants did not seem to have a tradition of bitter political and economic grievances against blacks, perhaps in part because they lacked the ethnic cohesiveness that characterized the Irish" (Senechal, *The Sociogenesis of a Race Riot*, 110).

[15] Heintzen, *Prairie School of the Prophets*, 87.

[16] Jeff G. Johnson, *Black Christians: The Untold Lutheran Story* (St. Louis: Concordia Publishing House, 1991) 163.

seminary. This group became the foundation of Springfield's black Lutheran congregation, Holy Trinity, organized in 1888. A year later, the congregation dedicated a church and parish hall, on 15th Street near Jefferson.[17] The effort to build and sustain a black Lutheran congregation was related to a wider mission effort begun in the 1870s by the Synodical Conference, an association of conservative Lutheran synods.

As Lutherans settled in the United States, they adjusted to the American religious environment by organizing themselves into a myriad of different synods. The word "synod" came from Greek, meaning "walking together." A Lutheran synod was typically united by geography and ethnicity as well as doctrine and church practice. Around the turn-of-the-century, there were scores of different Lutheran synods. Out of these various synods, the German Evangelical Synod of Missouri, Ohio, and Other States was one of the largest. Throughout the nineteenth century, there were various attempts to unify these disparate synods; the Synodical Conference represented the conservative, confessional version of these efforts.[18]

The Synodical Conference was a voluntary federation that grew out of theological discussions first initiated by Missouri's C. F. W. Walther in the 1850s. The Evangelical Lutheran Synodical Conference of North America was organized in 1872 and lasted, through various membership changes, for almost a century.[19] Members of the Synodical Conference recognized each

---

[17] "Holy Trinity Lutheran Church, 75th Anniversary, 1888–1963," Church files, Concordia Historical Institute, St. Louis MO.

[18] The General Synod and the General Council were other Lutheran federations operative during the nineteenth century. In the twentieth century, an array of mergers consolidated Lutherans so that today there are only three Lutheran church bodies in America of considerable size: The Evangelical Lutheran Church in America (ELCA), The Lutheran Church—Missouri Synod (LCMS), and The Wisconsin Evangelical Lutheran Synod (WELS).

[19] The Ohio Synod was one of the leaders behind the formation of the Synodical Conference. However, due to a Lutheran theological conflict known as the Predestination Controversy of the 1880s, Ohio was one of the first synods to leave the conference. A few of these synods, such as the Slovak Synod, were eventually incorporated into the larger Missouri Synod. The Wisconsin Synod and a smaller Norwegian Synod eventually broke off fellowship relations with the Missouri Synod. Relations with the Wisconsin Synod began to deteriorate in the 1930s and the

other as having sound doctrine and agreed to cooperate in areas such as education, missions, and publications. Part of the spirit behind the development of the Synodical Conference was the desire to reach out to other Americans, beyond the natural base of Lutherans in America: German and Scandinavian immigrants.[20]

Five years after its organization, in 1877, the year that also marked the end of the era of Reconstruction, the Synodical Conference embarked on a program of mission work among black Americans in the South. Other Protestant missionary groups were active in the South during the decades following the Civil War. However, Lutherans were not easily influenced by the trends of mainstream American Protestantism. The decision to support mission work in the South was a new and unexpected departure for the more conservative Lutherans. The work was prompted, in part, by the challenge of the president of the Norwegian Synod, Herman Amberg Preus, at the convention of the Synodical Conference at Fort Wayne, Indiana, in 1877. Preus questioned "whether the time had not come for the Synodical Conference to direct its attention to mission-work among the heathen and to start a mission, perhaps, among the Negroes and Indians of this country."[21] The Synodical Conference began this work by supporting John F. Doescher, a pioneer circuit preacher who had served the dispersed Lutherans of Dakota Territory, on a mission tour of several Southern

---

Wisconsin Synod formally suspended relations in 1961. For more on Wisconsin's decision to break with the Conference, see Mark Braun, "Changes within the Evangelical Lutheran Synodical Conference of North America which led to the Exit of the Wisconsin Evangelical Lutheran Synod" (Ph.D. diss., Concordia Seminary, St. Louis, 2000).

[20] Carl S. Meyer, "Ohio's Accord with Missouri, 1868," in *The Maturing of American Lutheranism*, ed. Herbert T. Neve and Benjamin A. Johnson (Minneapolis: Augsburg Publishing House, 1968) 193–94. For more on the Synodical Conference, Carl S. Meyer, ed., "The Missouri Synod and Other Lutherans Before 1918," in *Moving Frontiers: Readings in the History of the Lutheran Church—Missouri Synod*, ed. Carl S. Meyer (St. Louis: Concordia Publishing House, 1964).

[21] Christopher F. Drewes, *Half a Century of Lutheranism among Our Colored People, 1877–1927* (St. Louis: Concordia Publishing House, 1927) 11.

states.[22] This marked the beginning of the most consistent Lutheran mission effort among black Americans.

However, the history of black Lutheranism extended much further back than the work of the Synodical Conference. The history of black Lutheranism began during colonial days. In the North, there were sporadic contacts between Lutherans and free blacks since the mid-seventeenth century. In the South, blacks became Lutheran wherever Lutherans practiced slavery, in places such as Georgia, Virginia, and the Carolinas. But the number of Lutheran slaveholders and slaves was very small (except in the Danish West Indies, today's U.S. Virgin Islands). Following the Civil War, many black Lutherans left the churches of their masters and were most likely absorbed into black Baptist and Methodist congregations. The Lutheran presence in the South was small and Baptists and Methodists had much stronger roots in the black community.[23]

The Synodical Conference embarked on its outreach to black Americans in the South as if it were a "foreign" mission field. They began their task with little recognition that there was a prior history of black Lutheranism in America. As Jeff Johnson explained, "The Synodical Conference was blinded by its own conception of the task, viewing it as a mission 'to the heathen.' That perception precluded the possibility that some blacks were indeed Christian, and of those, some might even have been Lutheran."[24] The Lutheran synods that made up the Synodical Conference consisted of more recent Lutheran immigrants and still conducted the majority of their business in foreign languages. The black Americans whom they were aiming to reach had been in America longer than most of those who were members of the Synodical Conference.

---

[22] For a detailed description of the limited work and limited success of the Synodical Conference among African Americans in the South up through 1900, see Lueking, *Mission in the Making*, 83–118.

[23] Johnson, *Black Christians*, 21–148. "The Methodists and Baptists had worked with blacks from the middle of the 18th century, almost three quarters of a century before Lutherans even began discussing the possibility of working with blacks...the Methodists and Baptists had not only trained a considerable number of black leaders before the Civil War, their churches had become indigenous to the black community by that time" (Johnson, *Black Christians*, 148).

[24] Johnson, *Black Christians*, 153.

The Lutherans of the Synodical Conference prided themselves on confessing the pure Gospel of Jesus Christ. They were critical of more liberal Lutherans as well as Christians of other denominations. They held a particularly poor view of African-American churches. Lutherans generally had a well-educated and well-articulated faith and were critical of the emotionalism found in many African-American churches. Lutheran literature was especially critical of most African-American preachers. The English newsletter of the black Lutheran mission effort was *The Lutheran Pioneer*.[25] It explained that in addition to the many churchless black Americans in the South:

> countless numbers of those who are connected with some church nevertheless know nothing of the grace of God in Jesus Christ. Their preachers tell them nothing of this grace, but, instead these men, often illiterate and immoral, tell them their own dreams and pretended visions. It is almost incredible what all is done by these preachers in the name of the Christian religion.... Their chief aim seems to be to get as much money as possible out of the pockets of their people.... Most of them have never studied at a theological school.[26]

Of course, Lutherans were not alone in their criticisms; others were critical of the state of African-American churches. *The Lutheran Pioneer* agreed with

---

[25] Johnson compared the German and English periodicals covering the mission work in the South: "Two German periodicals widely circulated in the Missouri Synod, *Der Lutheraner* and *Die Missionstaube*, reported with some regularity on the progress of the new mission to the black community. The language of both journals was condescending, referring to the prospective converts as 'the children of Ham,' or 'the perishing darkie heathen,' and depicting blacks in highly negative racial terms.... Unlike *Der Lutheraner* and *Die Missionstaube*, *The Pioneer* regularly depicted the Negro as the hero of its stories and referred to him as 'the freedman of the South" (ibid., 156). Later, black Lutherans in Alabama, published *The Alabama Lutheran*, which soon became *The Colored Lutheran*. *The Colored Lutheran* was more devotional in nature and was written for the black constituency of the Synodical Conference (Johnson, *Black Christians*, 171).

[26] Christopher F. Drewes, "Twenty-first Report of the Board for Colored Missions," *The Lutheran Pioneer* 44 (October 1922): 75.

the opinion of the famous black educator, Booker T. Washington. It quoted Washington stating, "A large proportion of the church-members are just as ignorant of true Christianity, as taught by Christ, as any people in Africa or Japan, and just as much in need of missionary effort as those in foreign lands."[27]

The mission effort of the Synodical Conference began with the work of just a few individuals. In the first few decades of this mission effort, the Synodical Conference developed important bases in New Orleans and North Carolina.[28] Yet the efforts of the Synodical Conference met with rather limited success until the Synodical Conference was connected with Rosa J. Young. Rosa Young was a Methodist educator determined to improve educational opportunities for black children in Alabama. When boll weevils hit the Alabama cotton fields in 1915 and wiped out her financial support, Young contacted Booker T. Washington for support. Washington referred her to the Lutherans and Young soon herself became a Lutheran. Shortly after connecting with Young, Alabama became the fastest growing mission field of the Synodical Conference.[29] Young's work was based in Wilcox County, which became the center of black Lutheranism in Alabama. Wilcox County became the home of a significant number of black Lutheran churchworkers.[30] Still, in the mid-1920s, black Lutherans numbered just over 5,000, though an estimated 25,000 black Americans were in some way involved with Lutheran churches or schools.[31]

---

[27] Ibid., 75.

[28] In North Carolina, the Synodical Conference took over the Alpha Synod, a small, independent black synod formed in 1889. The Alpha Synod was a legacy of Lutheran slavery in North Carolina. It was made up of four pastors, five congregations, and about 180 members. See Thomas R. Noon, "The Alpha Synod of Lutheran Freedmen (1889–1891)," *Concordia Historical Institute Quarterly* 50 (Summer 1977): 64–70.

[29] See Rosa J. Young, *Light in the Dark Belt: The Story of Rosa Young as Told by Herself*, rev. ed. (St. Louis: Concordia Publishing House, 1950).

[30] For more on the Alabama Field, see Richard C. Dickinson, *Roses and Thorns: The Centennial Edition of Black Lutheran Mission and Ministry in The Lutheran Church—Missouri Synod* (St. Louis: Concordia Publishing House, 1977) 65–72.

[31] Drewes, *Half a Century of Lutheranism among Our Colored People*, 109.

At times, black Lutheranism met with resistance from local Baptists and Methodists, members of traditional African-American churches. The missionary efforts of the Synodical Conference often imposed a cultural bias against traditional African-American culture.[32] Lutheran hymns and chorales were traded for African-American spirituals. Still, some black Americans found Lutheranism appealing. The Christian day school was a particularly attractive and successful component of the Lutheran mission effort. The Synodical Conference took pride in its converts. *The Lutheran Pioneer* extolled the virtues of "our Negro Lutherans." *The Lutheran Pioneer* relayed positive, but also patronizing comments made about black Lutherans. As it described black Lutheran worship, it stated, "White Southerners, accustomed to the ordinary emotional and noisy Negro service, again and again express their great surprise at the quiet and decorous behavior of our Lutheran Negro worshipers."[33]

The fiftieth anniversary history of black Lutheran missions, published in 1927, gave special praise to its white Lutheran missionaries. They were described as "a band of real heroes. It was their lot to be misunderstood and treated with coldness and contempt by many of the whites. They and their families often suffered social ostracism. At times they were positively persecuted."[34] While there were many who were opposed to the interracial contact necessary for mission outreach among African Americans, mission outreach, in itself, was not a threat to ideas of racial superiority and inferiority. The Synodical Conference worked within the racial culture of the South and made no attempt to change the basic nature of race relations in America.

Springfield's Holy Trinity was different from most of the black congregations of the Synodical Conference because of its northern and

---

[32] "The Synodical Conference had attempted to convert black people to German culture.... Black congregations had to be organized like German Lutheran congregations. Black congregations had to sing German Lutheran hymns as German Lutherans sang them. Black Lutherans had to think in German theological categories as German Lutherans thought.... In order to be a 'good black Lutheran,' one had to become a 'good black German'" (Johnson, *Black Christians*, 196).

[33] Christopher F. Drewes, "Twenty-first Report of the Board for Colored Missions," *The Lutheran Pioneer* 44 (October 1922): 77.

[34] Drewes, *Half a Century of Lutheranism among Our Colored People*, 75.

urban location. However, the geographic location of black Lutheranism shifted between 1920 and 1950. During the 1920s, black Lutheranism began to spread to the northern, midwestern, and far western parts of the United States. Black Lutherans became more highly urbanized than the white constituency of the Missouri Synod.[35] This geographic shift was due to the Great Migration of black Americans from the South to the northern and western cities of the United States. The Great Migration began during World War I and continued through the next few decades of the twentieth century.[36]

The Great Migration was often viewed in economic terms as it was related to the decline of agriculture in the South and the rise of industry in the cities of the North and West. However, the Great Migration also had profound religious significance: "Participants framed it as more than a temporal response to economic and social forces; it was viewed as a religious event—another chapter in the ongoing salvation history of African Americans, rich in symbolic and metaphorical content."[37] The Great Migration transformed the religious geography of urban communities throughout the United States. As black Americans moved to the North and the West, they joined new churches and some switched denominations. Lutherans responded by opening thirty-four new black mission congregations between 1920 and 1950. Some of these congregations were organized around kinship groups of black Lutherans from the South.[38]

Though located in the North and West, black Lutheran congregations were organized on a segregated basis. Their "mission" status implied that they were not equal to white Lutheran congregations. It was often assumed that mission congregations were made up of new believers, and therefore

---

[35] Johnson, *Black Christians*, 172, 178.

[36] "Between 1910 and 1970, six and a half million black Americans moved from the South to the North…. In 1970, when the migration ended, black America was only half Southern, and less than a quarter rural…. The black migration was one of the largest and most rapid mass internal movements of people in history" (Nicholas Lemann, *The Promised Land: The Great Black Migration and How It Changed America* [New York: Alfred A. Knopf, 1991] 6–7).

[37] Milton Sernett, *Bound for the Promised Land: African American Religion and The Great Migration* (Durham NC: Duke University Press, 1997) 58.

[38] Johnson, *Black Christians*, 172–74.

they did not hold the same stature as mature Lutheran congregations. These congregations were not financially independent and operated with a financial subsidy from the Synodical Conference. Though a part of the mission effort of the Synodical Conference, black Lutherans did not share full membership in the Lutheran Church. As Jeff Johnson explained, "Black Lutheran congregations, like black pastors, could not join any of the constituent synods of the Synodical Conference. These were not just organizational problems, they were theological problems concerning the doctrine of the 'call' as well as the doctrine of the church."[39] Eventually, through his life and ministry, Andrew Schulze came to grapple with these theological problems.

Andrew Schulze was part of a group of twenty-two young men who made up Concordia Theological Seminary's Class of 1924.[40] At the seminaries of the Missouri Synod, students obtained a traditional seminary education in the areas of biblical studies, Christian doctrine, church history, and practical theology. Through his years of seminary study, Schulze developed a Lutheran theological outlook that guided him during his ministry. At the heart of Lutheran theology was and is the concept of justification by faith. This concept expressed the belief that Christians are saved not because of their good works, but solely because of faith in work of Jesus Christ. Lutheran thought and practice was and is also centered around Word and Sacrament, the belief that God continues to reveal himself to humankind through the Bible and through the sacraments of baptism and holy communion.

The basic ideas of Lutheran theology were declared in the Lutheran confessions of the sixteenth-century Reformation. The development of these confessions of faith was not originally meant to develop a particularist Christian tradition, but was seen as a way to unify Christians in the spirit of the ancient creeds of the church. Ever since the sixteenth century, Lutheran theological education put a considerable emphasis on the Lutheran confessions and on the history of Martin Luther and the Reformation. As Jaroslav Pelikan described, "Lutheranism found, and still finds, much of its genius in the figure of Luther, his struggle for faith, and his eventual

---

[39] Ibid., 195.
[40] Family photos, Schulze family papers, in the possession of Raymond Schulze.

discovery and declaration of that faith."[41] Since Luther and the other sixteenth-century Lutheran reformers did not comment on racial matters, race did not appear to be a particularly Lutheran topic. There was nothing in the Lutheran confessions that was especially helpful to Schulze as he later developed a commitment to racial justice in church and society.

However, there were aspects of the Lutheran tradition that Schulze drew on as he became committed to racial justice. Lutheran seminary training put a strong emphasis on personal pastoral care. Lutheran pastors were to be sensitive to the spiritual needs of their individual parishioners. This ethos of pastoral care helped Schulze to see the world through the eyes of some black parishioners. The Lutheran emphasis on the Bible also enabled Schulze to develop a theological framework that stressed the worth and dignity of all of humankind. Even though biblical principles supported the idea of human equality, these principles were long overlooked and ignored by most Lutherans and other Christians in America.

Looking back over almost fifty years, Schulze recalled that the race issue was seldom ever discussed during his seminary training, as though "a theological vacuum existed."[42] Schulze remembered that "segregation with all the concomitant ethical problems involved—the generally assumed innate superiority of one race and the inferiority of another, all running counter to the doctrine of creation as taught by the seminary...were not a matter of classroom discussion or debate."[43] A few people at the seminary, like Andrew Schulze, were involved in some way with Holy Trinity, Springfield's black congregation, but racial issues were generally ignored.

The Missouri Synod did take a stand against the popular Ku Klux Klan of the 1920s.[44] However, its reasons for doing so were not motivated by the

---

[41] Jaroslav Pelikan, "Lutheran Heritage," in *The Encyclopedia of American Religious Experience: Studies of Traditions and Movements*, ed. Charles H. Lippy and Peter W. Williams (New York: Scribner, 1988) 420.

[42] Schulze, *Race against Time*, 10.

[43] Ibid., 8.

[44] Though the Ku Klux Klan of the 1920s harbored the same racist ideology as earlier and later versions of the Klan, it couched its beliefs under an image which gained more widespread public acceptance. During the 1920s, the Klan presented itself as leading "a crusade for old-time fundamentalist religion, clean living, 100% Americanism, and law and order. Invocations of God, flag, and country, more than

ideals of racial justice. Many in the Missouri Synod denounced the Klan because they "were disturbed by its clandestine operations and were dissatisfied with the quality of its 'Christian' profession."[45] The Ku Klux Klan seemed far too similar to Masons and other lodges that held religious positions unacceptable to confessional Lutherans. Nonetheless significant numbers of individual Lutherans did join the Klan.[46] The Ku Klux Klan of the 1920s showed its greatest strength in the Midwest, the region of the country with the greatest proportion of Lutherans.

Schulze was taught with the understanding that Lutheranism, and the Missouri Synod version of Lutheranism in particular, was the truest exposition of the Christian faith. While members of other Christian denominations were recognized as fellow Christians, some of their theology and practices were considered suspect. Missouri Synod Lutherans wanted to distance themselves from the theology and practice of mainstream American Christianity. The Missouri Synod was particularly defensive about its tradition during the 1920s as the Missouri Synod was making the transition from a German-speaking church to an English-speaking church.[47]

---

white supremacy spurred its spectacular success" (Richard Tucker, *The Dragon and The Cross: The Rise and Fall of the Ku Klux Klan in Middle America* [Hamden CT: Archon Books, 1991] 2–3).

[45] Ralph Luther Moellering, "The Missouri Synod and Social Problems, A Theological and Sociological Analysis of the Relation to Industrial Tensions, War, and Race Relations from 1917 to 1941" (Ph.D. diss., Harvard University, 1964) 267. The Missouri Synod radio preacher, Walter A. Maier, took a particularly strong stand against the Klan, describing it as "un-American and un-Christian" (Moellering, "The Missouri Synod and Social Problems," 267).

[46] "Religious affiliations mirrored the whole of white Protestant society, including those who did not belong to any church" (Leonard Moore, *Citizen Klansmen: The Ku Klux Klan in Indiana, 1921–1928* [Chapel Hill: University of North Carolina Press, 1991] 9). "In every city where membership data are currently available, Lutherans joined the Klan in proportions comparable with Methodists, Baptists, or Disciples of Christ"(Moore, *Citizen Klansmen*, 52).

[47] See Alan Niehaus Graebner, "The Acculturation of an Immigrant Lutheran Church: The Lutheran Church—Missouri Synod" (Ph.D. diss., Columbia University, 1965).

Throughout the 1920s, most of the lectures and assigned readings at Missouri Synod seminaries were still in German.[48] Besides developing a working knowledge of German, Schulze also learned some Greek. Because Schulze was at the "practical" seminary, he was not required to study Hebrew and Greek, the original languages of the Bible. However, Schulze, on his own initiative, took private lessons in New Testament Greek. Schulze developed an important relationship with his Greek tutor, Professor O. P. Kretzmann.[49] Three decades later, Schulze was offered a position at Valparaiso University by its president, O. P. Kretzmann. Schulze also had a close relationship with Professor Theodore Engelder, who served for a time as pastor at Holy Trinity Lutheran Church and later as a professor at Concordia Seminary, St. Louis.[50]

Concordia's seminary training included one year of service as a vicar, ministering under the supervision of an experienced pastor. Schulze's vicarage was at St. Paul Lutheran Church in Westlake, Ohio, just outside of Cleveland.[51] At the time of Schulze's vicarage, in the early 1920s, the congregation was just beginning to make the transition from German to English.[52] At St. Paul Lutheran Church, Schulze was able to experience what was in many ways a typical Missouri Synod congregation. However, Schulze continued to be drawn to work among black Lutherans.

During their years of study, most of Concordia's seminary students were involved with Trinity Lutheran Church, Springfield's large and well-established Missouri Synod congregation. Trinity's beginnings dated back to 1841 and its large church building was dedicated in 1889. Trinity Lutheran Church was located on Second Street, in the heart of downtown. It was a church of some stature, sitting on a corner block across from the state

---

[48] Heintzen, *Prairie School of the Prophets*, 128–29.

[49] Karl Lutze, interview by author, 29 January 2000. "O. P. Kretzmann during these years was considered an excellent young teacher 'who stood in closest relationship to the student body'" (Heintzen, *Prairie School of the Prophets*, 125).

[50] Schulze, *Race against Time*, 7.

[51] Family photos, Schulze family papers.

[52] "'Our History' on St. Paul Lutheran Church, West Lake, Ohio." Church files, Concordia Historical Institute (CHI), St. Louis MO.

capitol.[53] During Andrew Schulze's study at Concordia, he became more and more involved at Holy Trinity Lutheran Church, Springfield's small black congregation. As Schulze remembered, "The more I became involved as a student in the work at Holy Trinity, the more I, with Holy Trinity, became isolated from Trinity congregation, its people, and its official district and synodical activities."[54]

Schulze did, however, have an important connection to Trinity Lutheran Church. Through a group of mutual friends, Schulze was introduced to his future wife and partner in ministry, Margaret Goering. The Goering family had long been members of Trinity Lutheran Church. Margaret's parents, Herman and Emma Goering, were also of German immigrant background. During their courtship, Margaret began attending Holy Trinity with Andrew, though she admitted she had never heard of Springfield's small black Lutheran congregation before she met him. Andrew and Margaret dated during his last years of seminary study at Concordia but waited to marry until after Andrew's graduation in the spring of 1924, in accordance with seminary regulations.[55]

Andrew and Margaret were married on 30 June 1924 at Margaret's home congregation of Trinity. They honeymooned on the *S. S. South American*, traveling on the Great Lakes to various port cities and to Niagara Falls.[56] After their honeymoon, Andrew and Margaret traveled to Cincinnati and spent some time with the Schulze family. On 20 July 1924 Andrew Schulze was ordained into the holy ministry by the Reverend Theodore Moellering, in his home congregation, Trinity Lutheran, in Cincinnati. The couple then returned to Springfield where Schulze was installed at Holy Trinity by H. A. Klein, President of Concordia Theological Seminary.

From the beginning of his ministry at Holy Trinity, Andrew Schulze proved to be different from most other white Lutheran pastors serving black

---

[53] "Trinity Lutheran Church to Mark Its 95th Anniversary with Three Services Today," Trinity Lutheran Church files, Sangamon Valley Collection, Lincoln Library, Springfield IL; "Trinity Lutheran Church Marks 125th Anniversary," Trinity Lutheran Church files, Sangamon Valley Collection, Lincoln Library, Springfield IL.

[54] Schulze, *Race against Time*, 6.

[55] Ibid., 6–7.

[56] Family photos, Schulze family papers.

congregations. Margaret also proved to be different from most of the other pastors' wives. When a white pastor served a black congregation, it was customary for a white pastor's wife and family to be members at a white congregation. As Schulze recalled concerning Holy Trinity, "My best friend on the seminary faculty, Dr. Theodore Engelder, who was the most liberal in racial matters and had identified himself with Holy Trinity more than any of his colleagues, advised me to have my wife retain her membership at Trinity Church. Margaret never entertained the idea."[57] Throughout Schulze's ministerial career, Margaret and the Schulze children were active members at the black congregations where Andrew served. The Schulze family also lived in homes that were located in the same neighborhood as many of their members. While this was the usual practice for white pastors with white congregations, white pastors of black congregations often commuted to their congregations from white neighborhoods.

Andrew and Margaret moved into the parsonage next to Holy Trinity. On 5 March 1926, they were joined by their first of three sons, Paul Schulze. Though the practice is less common today, Lutheran parsonages were usually provided for pastors and their families throughout the nineteenth century and through much of the twentieth century. Typically the parsonage sat right next to the church building. Residing next to the church, the pastor was able to keep a watchful eye on the church as well as the members who lived nearby. The parsonage system enabled the pastor to live among his people and minister to them as one of them. The parsonage was a place where members felt free to call upon their pastor in times of need. As Lutherans became more suburbanized in the twentieth century, pastors began purchasing their own homes, and the use of parsonages declined.[58] But in Springfield, St. Louis, and Chicago, Schulze and his family lived in homes in the midst of black neighborhoods. Schulze's commitment

---

[57] Schulze, *Race against Time*, 6–7.

[58] "The movement from city to suburb meant that the large concentration whose members 'lived in the shadow of the parsonage' was a thing of the past.... Once outside the shadow of the parsonage, the Missouri Synod Lutheran was also away from the close supervision of *Herr Pastor*, representative of the immigrant culture as well as spiritual mentor. The move to the suburbs thus weakened the mental as well as geographical ghetto" (Graebner, "The Acculturation of an Immigrant Lutheran Church," 183–84).

to live among his parishioners, even against the custom of the day, reflected something about his understanding of the ministry. Schulze's presence among his members gave him a personal understanding of his parishioners' daily struggles.

During his four years at Holy Trinity, Schulze was influential in re-opening Holy Trinity's parochial school. When Holy Trinity was built in 1889, it was built with an adjoining school building. However, Holy Trinity's school had only been in operation from 1896 to 1904. Under Schulze's leadership from 1924 to 1928, Holy Trinity made another attempt to support parochial education. But Holy Trinity's school was not very successful, and it closed when Schulze left to become pastor of St. Philip's Lutheran Church in St. Louis.[59] Later, Schulze attributed the failure of Holy Trinity's school to its segregated nature. At the time, Springfield's schools were integrated and most members did not wish to send their children to Holy Trinity's all-black school. Even during his years in Springfield, some were beginning to suggest that Schulze was "twenty five years ahead of his time" concerning race relations. But Schulze was not yet fully committed to integration. In his memoirs, Schulze quoted Psalm 25:7 ("Lord, remember not the sins of my youth.") as he expressed his regret over not attempting to integrate one of the other Lutheran schools in Springfield rather than re-starting Holy Trinity's school.[60] After Springfield, Schulze was never again as supportive of parochial schools.[61]

---

[59] "Holy Trinity Lutheran Church: Organized in 1888; Church Was Remodeled Six Years Ago," Holy Trinity Lutheran Church file, Sangamon Valley Collection, Lincoln Library, Springfield IL.

[60] Schulze, *Race against Time*, 28–30.

[61] In his memoirs, Schulze stated that parochial schools had "a latent potential for good," but raised many concerns as to how they had dealt with race relations and social concerns. This was a fairly controversial position to take in a church body with a rich history of parochial education. Even today, the Lutheran Church—Missouri Synod operates the largest system of parochial schools among Protestants. To support his position, Schulze cited the position of one of Missouri's founders, F. C. D. Wyneken, who also had reservations about parochial education. Wyneken's "concern was that the chief responsibility for the Christian training of the child is not that of the church nor the school, but the home" (Schulze, *Race against Time*, 39–40).

Though Andrew Schulze was not yet fully committed to the cause of integration, he quickly emerged as an advocate for black Lutherans. In 1926 he advocated on behalf of Holy Trinity's black schoolteacher, Phyllis Jones. She was interested in attending a Lutheran college in order to finish her degree. She had been refused admission to the Lutheran colleges in Seward, Nebraska, and New Ulm, Minnesota. Schulze wrote to the Synodical Conference's Director of Colored Missions, Christopher Drewes, about the situation. Regarding Miss Jones's refusals of admission, Schulze wrote, "You can well imagine that this action on the part of brethren of the faith cut very deeply. Many other denominational colleges and universities accept colored students. Why should the Lutherans not? This will continue to become an even more practical question as time goes on and our work in the North progresses." He asked Director Drewes to speak about admitting black students with Dr. W. H. T. Dau, the new president of Valparaiso University. Valparaiso University had recently become a Lutheran institution after being purchased by a group of Lutherans in Indiana in 1925. Schulze stated that "now, while the policies of the institution are being shaped, is the time to get those in authority to take definite action in establishing this truly Christian principle."[62] While President Dau was open to the idea of black students at the university, he concluded that the racial climate of the community made the prospect untenable.[63] Though Schulze's efforts were unsuccessful in this particular case, he later became involved in ending segregation in Lutheran education.

A few black men had studied for the ministry at Springfield's Concordia Theological Seminary in the late nineteenth century, but segregated higher education became the norm for Lutherans at the beginning of the twentieth century. Through the first half of the twentieth

---

[62] Andrew Schulze to Director Drewes, 9 March 1926 (copy), Andrew Schulze Papers, CHI, St. Louis MO.

[63] W. H. T. Dau to Rev. J. Shufelt, 9 July 1926 (copy), Andrew Schulze Papers, CHI, St. Louis MO. The Ku Klux Klan was especially strong in Indiana during the 1920s. When Valparaiso University ran into financial difficulties in 1923, "Indiana officials of the Ku Klux Klan reportedly reached an agreement to purchase the campus, but the offer was withdrawn when the national offices of the Klan failed to give its approval" (Richard W. Solberg, *Lutheran Higher Education in North America* [Minneapolis: Augsburg Publishing House, 1985] 924).

century, there were primarily two black institutions of higher education sponsored by the Synodical Conference. Immanuel Lutheran College opened in Concord, North Carolina, in 1903 and served as a seminary for those interested in serving as pastors in the Synodical Conference. In 1905 Immanuel moved to Greensboro, North Carolina, where it continued to operate until 1961. In 1922 the Synodical Conference opened Alabama Lutheran College in Selma for the education of black teachers in its growing Alabama mission field.[64] Today, Alabama Lutheran College continues to operate as Concordia University, Selma.

Over the years, Schulze was influenced by some of his parishioners. One of the most influential couples in Schulze's Springfield congregation was Mr. and Mrs. George Bates. George Bates was the man who had first invited Andrew Schulze to Holy Trinity for worship. During his time in Springfield, Schulze became well acquainted with the Bateses. Through fellowship with some of his members, Schulze began to view church and society from the perspective of black Americans. As Schulze later explained, "Through my contact with the Bateses I learned in the early days of my parish ministry what the seminary classroom lectures could not impart—a lesson that was to stand me in good stead for many years to come."[65] Mrs. Bates felt comfortable enough with her pastor to challenge his views and the church's position on race relations. On one occasion, Mrs. Bates asked Pastor Schulze why the Lutheran Church followed the practice of segregation. As Schulze recalled, "I was totally unsuccessful in convincing Mrs. Bates that the Church's task was 'to preach the Gospel....' I reasoned: 'The Gospel would in time change things.' I am not sure that I was able to convince myself completely of the validity of my argument."[66]

Schulze's response to Mrs. Bates was an expression of traditional Lutheran thought. Lutherans had a history of complicated attitudes toward political and social action. Martin Luther's theology included a distinction

---

[64] Johnson, *Black Christians*, 164–65, 170. Also see George J. Gude, "Training of African-American Church Workers in the LCMS/Synodical Conference," *Concordia Historical Institute Quarterly* 68 (Fall 1995): 103–18. Another black Lutheran college, Luther College, operated for a brief period during the early part of the twentieth century in New Orleans, Louisiana.

[65] Schulze, *Race against Time*, 142.

[66] Schulze, "That the Church May Lead," *The Vanguard* 4 (January 1957): 4.

between the "two kingdoms," the spiritual and secular realms.[67] Many Lutherans in America misunderstood this as promoting the idea of a complete separation of church and state. Compared to most American Protestants, Lutherans played a much more reserved role in political and social activism in American society.[68] As Johann Friedrich Pfotenhauer, president of the Missouri Synod from 1911–1935, expressed it, "The real business of the Church is to preach the Gospel. It is not the mission of the Church to abolish physical misery or to help men to earthly happiness."[69] Lutherans frequently expressed their concern for the spiritual welfare of others, but they were often silent when it came to political and social issues. When Andrew Schulze came to confront racial injustice, he often had to confront a false division of the spiritual and social dimensions of life.

When Lutherans did encounter ethical issues, "the focus of Lutheran interest was on personal rather than social ethics.... American Lutherans were in agreement that their church should concern itself with the salvation of the individual.... It was expected that social reform would result from the leavening effect in society of transformed individuals."[70] When this approach was applied to racial problems in America, it sounded similar to the accommodating, self-help philosophy of Booker T. Washington. For example, one column in *The Lutheran Pioneer* asked, "How Can the Negro Become Respected and Influential?" It reasoned:

the Negro...is to go on proving his worthiness, making himself, by industry, property, refinement, self-restraint, and Christian uprightness, a type of what the Negro can be, a proof of what he is

---

[67] See Martin Luther, *Selected Political Writing*, ed. J. M. Porter (Philadelphia: Fortress Press, 1974).

[68] See Paul Kuenning, *The Rise and Fall of American Lutheran Pietism: The Rejection of an Activist Heritage* (Macon GA: Mercer University Press, 1988). Kuenning noted the exceptions to Lutheran quietism on political and social issues. He gave significant attention to the abolitionist Franckean Synod.

[69] Niel M. Johnson, "Lutherans in American Economic Life," in *The Lutheran Church in North American Life*, ed. John E. Groh and Robert H. Smith (St. Louis: Clayton Publishing House, 1979) 142.

[70] Eugene L. Fevold, "Coming of Age, 1875–1900," in *The Lutherans in North America*, rev. ed., ed. E. Clifford Nelson (Philadelphia: Fortress Press, 1980) 356.

when given the right chance…. A public opinion can be created, a better and wiser spirit can be aroused…. Meanwhile our Lutheran Church will go on giving the Negro the Gospel and a truly Christian education in its mission-schools and help him to win the respect of even his enemies.[71]

Through its many decades of mission work, the Synodical Conference remained focused on preaching and teaching the Gospel.

Many black Americans, however, were becoming more assertive and more organized during the 1920s. The 1920s was the decade of the Harlem Renaissance, a period of exceptional vitality in black art, music, and literature. Marcus Garvey and his Universal Negro Improvement Association (UNIA) promoted ideas of black pride and pan-Africanism. Though Garvey's popularity and the UNIA were short-lived, other organizations proved more durable. The National Association for the Advancement of Colored People (NAACP) and the National Urban League, both begun in the first decade of the twentieth century continued their expansion. A local chapter of the Urban League was opened in Springfield in 1926.[72] The NAACP and the Urban League were Northern organizations, dedicated to improving racial conditions. While the NAACP concentrated on legal measures, the Urban League concentrated on social services.

Black Lutherans also organized in the 1920s. In 1920 the General Conference was formed, in recognition of "the need for fellowship, mutual education, and a mechanism through which all blacks in the Synodical Conference could tackle issues of mutual concern."[73] The General Conference was an organization made up of the black and white pastors and teachers who served in the black ministry efforts of the Synodical

---

[71] "How Can the Negro Become Respected and Influential?" *The Lutheran Pioneer* 53 (September 1931): 133.

[72] "Colored People of City Helped by Urban League," Urban League file, Sangamon Valley Collection, Lincoln Library, Springfield IL; "Urban League Aims Defined," Urban League file, Sangamon Valley Collection, Lincoln Library, Springfield IL.

[73] Johnson, *Black Christians*, 192. In 1925 the General Conference resolved to give special support to Lutheran missionary activities in Africa.

Conference. During the 1920s, the Synodical Conference had an equal number of black and white pastors involved in black mission work.[74] As the white churchworkers of the Synodical Conference were recognized as members of their constituent synods, the General Conference was specifically intended to give organization to the black churchworkers and black congregations of the Synodical Conference. The General Conference, however, was a grassroots organization that had no official standing or power within the structure of the Synodical Conference. The black mission efforts of the Synodical Conference were under the control and supervision of the Board for Colored Missions, based in St. Louis.[75]

As pastor of a black congregation, Andrew Schulze attended meetings of the General Conference that were held every other year beginning in 1925. At the 1925 meeting of the General Conference, held in North Carolina, members discussed their hope that "the colored churches will be in a position to form their own synodical body, which will then be able to become a member of the Synodical Conference, even as Missouri, Wisconsin, and others are members of that body."[76] The motivation behind the formation of a black synod was not separatist in nature; rather, the idea was that black Lutherans could become full members of the Synodical Conference. This discussion turned into a more formal proposal at the 1927 meeting of the General Conference held in Selma, Alabama.

Andrew Schulze enjoyed the meetings of the General Conference and made important contacts for his future work in the church. He quickly emerged as a leader among Lutherans involved in black ministry. Schulze was eventually chosen to write the proposal for the formation of a black synod. In the proposal to the Board for Colored Missions, Schulze pointed out the isolation of many black Lutheran congregations.

---

[74] Drewes, *Half a Century of Lutheranism among Our Colored People*, 100–107. The 1927 anniversary history of black mission work listed brief biographies of twenty-two white churchworkers and twenty-two black churchworkers then serving the Synodical Conference. The lists included pastors and professors but not teachers.

[75] Johnson, *Black Christians*, 192–93.

[76] Description of the second meeting of the General Conference, Andrew Schulze Papers, CHI, St. Louis MO.

Our congregation in Chicago is literally surrounded by fifty or more orthodox Lutheran congregations; our two congregations in St. Louis likewise. Yet, aside from the financial assistance which the congregations of our mission receive from these surrounding congregations there is almost no contact whatsoever...Without entering into a discussion of social conditions that obtain, thus avoiding a very unpleasant, and (humanly speaking) unprofitable conflict of opinions on the question, the formation of a separate organization, which in turn might be connected with these surrounding orthodox Lutheran congregations, through membership in the Synodical Conference, would aid in bringing about a better feeling on the part of the members of the congregations of our mission.[77]

While Schulze acknowledged that black mission congregations were financially dependent on the Missionary Board, he noted that financially dependent white congregations of the Missouri Synod had the same privileges of self-supporting congregations. But the formation of a black synod was not in the making.

The Missionary Board of the Synodical Conference maintained considerable control over its program of black missions. While white congregations of the Synodical Conference called their own pastors and determined their own affairs, black congregations lacked such autonomy. The Missionary Board of the Synodical Conference was responsible for the placement and the payment of churchworkers involved in black ministry. In the spring of 1928, the Missionary Board transferred Schulze to St. Philip's

---

[77] Andrew Schulze to the members of the Board for Colored Missions, 3 April 1928 (copy), Andrew Schulze Papers, CHI, St. Louis MO, 5–7, 9. Schulze explained, "We are inclined...to underestimate the true worth of our missions. We remember that the members of our churches are only a few decades removed from a long period of slavery, that for this and perhaps other reasons...a large number of them are ignorant with respect to the knowledge of this world.... But the church of the first Christian era was made up largely of slaves...and of people of the humbler walks of life. All Christians, regardless of their station in life, their knowledge, and their material possessions, are in possession of gifts of the Holy Spirit" (Schulze to Board for Colored Missions, 3–4).

Lutheran Church in St. Louis, the administrative center of Missouri Synod Lutheranism. As Schulze recalled, "The Missionary Board very likely did not have the slightest idea of the trouble I was to cause them."[78]

---

[78] Schulze, *Race against Time*, 11.

Chapter 3

St. Louis, 1928–1947

In the winter of 1838–1839, a charismatic Lutheran preacher from Dresden, Saxony, Martin Stephan, led a group of about 600 followers to the frontier state of Missouri.[1] The Saxon emigrants were not only captured by the personality of their leader but also with the idea that they could establish an orthodox Lutheran community away from the rationalism of the Saxon Lutheran Church. The Saxon emigrants landed in New Orleans and then traveled by steamboat up the Mississippi to St. Louis. A few of the Saxons settled in St. Louis, but most moved to land about 100 miles south of the city in Perry County, Missouri. The Lutheran colony intentionally chose to build a settlement away from the influences of the city.[2]

---

[1] The decision to settle in Missouri was based on Gottfried Duden's description of it: "Missouri was tentatively but unanimously regarded by those present as the most suitable destination. This attitude was largely a reflection of their reaction to Duden's account of life there and makes its contribution toward justifying M. L. Hansen's characterization of Duden's work as 'the most important piece of literature in the history of German emigration'" (Walter O. Forster, *Zion on the Mississippi: The Settlement of the Saxon Lutherans in Missouri, 1839–1941* [St. Louis: Concordia Publishing House, 1953] 97–98).

[2] Ibid., 98. Though there were some farmers among the Saxons, the majority were craftsmen and professional men. The reason for settling away from the city had less to do with occupation and more to do with creating a self-sufficient religious community. "'The German farmer,' observed Wittke, 'usually was shrewd in selecting the best farming country available.' Not so the Stephanites. It was on impractical grounds, such as topography and the desire to build a 'Zion' far removed from the distracting influences of a robust and young West, and by a committee of questionable competence and independence, that the eventual site of the colony was determined" (Forster, *Zion on the Mississippi*, 232, 376–77).

A few months after their arrival in May 1839, the Saxons discovered that the leader to whom they had pledged obedience was involved in sexual and financial misconduct. The Saxons disposed of Martin Stephan by sending him into exile across the Mississippi River. The Lutheran colony was left disillusioned and disorientated for nearly two years. Then in April 1841 the Perry County settlers held a debate in their log cabin seminary at Altenburg. There Franz Adolph Marbach and Carl F. W. Walther debated the nature of church and ministry and whether the spiritual endeavor begun by the Saxon immigrants was legitimate. The young pastor, C. F. W. Walther, won the debate, basing his arguments on the Bible and the works of Martin Luther. Walther argued that the Saxon immigrants were a part of the true Christian Church. As he stated, "The name of the true Church belongs also to all those visible companies of men among whom God's Word is purely taught and the holy Sacraments are administered according to the institution of Christ." After restoring the shattered confidence of the immigrant community, Walther left for his new calling as pastor of the Saxon congregation in St. Louis.[3]

From St. Louis, Walther articulated a congregational polity and a conservative, confessional theology to other Lutherans throughout America. In 1847 the Saxon immigrants joined with other conservative Lutherans to form the Evangelical Lutheran Synod of Missouri, Ohio, and Other States. In the decades before his death in 1887, C. F. W. Walther served as pastor of Trinity Lutheran Church, editor of *Der Lutheraner*, professor and president of Concordia Seminary, and president of the Evangelical Lutheran Synod of Missouri, Ohio, and Other States. Walther emerged as one of the most significant figures in American Lutheranism. Just as Henry Melchior Muhlenberg organized Lutherans in the East during the colonial period, C. F. W. Walther organized Lutherans in the West during the nineteenth

---

[3] Forster, *Zion on the Mississippi*, 524. "The victory in the Altenburg Debate laid the foundations for the ecclesiastical edifice which Walther was to spend his life in building.... Other factors, such as his transfer to St. Louis, were also instrumental in changing his station. But his prestige rested upon the fact that he emerged from the chaos of two years of controversy with the most lucid presentation of what the majority of people felt to be a Scriptural solution for their emotional-doctrinal dilemma and the only plan for a church polity which was workable under the circumstances" (Forster, *Zion on the Mississippi*, 526).

century. Though the constituency of the young Missouri Synod was predominantly rural in character, its center was based in the frontier city of St. Louis.

By the time Andrew Schulze arrived in St. Louis, the Missouri Synod operated a vast organizational network that included a comprehensive school system, a publishing house, and a radio station. In the 1920s the Missouri Synod invested in a new Gothic campus for the home of Concordia Seminary on the outskirts of St. Louis. As Alan Graebner described, "In many ways the new buildings reflected in microcosm the aims and aspirations of the Missouri Synod.... The dedication of the largest Lutheran seminary in America in 1926 brought the largest crowd in Synodical history."[4] The Missouri Synod was a unique entity on the American religious scene. As the leading Protestant magazine, *The Christian Century*, described it in 1926:

> The Missouri Lutheran church has its strength in the middle west and its large theological seminary in St. Louis, Missouri. It represents a distinctively American development in Lutheranism for which there is practically no parallel in Europe. It has isolated itself from other churches with an effectiveness which may be equaled by the southern Baptists but is not surpassed by any other body.... Like Catholicism it perpetuates itself through the parochial school. The rigid discipline of the church seems to be under the control of the theological seminary faculty which has become a kind of corporate pope. Curiously enough anti-Catholic feeling runs very high in this denomination which is in many of its characteristics deeply akin to Catholicism not excepting any other protestant body, not excepting Anglicanism. The denomination has had remarkable growth in

---

[4] Alan Niehaus Graebner, "The Acculturation of an Immigrant Lutheran Church: The Lutheran Church—Missouri Synod, 1917–1929" (Ph.D. diss., Columbia University, 1965) 268–70. "At the dedication ceremonies of the Seminary, the Rev. J. W. Behnken lashed out against 'modernist, evolutionist, and higher critics' and asked for a 'strict adherence to the truths of God's Word'" (Carl S. Meyer, *Log Cabin to Luther Tower: Concordia Seminary During 125 Years Toward a More Excellent Ministry, 1839–1964* [St. Louis: Concordia Publishing House, 1965] 113).

America and numbers almost a million.... Its social influence upon American life is very slight and its ministers are prevented by the many restrictions which hedge about from assuming positive social leadership in the various communities where they labor.[5]

Despite its difficult beginnings, the Missouri Synod had emerged as one of the largest and most significant Lutheran synods in America.

The years between World War I and the Great Depression were another difficult period for the Missouri Synod. The decade of the 1920s brought considerable challenges for this German synod fast becoming Americanized.[6] The transition from German to English was the most dramatic change of the decade. Language facility helped determine careers within the church: "The men on their way up in the Synod during the Twenties were using English. Two good illustrations [were] the future Synodical president, John W. Behnken, and radio evangelist Walter A. Maier."[7] German language and culture provided a significant measure of insulation and identity for the Missouri Synod. With the use of English, the synod needed to define itself more clearly against the trends of American religion and society.[8]

During the 1920s, the American religious scene was engaged in a debate between modernist and fundamentalist interpretations of the Bible. The Missouri Synod viewed the modernist approach to the Bible as little

---

[5] "What Is Disturbing the Lutherans?" *The Christian Century* 43 (22 July 1926): 909–11.

[6] See Everette Meier and Herbert T. Mayer, ed., "The Process of Americanization," in *Moving Frontiers: Readings in the History of the Lutheran Church—Missouri Synod*, ed. Carl S. Meyer (St. Louis: Concordia Publishing House, 1964) 344–85.

[7] Graebner, "The Acculturation of an Immigrant Lutheran Church," 140.

[8] The *Lutheran Witness* became the primary periodical of the synod as *Der Lutheraner* declined in circulation. The *Witness* "tried to regain the denominational identity lost with the German by substituting new boundaries for the former boundaries of language, by replacing linguistic barriers with those of explicit proscription. In other words, the *Lutheran Witness* effectively translated into English the siege mentality so marked in previous Missouri Synod history, as also in the history of other immigrant groups" (Graebner, "The Acculturation of an Immigrant Lutheran Church, 129–30).

different from the rationalism that they had opposed in Europe. As *Lutheran Witness* editor, Theodore Graebner, explained, modernism was equivalent to "the old rationalism which rejects the authority of the Bible and substitutes for it the authority of reason."[9] Yet the Missouri Synod could not fully identify itself with the Fundamentalists who put forth five fundamentals of Christian belief. The Missouri Synod regarded all of Christian doctrine as essential, not simply five fundamentals: "Aspects of the Fundamentalist hermeneutics, their treatment of the sacraments, their unionism, and their Sabbatarianism and Prohibition made the Fundamentalists another of the groups from which the Synod disassociated itself."[10] Lutherans generally continued to follow their own particular doctrine and traditions, outside of the mainstream of American Protestantism.[11] However, Lutherans had to confront the issues of race relations just like the rest of American denominations.

St. Louis was a case in point as a city with a relatively large Lutheran population and a relatively large black population. Most of the city's Lutherans were of German ancestry. Like most Midwestern cities, St. Louis attracted numerous German and Irish immigrants during the nineteenth century. Like German Americans in other Midwestern cites, St. Louis Germans were marked by their variety. However, St. Louis Germans also tended to be more open to assimilation because of their dispersed patterns of settlement. Unlike the German settlers in Cincinnati or Milwaukee, German-Americans in St. Louis were spread throughout the city with concentrations of residences in both northern and southern parts of the city.[12]

---

[9] Theodore Graebner, "New Theology and Higher Criticism," *Lutheran Witness* 41 (12 September 1922): 295.

[10] Graebner, "The Acculturation of an Immigrant Lutheran Church," 364–65.

[11] Mark Granquist, "Lutherans in the United States, 1930–1960: Searching for the 'Center,'" in *Reforming the Center: American Protestantism, 1900 to the Present*, ed. Douglas Jacobsen and William Vance Trollinger, Jr. (Grand Rapids: Wm. B. Eerdmans Publishing Co., 1998) 234–51. Also see Milton L. Rudnick, *Fundamentalism and the Missouri Synod: A Historical Study of Their Interaction and Mutual Influence* (St. Louis: Concordia Publishing House, 1966).

[12] Audrey Olson, "The Nature of an Immigrant Community: St. Louis Germans, 1850–1920," *Missouri Historical Review* 66 (April 1972): 345–46.

St. Louis began to be home to a significant number of black Americans after the Civil War. By the late nineteenth century, St. Louis had the third largest concentration of urban black Americans, following Baltimore and Philadelphia.[13] St. Louis's black population continued to grow in the twentieth century. St. Louis played an important role in the Great Migration of black Americans to cities in the North. Many black Americans traveled north through St. Louis, both because of its location on the Mississippi River and because it served as an important railway hub. Some of the migrants heading north ended up staying in St. Louis.[14] By 1940 black citizens made up 18 percent of the population.[15]

Residential patterns showed that immigrants from Germany and Ireland were able to settle wherever they pleased. But the black population in St. Louis developed a concentrated settlement pattern due to residential restrictions.[16] In 1916 St. Louis became the first city where people initiated the vote to formalize *de facto* residential segregation into law. While the Supreme Court determined that this law was unconstitutional, residential segregation continued until after World War II through the use of restrictive covenants, private agreements between property owners.[17] Segregation extended far beyond housing to areas such as education, health care, and recreation. While segregationist law was not as uniform in Missouri as in Southern states, segregation persisted through custom. Segregation,

---

[13] James Neal Primm, *Lion of the Valley: St. Louis, Missouri, 1764–1980*, 3rd ed. (St. Louis: Missouri Historical Press, 1998).

[14] Lawrence Oland Christensen, "Black St. Louis: A Study in Race Relations, 1865–1916" (Ph.D. diss., University of Missouri—Columbia, 1972) 67.

[15] Primm, *Lion of the Valley*, 475. "The black population of St. Louis nearly tripled between 1900 and 1940, from 35,000 to over 100,000 but the area where blacks could buy or rent expanded only slightly" (Katharine T. Corbett and Mary E. Seematter, "No Crystal Stair: Black St. Louis, 1920–1940," *Gateway Heritage* 8 [Fall 1987]: 9).

[16] Christensen, "Black St. Louis," 95.

[17] Parts of the law also placed racial restrictions on churches and dance halls. Daniel T. Kelleher, "St. Louis' 1916 Residential Segregation Ordinance," *The Missouri Historical Society Bulletin* 26 (April 1970) 239–48. "After World War II, the highest court in the land would declare such covenants un-enforceable in the courts, and St. Louis would again play a central role in this fight of a generation later" (Kelleher, "St. Louis' 1916 Residential Segregation Ordinance," 248).

intended to create social distance, made extensive contacts between the races relatively rare occurrences.

The specific reasons for Schulze's transfer to St. Philip's Lutheran Church in St. Louis are not known, but there had been a link between the black Lutheran congregations in Springfield and St. Louis. For a time during the early part of the twentieth century, the two congregations, about ninety miles apart, shared a pastor. Their locations in cities that were home to Missouri Synod seminaries meant that seminary students often served as assistants. The congregations also shared some similar characteristics in their northern location and their appeal to middle-class members. However, St. Philip's Lutheran Church had its own unique role to play in Lutheran history.

St. Philip's Lutheran Church grew out of nearly a quarter of a century of black Lutheran mission work in St. Louis. Mission efforts among black Americans in St. Louis began based on the initiative of a few individuals. In 1903 Mrs. M. Bailey began holding Sunday school classes and City Missionary F. W. Herzberger began holding services not far from downtown St. Louis. These efforts marked the beginning of Grace Colored Lutheran Church. Over the next two decades, the small mission struggled without a permanent location until a large lot of land was purchased in 1926 on the corner of Goode and St. Ferdinand. The Synodical Conference Missionary Board continued to sponsor "colored" services near downtown, but a new church was constructed on Goode and St. Ferdinand, in a black middle-class neighborhood situated to the northwest of downtown St. Louis. This was a new venture for the Synodical Conference as it intentionally chose to locate the church in a black middle-class neighborhood, with the hope that the congregation would eventually become self-supporting.[18]

The construction of this new church was made possible in part due to the determination of a unique group among Lutherans, the St. Louis-based Lutheran Ladies' Aid for Colored Missions. The Lutheran Ladies' Aid for

---

[18] "Rev. Gose's Report," *The Missionary News* 11 (April/May 1926): 11–12. "St. Philip's Church Began as Negro Missions Experiment," *The St. Louis Lutheran*, 1 December 1956, Lutheran Churches of Greater St. Louis ser. 50, Church files, Concordia Historical Institute, St. Louis MO.

Colored Missions began in 1915 "to further the cause of Colored Missions in general and that of the local colored congregations in particular."[19] The Lutheran Ladies' Aid for Colored Missions donated nearly half of the money necessary for the construction of St. Philip's Lutheran Church. This contribution along with a fund from Grace and money from the Synodical Conference enabled the construction of what was considered to be one of the most beautiful churches built for a black Lutheran mission.

The new church was named St. Philip's, the most common name for black mission churches, based on the story of St. Philip and the Ethiopian in Acts 8:26–40. St. Philip's Lutheran Church was dedicated on 7 May 1927 with a large crowd of well-wishers in attendance. The Rev. Marmaduke Nathanael Carter, a well-known black pastor of St. Philip's Lutheran Church in Chicago served as a guest preacher. Andrew and Margaret Schulze were among those in attendance, not knowing that in little over a year this would be their new church home.[20]

St. Philip's enjoyed immediate success. Though there were only seventeen charter members, the congregation quickly grew. Under the one-year pastorate of the Rev. Paul E. Gose, the congregation grew to about one hundred members. The congregation continued its remarkable growth during the years of Andrew Schulze's pastorate from 1928 to 1947. Schulze was a strict, but loving pastor. As he explained, he was "extremely careful in accepting members into the church. At least 25 lessons are given over a period of six months to each prospect.... The catechumens intending to become members are expected to attend divine services, unless they have a good excuse to explain their absence."[21] Yet many wanted Schulze as their pastor. When Schulze left for Chicago in 1947, the congregation had over 500 adult members. In addition, some of St. Philip's members had been

---

[19] "History of the Lutheran Ladies' Aid for Colored Missions," in "Lutheran's Women's Work in Greater St. Louis," box on General Citywide Lutheran Activities, St. Louis Papers, Concordia Historical Institute (CHI), St. Louis MO, 36, 37.

[20] Andrew Schulze, *Race against Time: A History of Race Relations in the Lutheran Church—Missouri Synod from the Perspective of the Author's Involvement, 1920–1970* (Valparaiso IN: The Lutheran Human Relations Association of America, 1972) 11–12.

[21] [Andrew Schulze], "A Negro Lutheran Church Unusual in its Development and in its Prospects," Church files, CHI, St. Louis MO, 2.

released in the early 1940s to begin two new daughter congregations, Holy Sacraments on West Belle Place and St. Michael in Kinloch.[22]

Schulze attributed the growth of St. Philip's to three factors.[23] One was related to a nearby African Methodist Episcopal congregation. The AME congregation experienced a period of strife that caused some members to leave for other congregations. St. Philip's attracted some of these members as well as others who were dissatisfied with traditional African-American churches. Another factor in the growth of St. Philip's was the popularity of KFUO, the local radio station owned and operated by the Missouri Synod. KFUO was the first religious broadcasting station in existence and the original home of Walter A. Maier's popular radio program, "The Lutheran Hour." During the golden era of radio, Walter A. Maier's fame reached far outside the synod; some compared him to Billy Sunday before him and Billy Graham after him.[24] Schulze discovered that some of his new members had become interested in the Lutheran Church through "The Lutheran Hour."[25] Additionally, Schulze and others also credited the attractive, churchly edifice built as the home of St. Philip's Lutheran Church.[26]

---

[22] Schulze, *Race against Time*, 12–13. "Holy Sacraments Started to Expand Negro Missions," *The St. Louis Lutheran*, 4 May 1957, Lutheran Churches of Greater St. Louis ser. 62; "St Philip's Church Members Start Kinloch Park Mission," *The St. Louis Lutheran*, 27 July 1957, Lutheran Churches of Greater St. Louis ser. 68, Church files, CHI, St. Louis MO.

[23] Schulze, *Race against Time*, 12.

[24] Alan Graebner, *Uncertain Saints: The Laity in the Lutheran Church—Missouri Synod, 1900–1970* (Westport CT: Greenwood Press, 1975) 142. Ralph Luther Moellering disliked this comparison. Walter A. Maier "does not form a real connecting link between Billy Sunday and Billy Graham.... His Harvard-acquired intellectualism and the heavy doctrinal content of his sermons distinguish him from most of the revivalist tradition" (Ralph Luther Moellering, "The Missouri Synod and Social Problems, A Theological and Sociological Analysis of the Reaction to Industrial Tensions, War, and Race Relations from 1917 to 1941" [Ph.D. diss., Harvard University, 1964] 27). For more on Maier, see Paul L. Maier, *A Man Spoke, A World Listened: The Story of Walter A. Maier* (St. Louis: Concordia Publishing House, 1963).

[25] Andrew Schulze, "The First Colored Mission Congregation to Become Self-Supporting," *The Lutheran Pioneer* 55 (July 1933): 98.

[26] Theodore Graebner, editorial note with "St. Philip's (Colored)—And Its Lessons," *Lutheran Witness* 46 (9 August 1927): 275.

Schulze became convinced of the need for attractive church buildings. He thought that it was particularly important for black Lutheran missions to distinguish themselves from storefront churches, which multiplied with the Great Migration of black Americans to urban areas. Storefront congregations met in facilities not originally designated for religious purposes. Storefronts were often known for their "independence from mainline denominations, institutional instability, the lack of formal training for clergy, the preponderance of women among members, and a proclivity for Pentecostal ritual and Holiness doctrine."[27] After his experiences in St. Louis, Schulze concluded, "The intelligent Negro, to whom our church with its dignified sermon and service appeals, knows these store-front missions and preachers. Were we to begin in a store—as many of our missions have been begun—we would fall into the store-front category, the name Lutheran not-withstanding."[28]

St. Philip's was benefited by its location in the premiere black neighborhood of St. Louis, "The Ville." The Ville was a shortened name for Elleardsville, a tract of land once owned by a horticulturist Charles M. Elleard and later annexed to the city of St. Louis in 1876. In the late nineteenth century, the neighborhood was home to a mix of German, Irish, and African American residents. In 1874 the neighborhood's first colored school opened, later renamed Simmons School. In the 1880s two black churches organized, Antioch Baptist Church and St. James African Methodist Episcopal Church. The development of black institutions reflected the mixed and changing neighborhood. The percentage of black residents of the neighborhood jumped from 8 percent in 1920 to 95 percent in 1950.[29] St. Philip's Lutheran Church was built near the center of the Ville. On the corner of Goode and St. Ferdinand, St. Philip's was only a

---

[27] Milton C. Sernett, *Bound for the Promised Land: African American Religion and the Great Migration* (Durham NC: Duke University Press, 1997) 188.

[28] [Schulze], "A Negro Lutheran Church Unusual in its Development and in its Prospects," 4.

[29] Charles Bailey, "The Ville: A Study of a Symbolic Community in St. Louis" (Ph.D. diss., Washington University, 1978) 41.

block away from Antioch Baptist on Goode and a couple of blocks away from St. James AME on St. Ferdinand.[30]

In 1910 Sumner High School, named after the emancipationist senator Charles Sumner, moved to the Ville. Opened in downtown St. Louis in 1875, Sumner High School was the first black high school west of the Mississippi River. It attracted an excellent faculty and educated many successful students. Sumner graduates included Arthur Ashe, Tina Turner, and Dick Gregory. As Charles Bailey described, "Building on the suburban atmosphere, the educational, social, and cultural significance of Sumner High School, as well as, on the roots of Simmons Elementary School, the Antioch Baptist and the St. James AME Churches, 'the Ville' became a symbolically elite referent for black people in St. Louis—particularly from 1910 to 1955."[31]

In the 1930s another neighborhood anchor was added to the community. Homer G. Phillips Hospital was completed in 1937, using money from the New Deal and labor from white construction unions. Homer G. Philips Hospital sat right across the street from St. Philip's Lutheran Church. Until its controversial closing in 1979, Homer G. Philips Hospital was considered one of the finest hospitals dedicated to serving black patients and training black doctors and nurses. Amid racial tensions and hostilities, the Ville was an incredible example of "black resiliency and commitment to cultural integrity.... Ville residents prided themselves on

---

[30] Goode Avenue was later named Annie Malone Drive after the nation's first black woman millionaire. Annie Malone made her money from a successful haircare and beauty business. She was also known for her philanthropy. For a brief description and map of the neighborhood's institutions, see "The Ville," in *Where We Live: A Guide to St. Louis Communities*, ed. Tim Fox (St. Louis: Missouri Historical Society Press, 1995) 152–57.

[31] Bailey, "The Ville," 37. The Ville began to deteriorate in the 1950s and 1960s as many middle class blacks moved to the suburbs. With suburbanization, St. Louis, never a stellar city, became "a premier example of urban abandonment" (Kenneth T. Jackson, *Crabgrass Frontier: The Suburbanization of the United States* [New York: Oxford University Press, 1985] 217).

their middle-class values and on the strength of their sustaining institutions."[32]

During the heart of Andrew Schulze's time in the parish ministry, Schulze and his family lived in the vibrant neighborhood of "The Ville." Schulze's sons recalled in fondness "the joy, the excitement, and the beauty of that neighborhood."[33] During their years in St. Louis, Margaret and Andrew were busy raising their three sons. Herbert Schulze was born on 19 April 1930, and Raymond Schulze was born on 3 October 1932. The Schulzes' immersion in the black community was illustrated by a family anecdote. When Andrew and Margaret's youngest son Raymond was born, Paul was anxious to know whether the baby was black or white.

Editor Martin Simon of the *Christian Parent* interviewed Andrew and Margaret in the 1950s about their experiences raising their sons in black neighborhoods. Margaret was quick to point out that their experiences were "the same as if they had been brought up with white children. They found some whom they liked, some whom they disliked."[34] However, the Schulzes were not always well received by their fellow white Lutherans. Herb Schulze remembered the parochial school teachers at his school making fun of the fact that his family was so closely involved with a black church and community.[35]

Schulze's work isolated him from other white Lutheran pastors, but he continued to develop contacts with others involved in black Lutheran ministry. In 1931 the black educator and leader in Alabama missions, Rosa Young, began her first trip North to lecture to various church groups.

---

[32] Lorenzo J. Greene, Gary R. Kremer, and Antonio F. Holland, *Missouri's Black Heritage*, rev. ed. (Columbia: University of Missouri Press, 1993) 144. "Ironically, in spite of the fact that the Homer G. Phillips Hospital was to be a facility for blacks, white unions kept black laborers from helping to build this structure" (Greene et al., *Missouri's Black Heritage*, 152).

[33] Paul Schulze, interview by author, 14 June 2000, telephone; Herb Schulze, interview by author, 10 June 2000, telephone; Raymond Schulze, interview by author, 10 July 1999, telephone.

[34] Martin P. Simon, ed., "They Lived among Negroes," *The Christian Parent* 20 (December 1956): 7. Martin Simon was the father of the politician Paul Simon and the pastor Arthur Simon.

[35] Herb Schulze, interview by author, 10 June 2000, telephone.

Andrew Schulze hosted Young while she was in St. Louis. Schulze made arrangements for Young to speak at his church as well as another and showed Young some of the sights of St. Louis.[36] There was no indication that these two Lutheran leaders of race relations would be at odds thirty years later over the fate of Alabama Lutheran Academy and College in Selma. However, already in the 1930s, they served in fields with vast differences, the one, Northern and urban, and the other, Southern and rural.

Schulze's experiences with Holy Trinity and St. Philip's shaped much of his outlook with regards to black ministry. Both of Schulze's congregations were a part of the Northern Conference, one of four regional divisions of the General Conference.[37] The other three conferences that made up the General Conference were based in the South, named for the states of Louisiana, Alabama, and North Carolina. Schulze and other pastors of the Northern Conference became specifically interested in reaching out to middle-class blacks. A 1929 meeting of the Northern Conference resolved "that our missionaries be encouraged to appeal to and to center their missionary efforts more strongly upon the responsible, intelligent and progressive element of Colored people, than upon the less stable and more transient class."[38] While this approach involved class bias, it was related to the practical experiences of those involved with black Lutheran ministry in the North.

There was some validity in the attempt to reach middle-class blacks as Lutherans had a well-educated clergy that was more appealing to those who were more educated. Contemporary observers noted that as blacks became more educated some became interested in more solemn and liturgical

---

[36] Rosa Young, *Light in the Dark Belt: The Story of Rosa Young as Told by Herself*, rev. ed. (St. Louis: Concordia Publishing House, 1950) 171–74.

[37] "The origin of the N. Conference was the result of a conversation held between Pastor Carter and Pastor Schulze during a noon-day walk...in Concord, North Carolina at the time of the General Conference in 1925. One year later the first meeting was held in Springfield, Illinois." Four pastors and the Director of Missions, the Rev. Christopher Drewes, were present at the first meeting (Minutes of the Northern Conference, 17 July 1934, Cleveland, OH, Andrew Schulze Papers, CHI, St. Louis MO, 1).

[38] Minutes of the Northern Pastoral Conference, 18 and 19 June 1929, Chicago IL, Andrew Schulze Papers, CHI, St. Louis MO, 3.

churches, such as the Catholic, Episcopal, and Lutheran. "The Trend of the Negro away from his Traditional Churches" was the featured topic of discussion at a meeting of the Northern Conference.[39] Some blacks who chose to become Lutheran explained their decision in a similar manner. As a black Lutheran explained, "Lutheranism, although the oldest of the Protestant religions, is comparatively new to our group. It appeals to the thinking class of our race. The Negro is naturally religious, and as he gains education he is seeking a quiet and dignified form of it."[40]

However, the Christian Church was intended for all people and Christianity includes an obligation to the poor and the needy. Schulze explained his ministry at St. Philip's in this way:

> It should be our desire to bring into the Church the poor, the lame, and the blind, the publican and the sinner, the outcasts of human society. While stressing our obligations over against the lowly, however, we must not forget that Christ died also for the wise and those on a higher social plane. And while it remains true to this day what the Apostle Paul once wrote to the Corinthians, that "not many wise men after the flesh, not many mighty, not many noble are called," nevertheless there are always some wise, some mighty, and some noble that are.[41]

Schulze's ministry among black parishioners who were not only faithful, but also successful by the world's measures was a challenge to Schulze and to others. The "high intellectual level" of St. Philip's members "exceeded that of most Lutheran congregations in this period, shattered white presuppositions about Negro illiteracy and incompetence."[42]

---

[39] W. Fields, "Negro Mission Workers' Conference," *The Lutheran Witness* 61 (7 July 1942): 242.

[40] Andrew Schulze, "Saint Philip's Is Unique," *The Walther League Messenger* 43 (November 1934): 145.

[41] Ibid., 145.

[42] Moellering, "The Missouri Synod and Social Problems," 269. Andrew Schulze wrote, "At one time during my pastorate I counted 32 members who had college degrees, no mean number for any congregation in the thirties of this century, doubly

In 1933 St. Philip's Lutheran Church became the first black congregation begun under the auspices of the Synodical Conference to become financially self-sufficient. As Schulze described it, "That St. Philip's has become self-supporting at this time is a strange happening and perhaps an outstanding fact in the history of our Lutheran Church in America."[43] What was particularly remarkable about the accomplishment was that it occurred in the midst of the Great Depression. Schulze later recalled, "The economic depression of the thirties struck a devastating blow to the black communities of the industrial centers of the nation. St. Philip's congergation, with perhaps a third of its employable members unemployed, became…self-supporting."[44] The fact that Schulze's salary was now paid for by St. Philip's rather than the Synodical Conference provided Schulze with a measure of independence. Shortly after the St. Louis congregation became independent, St. Philip's in Chicago, under the pastorate of Marmaduke N. Carter, also became self-sufficient.

Andrew Schulze had a very pastoral nature; he had a great deal of concern and empathy for those within his care. He gradually became convinced of the need for integration as he realized how members of his own congregation were treated when they encountered other Lutheran congregations. Raymond Schulze remembered the one time he really saw his father cry was after reading a letter from a member of his congregation, Otis Finley, who spent part of his military service during World War II in Texas. Finley wrote that one Sunday he traveled to another town to find a Lutheran congregation so he could partake of Holy Communion. He spoke with the pastor before the service as was customary for Lutherans visiting other congregations. The pastor was willing to communion Schulze's parishioner but had him sit in the sacristy during the whole service so that he would be out of sight from the rest of the congregation. The pastor

---

true of The Lutheran Church—Missouri Synod of that time" (Schulze, *Race against Time*, 14).

[43] Schulze, "The First Colored Mission Congregation to Become Self-Supporting," 98.

[44] Schulze, *Race against Time*, 12.

communed the congregation and then entered the sacristy to commune Schulze's member last.[45]

During the first part of Schulze's ministry, he wanted there to be exceptions to the pattern of segregation. For example, if there was no black Lutheran congregation in a city where one of his members transferred, he wanted them to be accepted by a white Lutheran congregation. But when even exceptions to segregation met solid resistance, Schulze gradually became convinced that segregation as a whole had to come to an end.[46] As Schulze wrote to one pastor, "The impression cannot escape me, that something is wrong somewhere in our Christianity if a Christian congregation...cannot welcome a fellow Christian...into its midst to hear the Gospel simply because the person in mind is of another race."[47]

The mid-to-late 1930s was a pivotal time for Andrew Schulze. Schulze had long considered black Americans to be his among his friends and neighbors, but he now began to see racial problems from a larger perspective. Besides the commitment that he had to his individual parishioners, Schulze now became concerned and committed to the idea of racial justice for all. Schulze began to look beyond his own parishioners and became concerned with the dilemma facing the synod and the church at large. As a prophet to the synod, Schulze called the church to be the Church, open to all irrespective of racial boundaries.[48]

But before Andrew Schulze really struggled against the church hierarchy, he struggled with himself. This was a struggle that was not fully

---

[45] Raymond Schulze, interview by author, 10 July 1999.

[46] Even during the beginning of the Montgomery Bus Boycott of 1955–1956, the first major event of the civil rights movement, organizers tried at first to compromise with segregation. Only after their compromise met continued resistance did the leaders of the Montgomery Bus Boycott push for full integration of Montgomery's buses.

[47] From correspondence between Andrew Schulze and Rev. J. M. Bailey in 1935. Quoted by Moellering, "The Missouri Synod and Social Problems," 274.

[48] Ralph Luther Moellering described Schulze's role as prophet to the synod. "The role of a prophet who feels constrained to pass judgment is never easy.... He sensitized calloused ecclesiastical consciences, and he paid the price in the ridicule and persecution that confronted him for many years. Ultimately though, his views were recognized as valid and adopted" (Moellering, "The Missouri Synod and Social Problems," 280).

resolved until the writing and publication of his first book, *My Neighbor of Another Color*, which first appeared in print in 1941. Schulze's oldest son, Paul, remembered this period of "storm and stress." Paul Schulze recalled that once on a streetcar ride, his father "compared his tests and trials to 'something of what Martin Luther' went through. As a youngster, I thought this was a little exaggerated at the time, but later I came to understand the immensity of his own inner struggles." Schulze identified with the pain of Luther's struggle. Schulze had to ask whether he could "imagine himself opposing the Church he had loved from infancy? Could he be right and the Church be wrong?"[49]

In 1935 John W. Behnken was elected president of the Missouri Synod and served in that office until 1962. John W. Behnken was the first American-born president of the Missouri Synod. He presided over the synod during a time of great growth in terms of membership and administrative bureaucracy.[50] Behnken was the great Americanizer of this German-American church, but on the race issue, he was not only American, but Texan.[51] Behnken consistently referred to his Texas roots as a means of explaining his position on racial issues. If Schulze was an example of an early integrationist, Behnken was an example of an early reactionary. As Schulze remembered, "During the crucial years that followed his first election, when race was an important element of the criteria by which the church was to be judged by people of understanding and good will, the president, who was re-elected eight times, was very slow in moving toward a viewpoint that is truly reflective of the Head of the church."[52]

---

[49] Paul Schulze to the author, 5 June 2000.

[50] For more on this dynamic period of the synod's history, see Thomas Coates and Erwin L. Lueker, ed., "Four Decades of Expansion," in *Moving Frontiers: Readings in the History of the Lutheran Church—Missouri Synod*, ed. Carl S. Meyer (St. Louis: Concordia Publishing House, 1964) 386–435.

[51] In the opening of John W. Behnken's autobiography, Behnken described the importance of his Texas upbringing. He mentioned the commencement speech he gave at his graduation from St. John's College in Winfield, Kansas: "Since I was the proud Southerner of the class, I chose 'Robert E. Lee' as my topic" (*This I Recall* [St. Louis: Concordia Publishing House, 1964] 16.

[52] Schulze, *Race against Time*, 45.

In the early 1920s, while Schulze was still a seminary student and assistant at Holy Trinity in Springfield, John Behnken already made a stand against integration. Holy Trinity's youth society came under the administration of the local branch of the Missouri Synod youth organization, the Walther League, named in honor of C. F. W. Walther. Behnken, then a pastor in Texas, wrote a letter of protest to the Executive Board of the International Walther League. Behnken wrote, "If further Negro societies will be received into the league, it will eventually mean the withdrawal of all Walther Leagues below the Mason and Dixon line…. As far as mission work among the Negroes is concerned, our Southern people try to do their part, but we know that it is absolutely impossible for us to sanction social equality."[53]

In 1936, shortly after John Behnken was elected president, he made very clear his position on integration. The biennial convention of the Synodical Conference in 1936 discussed the status of its two self-supporting black Lutheran congregations, St. Philips, St. Louis and St. Philips, Chicago. It was proposed that self-supporting congregations become a part of the synodical districts in which they were located. The proposal did not mean real integration at the parish level, rather it meant merely administrative integration. Behnken reminded the convention that he was from the South and stated that the proposal "will never do."[54] It took another ten years before a resolution was passed that allowed black Lutheran congregations to join their local synodical districts.

In the late 1930s, Andrew Schulze became increasingly active in his promotion of better race relations within the church. Schulze began "quiet and peaceful agitation on all fronts. All the while he remained a faithful and beloved pastor who identified himself unreservedly with the Negro cause and gained the uninhibited confidence and allegiance of his parishioners."[55] Though Schulze began walking a lonely path, he found support along the way. As he recalled in his memoirs, "In the dry and thirsty land of the thirties and early forties, my loneliness was seldom if ever spelled out. Those

---

[53] Ibid., 45. J. W. Behnken to the executive board of the International Walther League, 27 April 1922 (copy), Andrew Schulze Papers, CHI, St. Louis MO.

[54] Schulze, *Race against Time*, 42.

[55] Moellering, "The Missouri Synod and Social Problems," 270.

who at that time were speaking against racism in the world and ignorance in the church toward racism were indeed following a lonely path, and 'a cup of cold water' offered by some friend who understood was like the 'balm of Gilead.'"[56] Schulze mentioned some of the friends that supported him and his ministry in the last chapter of his memoirs, but his sons emphasized that it was his relationship with Jesus Christ that gave Schulze the strength to carry on. Schulze had a very active prayer life and even when he was attacked for his views, Schulze prayed for his enemies.[57]

There appeared to be no particular reason for Schulze's growing activism, but he did mention being inspired by his reading of Booker T. Washington's famous autobiography, *Up from Slavery*.[58] Schulze referred to Booker T. Washington's book in a letter he wrote to Edmund Seuel, the manager of the Missouri Synod's publishing agency, Concordia Publishing House (CPH). In Schulze's 1937 letter, he requested that Concordia Publishing House, located in a mixed neighborhood just south of downtown St. Louis, make an effort to employ black Lutherans.[59] A couple of weeks later Schulze received the response that "it was the unanimous opinion of our Board that it would be unwise to employ colored people in our offices or

---

[56] Schulze, *Race against Time*, 137.

[57] Raymond Schulze, interview by author, 10 July 1999, telephone; Herb Schulze, interview by author, 10 June 2000, telephone; Paul Schulze, interview by author, 14 June 2000, telephone.

[58] Andrew Schulze to Mr. E. Seuel, 23 August 1937 (copy), Andrew Schulze Papers, CHI, St. Louis MO. Schulze and those of his generation were not that far removed from the era of slavery. Some of Schulze's members were former slaves. Schulze served one member who had known the famous abolitionist John Brown. As Schulze remembered, "When I met Mrs. Bettie Washington in 1928 as I became the pastor of St. Philip's Church in St. Louis, she was about 80 years old. She told me that as a slave girl in Virginia, in the house of her master, she had on more than one occasion served John Brown, the great abolitionist, at table. If my memory serves me correctly, she told me her master cooperated with the Underground Railroad movement which had as its purpose smuggling slaves out of the South. It was in that capacity, according to Mrs. Washington, that her master had clandestinely acted as host to John Brown" (Schulze, *Race against Time*, 143).

[59] Andrew Schulze to Mr. E. Seuel, 23 August 1937 (copy), Andrew Schulze Papers, CHI, St. Louis MO.

in our workrooms, at least for the present."[60] Schulze replied that he hoped to make his case personally before the board and continued to remind Concordia Publishing House of his request.[61]

Schulze was not only concerned with the treatment of black Lutheran laypeople, but was also concerned with the treatment of black Lutheran pastors. Schulze had a close enough relationship with the Rev. Dr. Marmaduke Carter so that Carter felt comfortable in confiding in him. In the North, Carter had "charmed Midwest congregations with German sermons and hustled his own support to form the first LCMS congregation headed by a black clergyman."[62] Yet Carter was not spared from discrimination. Carter was offended with how many people in the Missouri Synod communicated with him. Carter objected "to receiving mail with the 'superfluous' identification 'colored' in brackets after his name. Despite his advanced academic training...he [was] convinced that some of the Lutheran clergy think of him 'as a shoe shine boy.' He [resented] their efforts to address him in Negro dialect."[63]

Andrew Schulze also became very close to another black Lutheran pastor, Clemonce Sabourin. In 1944 Sabourin became pastor of Mount Zion Lutheran Church in Harlem. Over the years, "Clem" became one of Andrew Schulze's most important friends and partners in promoting racial integration in the church. Schulze connected with Sabourin after he raised the issue of salaries at the meeting of the General Conference in 1938 at Greensboro, North Carolina.[64] The Synodical Conference had a vastly

---

[60] Edmund Seuel to Rev. Andrew Schulze, 17 September 1937, Andrew Schulze Papers, CHI, St. Louis MO.

[61] In 1939 Schulze sent Seuel clippings from a black newspaper that featured a commercial organization that hired a black executive. Andrew Schulze to Mr. E. Seuel, 3 July 1939 (copy), Andrew Schulze Papers, CHI, St. Louis MO.

[62] Richard Luecke, "Themes of Lutheran Urban Ministry" in *Churches, Cities, and Human Community: Urban Ministry in the United States, 1945–1985*, ed. Clifford J. Green (Grand Rapids: William B. Eerdmans Publishing Company, 1996) 139.

[63] Moellering, "The Missouri Synod and Social Problems," 263.

[64] Clemonce Sabourin, interview by Karl E. Lutze, 21–22 April 1983, Oral History Collection from the Archives of Cooperative Lutheranism, Evangelical Lutheran Church in America (ELCA) Archives, Chicago IL, 50–56. Sabourin recalled, "Andrew Schulze and I became bosom buddies and worked forever after that. But up to that time he was the only white man I knew in the church...who also

different pay scale for its white and black pastors. Schulze became convinced that "this salary differential was a major reason why our work among Negroes had been discouragingly slow in developing."[65] No doubt this was related to the Synodical Conference's difficulties in recruiting and retaining black pastors during this period.[66]

In the spring of 1938, Andrew Schulze received a letter from Albert J. C. Moeller of St. Paul's College in Concordia, Missouri. Moeller sent out a letter to pastors requesting that they encourage Lutheran students to attend Lutheran institutions of higher education such as St. Paul's College. Schulze wrote back and asked if St. Paul's College would enroll some students whom he could recommend from his black congregation in St. Louis.[67] The board of St. Paul's College was uncertain how to handle this question and sought the opinion of the Board of Directors of the Missouri Synod. During its 18 May 1938 meeting, the synod's board of directors resolved to continue a policy of segregated schools for its black high school, college, and seminary students. The board's decision was "an endorsement of the answer which President Behnken had already given in the matter."[68]

Schulze wrote to the Board of Directors of the Missouri Synod and stated that he believed the resolution to be "a blanket discrimination against our workers, our work, and our Negro Christians regardless of locality and

---

identified the race question as being the crux of all of our problems and a hindrance to all of our mission work" (Sabourin, interview by Lutze, 56).

[65] Schulze, *Race against Time*, 64.

[66] Jeff G. Johnson, *Black Christians: The Untold Lutheran Story* (St. Louis: Concordia Publishing House, 1991).

[67] Andrew Schulze to Rev. Prof. Albert J. C. Moeller, 12 May 1938 (copy), Andrew Schulze Papers, CHI, St. Louis MO.

[68] Resolution 380518-AA, Board of Directors Meeting Minutes, 18 May 1938, CHI, St. Louis MO. Nothing was stated about the synod's rather extensive system of parochial grade schools. This was probably due to the fact that they were under local control and to the fact that racial mixing was less controversial among children. As Pastor F. J. Seltz of St. Stephanus Lutheran in St. Paul, Minnesota wrote to Andrew Schulze in May 1939, "To have colored children enrolled in Sunday School or day school, up north here works out well, but it becomes a real problem when these people grow into man or womanhood" (Andrew Schulze Papers, CHI).

circumstances."[69] He also sent a copy of the letter to Rev. L. A. Wisler, the Executive Secretary of Colored Missions for the Synodical Conference. This correspondence must have raised some concern, as shortly thereafter, Schulze was asked to provide the Rev. Wisler with a statement of his views on race relations. Schulze's response to the Rev. Wisler marked Schulze's clearest expression to that date of his commitment to the cause of racial justice within the church.

Schulze's letter to Wisler was written ten years before President Truman ordered the military to desegregate, sixteen years before the Supreme Court ruled against segregation in *Brown v. Board of Education*, and twenty-five years before the plight of Southern blacks was dramatized in Birmingham, Alabama. Schulze's views had shown that he had moved ahead of mainstream American views on race. Schulze certainly had more contact with blacks than most whites because of his ministry at black congregations. However, Schulze emerged as someone distinct in his attitudes even compared to other white pastors of black congregations.

At the heart of Schulze's letter to Wisler, he wrote with the conviction that "the attitude held generally toward the Negro has its origin to a great extent in a wrong interpretation and application of Genesis 9. To me it seems that this very attitude assumed by our Lutheran pastors and congregations is altogether contrary to Christian universalism."[70] Schulze's reference to Genesis 9 was reference to the Curse of Ham, an Old Testament account that had long been used to justify racial prejudice. In Genesis 9:25, Noah cursed the descendants of Ham, saying, "The lowest of slaves will he be to his brothers." These verses were often used to explain and justify the inferior status of black Americans.

Martin Luther's interpretation of Genesis 9 did not have any racist overtones, but later Lutheran theologians did embrace a racist interpretation. Even some African-American Christians internalized this

---

[69] Andrew Schulze to Rev. M. F. Kretzmann, Secretary of the Board of Directors of the Missouri Synod, 25 May 1938, Andrew Schulze Papers, CHI, St. Louis MO.

[70] Andrew Schulze to L. A. Wisler, 27 May 1938 (copy), Andrew Schulze Papers, CHI, St. Louis MO.

view.[71] The great black Lutheran preacher, the Rev. Dr. Marmaduke Carter, believed in the Curse of Ham.[72] It was during this period that Schulze became convinced of the need for a new examination of race relations based on the New Testament.[73] Andrew Schulze not only criticized old racial concepts, but was interested in developing a new theological outlook that embraced the ideal of Christian equality.

In the fall of 1938, Schulze presented a paper on the church and the race issue to a pastoral conference of the Western District of the Evangelical Lutheran Synod of Missouri, Ohio, and Other States.[74] There were about 100 pastors in attendance, including a few faculty members from Concordia Seminary, St. Louis. The presentation generated a great deal of discussion and Schulze was surprised that there was as much positive reaction as there was negative reaction. While seminary professor Dr. Theodore Laetsch spoke out in opposition to Schulze's position, seminary professor Dr. Alfred M. Rehwinkel spoke in praise of Schulze's position. During the preceding years, various individuals in the church had encouraged Schulze to publish his views on race. However, it was the response to this conference presentation that finalized Schulze's decision to write his first book, *My Neighbor of Another Color.*[75]

Over the next couple of years, Schulze devoted considerable time and effort to writing and publishing his first book. All the while, he received considerable assistance from his wife, Margaret. Throughout his career, Margaret not only provided steadfast support but also served as his personal

---

[71] Robert E. Hood, *Begrimed and Black: Christian Traditions on Black and Blackness* (Philadelphia: Fortress Press, 1994) 129–30, 180.

[72] M. N. Carter, "Why Negro Lutherans Should Joyfully Participate in the Centennial Celebration of the Saxon Immigration," in Proceedings of the Fifth General Conference of Lutheran Negro Mission Workers, 25 to 28 August 1938, Clemonce Sabourin Papers, in the possession of William Carr, 26.

[73] Andrew Schulze and O. P. Kretzmann, correspondence, June 1938, Andrew Schulze Papers, CHI, St. Louis MO.

[74] In the 1850s, it was resolved to divide the synod into four administrative districts: Northern, Central, Eastern, and Western. From these original four districts grew the current thirty-five districts of the Lutheran Church—Missouri Synod. See August R. Suelflow, *The Heart of Missouri: A History of the Western District of the LCMS, 1854–1954* (St. Louis: Concordia Publishing House, 1954).

[75] Schulze, *Race against Time*, 93–94.

secretary. Margaret took dictation, typed, and helped edit much of Andrew's work. Margaret's assistance was essential to Andrew's ability to keep up with parish duties, wide correspondence, and publications of his writings. Though she remained in the background, it is difficult to picture Schulze's career without her.[76] A colleague at Valparaiso remembered that Schulze was not particularly gifted at organization. As John Strietelmeier explained, "It's difficult to be a bookkeeper when you are a prophet."[77] Margaret was the one who really helped to keep Andrew organized.

In the meantime, Schulze continued to be concerned about segregation in Missouri Synod schools. In 1940 Schulze wrote a stronger letter to the Missouri Synod's board of directors asking them to change their position on their policy of segregated schools. Schulze explained that the 1938 resolution had been discussed at a recent meeting of the Northern Pastoral Conference and met with unanimous disapproval. Schulze concluded, "Were it to be known generally among our Negro Christians that this resolution stands on the minutes of the Board of Directors of the Missouri Synod, their confidence would be shattered. And what is more, were the resolution to remain, our Church would never grow…among Negroes."[78]

Schulze's letter to the board of directors also included a theme that Schulze continued to stress over the next decades of his career. He wrote, "It seems to me that this resolution puts the Church behind the world in its attitude toward other races." Schulze explained that most state schools located in the North accepted black students and offered examples of other religious schools that accepted black students. Schulze also discussed the 1939 Gaines case in which the Supreme Court ruled that the law school of the University of Missouri must admit black students or provide a school of equal sature within state borders. The idea of "separate but equal" was still the dominant idea of the day. Schulze received the response that since the

---

[76] Raymond Schulze referred to his father as a "spiritual genius" and his mother as a "practical genius." Interview with Raymond Schulze, 10 July 1999.

[77] John Strietelmeier, interview by author, 8 February 2000.

[78] Andrew Schulze to the board of directors of the Missouri Synod, 29 March 1940 (copy), Andrew Schulze Papers, CHI, St. Louis MO.

Synodical Conference provided educational facilities for "colored" students, it therefore did not consider its policy to be "unfair discrimination."[79]

Segregation was fast becoming a major issue in the courts. The National Association for the Advancement of Colored People was active during this period, building legal groundwork that culminated in their 1954 victory in *Brown v. Board of Education*, which declared that segregation was inherently unequal. A growing number of individuals and organizations were becoming committed to the ideal of racial equality in the 1930s and 1940s. Despite the overwhelming nature of racism in America, a few prominent individuals were becoming more and more concerned about the need for improved race relations. In the late 1930s, the first lady, Eleanor Roosevelt, made symbolic gestures of support to the African-American community. In one instance in 1939, after the Daughters of the American Revolution refused to let the renowned black opera singer Marian Anderson perform in their auditorium, Roosevelt gave up her membership in the organization and made arrangements for Anderson to sing at a concert at the Lincoln Memorial.[80]

In his correspondence, Andrew Schulze repeatedly rejected the idea that he was "ahead of his times." In the late 1930s and 1940s, there were a growing minority of individuals in American society who developed sensitivities to racial matters and who understood that racial issues needed to be put on the public agenda. Why Schulze measured himself against this minority rather than majority culture is part of what made him unique. As Ralph Luther Moellering described Schulze, "This humble parish pastor read the signs of the times more accurately than most of his Missouri Synod 'superiors.' The 'radical' opinions he voiced in the Thirties and early Forties would be regarded as commonplace and mild by the early Sixties."[81] Schulze

---

[79] M. F. Kretzmann to Andrew Schulze, 19 April 1940. Andrew Schulze Papers, CHI, St. Louis MO.

[80] In 1960, when Marian Anderson was at the climax of her singing career she gave a special performance and interview for the Lutheran radio program, "The Lutheran Hour." See Oswald C. J. Hoffmann, *What More Is There To Say But Amen: The Autobiography of Dr. Oswald C. J. Hoffmann*, as told to Ronald J. Schlegel (St. Louis: Concordia Publishing House, 1996) 183–86.

[81] Moellering, "The Missouri Synod and Social Problems," 274.

repeatedly challenged the church to be ahead of society when it came to race relations.

Andrew and Margaret wanted their sons to attend Lutheran schools, but they also began to choose schools based on their position with regards to integration. The Schulze boys attended Lutheran grade school as the Schulzes were not then aware of the fact that state segregation laws could not be applied to parochial schools.[82] By the time that the Schulzes' youngest son began attending high school in 1946, a Lutheran high school had opened in St. Louis. When the high school refused to admit a black student from St. Philip's, the Schulzes sent their son to segregated public high school in protest. Andrew Schulze viewed segregation in a Christian school as worse than segregation in a secular school.[83] The Schulzes decided on colleges with race relations in mind. Paul attended Concordia College, Milwaukee as its president Leroy Rincker assured the Schulzes that he would not comply with the 1938 board of directors resolution if black students wished to attend Concordia Milwaukee.[84]

During these years, Schulze wrote to influential persons in the Missouri Synod, such as radio preacher and seminary professor Walter A. Maier and the new president of Valparaiso University, O. P. Kretzmann. Schulze wanted get them involved in making the church more sensitive to racial matters. Over the next couple of decades, O. P. Kretzmann emerged as one of Schulze's strongest supporters. The mission-minded Walter A. Maier was open to issues of racial concern and became somewhat involved with racial matters. However, he was not always a consistent spokesperson when it came to race.[85] Nonetheless, Schulze had a good relationship with Maier. In Schulze's letter to Maier, Schulze mentioned the temptation to stop his lobbying efforts. As he explained, "Were I to lend myself to my desire for ease and quiet and peace, I would 'shut up' as I have been tempted

---

[82] Schulze, *Race against Time*, 31.

[83] Raymond Schulze, interview by author, 10 July 2000.

[84] Schulze, *Race against Time*, 19. Herb and Ray Schulze attended Concordia College, Portland. The president of Concordia Portland, Thomas Coates, was also interested in improved race relations in the church and later was actively involved with the Lutheran Human Relations Association of America.

[85] Ibid., 138–39.

to do a thousand times; but despite the many complexes that lay hold of me, I still believe that I must speak out."[86]

When Schulze set out to publish his views on race relations in the church, he found only two other books that dealt exclusively with the subject. As he described in the introduction to his book, Trevor Bowen's *Divine White Right* approached race relations from a social gospel perspective, and Francis J. Gilligan's *The Morality of the Color Line* approached race relations from a Roman Catholic perspective. Schulze became determined to be a voice for an evangelical Christian perspective on race relations. Schulze organized the St. Louis Lutheran Society for Better Race Relations in 1943 with a similar outlook. He recognized that there were leaders in liberal and Catholic circles on the issue of race and now he wanted to have an interracial organization for evangelical Christians.[87]

Schulze's message in *My Neighbor of Another Color* was to show that there were discrepancies in the church's handling of race relations when measured against the gospel message of the New Testament. While the New Testament parable of the Good Samaritan (Luke 10:25–37) was only briefly mentioned in *My Neighbor of Another Color*, it was the obvious inspiration for the title. It was a title laden with theological meaning. The parable of the Good Samaritan demonstrated that Christians have neighbors across national and racial boundaries. To friends and acquaintances, Schulze said with pride that he was a "neighbor-lover"; that was his response to the epithet, "nigger-lover."[88]

My Neighbor of Another Color criticized the attitude and behavior of Christians who wanted "to bring the colored into the Church of Christ...but

---

[86] Andrew Schulze to President O. P. Kretzmann, 30 January 1941 (copy) Andrew Schulze Papers, CHI, St. Louis MO; Andrew Schulze to Professor Walter A. Maier, 26 March 1941 (copy), Andrew Schulze Papers, CHI, St. Louis MO.

[87] The St. Louis Lutheran Society for Better Race Relations recognized that there were leaders working to improve race relations among the academic community, modernistic churches, the Roman Catholic Church, and atheistic communists. The St. Louis Lutheran Society for Better Race Relations was dedicated to a discussion of race relations from an evangelical Christian point of view. [Andrew Schulze], "Resolution Relative to a Christian Racial Understanding," *Focus: Lutheran Race Relations Bulletin* 2 (April 1946): 2–4.

[88] Will Herzfeld, interview by author, 26 January 2000.

not too close."[89] As Schulze pointed out, while the church was not opposed "to bringing Christianity to the Negro, it is opposed to the social contact which the bringing of the Gospel to the Negro often implies." Schulze wrote based on his observations within his own Lutheran synod. While white Lutherans were willing to pray and pay for black missions, they generally did not welcome black Lutherans into mutual fellowship. This was true on a structural and administrative level, as black missions and congregations were not a part of synodical districts. However, Schulze gave examples of how this affected individual black Lutherans. Some were denied invitations to worship and others were given communion only under restricted circumstances, such as partaking of the Lord's Supper after all of the white communicants had.[90]

Schulze stressed the fact that Christians needed to have a lowly spirit, noting that Christ was accused of "savoring the gutter." Schulze highlighted the example of St. Peter who broke Jewish custom to associate with the Gentile Cornelius (Acts 10:23-48). He quoted an essay by former St. Louis Seminary professor, W. H. T. Dau, that described the account of Peter and Cornelius as rejecting "pharisaism" and "all exclusiveness which looks down on classes and races." In a footnote, he quoted James Weldon Johnson's *The Autobiography of an Ex-Coloured Man*, that stated, "Let us grant for the sake of argument that the Negro is inferior in every respect to the white man; that fact only increases our moral responsibility in regard to our action toward him."[91]

My Neighbor of Another Color expressed concerns that Schulze expanded upon over the next three decades of his career. Schulze stated his belief that the church should be in the forefront of racial change. The same attitude was shown years later in his decision to name the newsletter of the Lutheran Human Relations Association, "The Vanguard." Another concern was that

---

[89] This was a quotation from M. L. Kretzmann, a missionary to India. Quoted by Andrew Schulze, *My Neighbor of Another Color* (St. Louis MO: Andrew Schulze, 1941) 29. Schulze pointed out in his 1938 letter to Wisler, "We never have studied race relations as they affect the Church, unless the difficulties in India be considered a case in point" (Andrew Schulze to L. A. Wisler, 27 May 1938 [copy], Andrew Schulze Papers, CHI, St. Louis MO).

[90] Schulze, *My Neighbor of Another Color*, 15, 4–7.

[91] Ibid., 23, 15–16, 118.

racial discrimination in America was impeding the Christian mission effort worldwide. Just as American statesmen realized the foreign impact of domestic racism during World War II and the Cold War, American churchmen, such as Schulze, realized the negative impact of domestic racism in foreign missions. Finally Schulze stressed the power of the Gospel. He believed that "a Church of the pure and unadulterated Gospel has a perfect means for a perfect relation between the races."[92]

Schulze first tried to publish his book through Concordia Publishing House, the official publishing agency of the Missouri Synod. Schulze met with the response that "since the subject matter treated in your manuscript is in some circles controversial, we deem it unwise for Concordia Publishing House to publish it. This does not mean that the subject should not be discussed." Schulze tried to get his book published elsewhere, but in the end, it was self-published. He borrowed money from members of his congregation to pay the printing costs.[93] *My Neighbor of Another Color* was a small book of 147 pages. It was not a book that had great literary merit. However, Schulze did get his message across as was apparent in the book's reception.

The first printing of 2,000 copies of *My Neighbor of Another Color* began to be circulated by Schulze and his colleagues in the last months of 1941. The first responses that Schulze received were generally positive. The book was discussed in a couple of St. Louis's black newspapers.[94] Otto H. Theiss, the executive secretary of the Walther League (1941–1952), the synod's youth organization, was the first to review the book. Theiss's complimentary review appeared in the December 1941 edition of *The Cresset*, then a publication of the Walther League.[95] This warm reception led to an arrangement by which the Walther League advertised and sold copies of the book. Several of Schulze's early supporters were associated with the Walther

---

[92] Ibid., chapter 11, chapter 6, 71.

[93] Schulze, *Race against Time*, 95.

[94] Newspaper clippings, Andrew Schulze Papers, CHI, St. Louis MO.

[95] For a history of the Walther League, see John Pahl, *Hopes and Dreams of All: The International Walther League and Lutheran Youth in American Culture, 1893–1993* (Chicago: Wheat Ridge Ministries, 1993). *The Cresset* was a publication of the Walther League from 1937 to 1956 and then it became a publication of Valparaiso University.

League or were among the synod's military chaplains. Just as American youth and the American military generally had better records on race than the general public, similar tendencies existed in the church.

Over the next few months, individuals worked through Christian publications, African-American publications, and private contacts to help *My Neighbor of Another Color* receive increased attention. *The Christian Century*, a leading Protestant magazine, gave a brief review of the book. It stated that the author "discusses many aspects of race relations, always with intelligence and a deeply Christian spirit."[96] H. R. Niebuhr, professor of Christian Ethics at Yale University, received a copy of the book from Clemonce Sabourin, an alumnus of the black Lutheran seminary in Greensboro, North Carolina. Niebuhr replied that "the idea of the book is excellent, the spirit of the author admirable, the cause he pleads is thoroughly Christian." However, he also noted that the book was "somewhat limited by the fact that he envisions the problem as it presents itself to his denomination. All white Protestant denominations have the same problems."[97] But the fact that Schulze's book did receive wider attention was remarkable considering that Schulze came from a rather conservative and insular church body. It reflected that race relations was a concern shared across some of the strictest denominational lines.

Despite the book's positive reception in wider circles, it was not well received by official "Missouri." According to word-of-mouth sources, President Behnken described the book as "vicious." The book never received any mention in *The Lutheran Witness*, the official publication of the synod. The editor, Theodore Graebner, consciously omitted any mention of the book.[98] St. Louis Seminary professor, Theodore Engelder, who had worked with Andrew in Springfield, gave the book a mixed review in the *Concordia Theological Monthly*. Engelder believed that the book was written

---

[96] "Books Received," *The Christian Century* 59 (18 February 1942): 219.

[97] H. R. Niebuhr to Clemonce Sabourin, 2 February 1942, Andrew Schulze Papers, CHI, St. Louis MO. Denominational differences were a concern of H. R. Niebuhr; he wrote *The Social Sources of Denominations* in 1929.

[98] Schulze, *Race against Time*, 98.

out of genuine concern for "our colored brethren…even though we do not agree with all of its conclusions and judgments."[99]

But the greatest criticism of *My Neighbor of Another Color* came from the Missionary Board of the Synodical Conference. The fact that Schulze was now pastor of a self-supporting congregation rather than a missionary pastor assigned by the Synodical Conference did give him a measure of independence. But Schulze was still deeply involved with the work of the Synodical Conference. As chairman of the General Conference, he was a spokesperson for the interests of those involved with black ministry. Schulze did have an interest in the work of the Synodical Conference and was deeply hurt by the criticism of the Missionary Board.

In August 1942 St. Louis Seminary professor and Missionary Board member, John Theodore Mueller wrote "A Review and Opinion on My Neighbor of Another Color" based on a request from the Missionary Board. J. T. Mueller was one of the Missouri Synod's most active theologians in the first half of the twentieth century. He was fluent in both German and English and was able to assist the synod's transition from German to English. He was part of a group of theologians who "continued to stress strongly the biblical character of Lutheran confessionalism and to resist unequivocally many of the contemporary trends in theology."[100] He wrote many books and articles but was best known for *Christian Dogmatics*, a condensed version of Franz Pieper's three-volume work by the same title. He was respected in the Missouri Synod for his orthodox theology, but he could be considered more of a popular theologian within the Missouri Synod. His work did not reveal theological depth and instead tended to simplify more complex theological ideas.

---

[99] Engelder attempted to take a middle position. "It means…a white congregation will, as occasion demands it, have a colored pastor in the pulpit of its church as a guest preacher and, if the need arises, have a colored Christian receive the Holy Communion at its altar. It does not mean that the Church must establish mixed congregations. The Lord of the Church has left the ordering of this matter to the wisdom of His Christians. He has given no regulation either forbidding or demanding it" (Theodore Engelder, *Concordia Theological Monthly* 13 [April 1942]: 318).

[100] Charles P. Arand, *Testing the Boundaries: Windows to Lutheran Identity* (St. Louis: Concordia Publishing House, 1995) 207.

The Missionary Board sent Mueller's "A Review and Opinion on My Neighbor of Another Color" to select individuals. Andrew Schulze received a copy, but copies were not made available for certain individuals such as those at Immanuel Lutheran College, the black Lutheran seminary of the Synodical Conference.[101] Both the president of Immanuel, Henry Nau, and one of the seminary's graduates, Clemonce Sabourin, requested copies of Mueller's review and were initially denied.[102]

The first complaint that Mueller made in his review was that Schulze wrote his book without the consent of the Missionary Board. Mueller even criticized the fact that St. Louis Seminary professor A. M. Rehwinkel wrote the foreword to Schulze's book rather than a member of the mission board.[103] Schulze was, on the one hand, taken by surprise at this criticism. As he explained in some of his correspondence, the mission board never voiced any kind of reaction to his 1938 statement on race relations that he sent to the executive secretary of the mission board, the Rev. Wisler. Schulze also stated that he had been encouraged by the response of Concordia Publishing House (CPH) to his publishing request. While CPH had voiced some concern about his manuscript, they also said that race relations was a topic

---

[101] Immanuel Lutheran College operated from 1903–1961. For more on Immanuel Lutheran College, see Richard Dickinson, *Roses and Thorns: The Centennial Edition of Black Lutheran Mission and Ministry in The Lutheran Church—Missouri Synod* (St. Louis: Concordia Publishing House, 1977).

[102] H. Nau to Andrew Schulze, 21 November 1942. Letter from Clemonce Sabourin to Andrew Schulze, 31 October 1942. Sabourin wrote that Wisler response's stated, "Dr. Mueller's review of My Neighbor of Another Color, thus far, has appeared in limited numbers and mailing to date has been per instructions. In due time your request will be granted" (Andrew Schulze Papers, CHI). Clemonce Sabourin did eventually get a chance to examine a copy of Mueller's review. While many of Schulze's colleagues were upset by Mueller's review, Sabourin also saw it as "a beam of light." As Sabourin pointed out years later, "In the course of [Mueller's] discussion of Andy's book, he did admit that Andy was right on a discussion of the curse of Ham.... I grabbed that one little statement out of the whole thing...and used that as...a beam of light that might show us the way to the future" (Clemonce Sabourin, Oral History Collection, 4).

[103] John Theodore Mueller, "A Review and Opinion on My Neighbor of Another Color," August 1942, Andrew Schulze Papers, CHI, St. Louis MO, 1. "A Review" can also be found in the John Theodore Mueller Papers, CHI.

that needed to be discussed. But, on the other hand, Schulze suspected, based on his experiences, that the mission board held other views. As he concluded, "now it is manifest."[104]

Mueller's review objected to the sources Schulze used in his book. Mueller complained about Schulze's "constant quotation from unchristian Modernist and fanatic Negro writers, as if these were setting forth the Christian truth underlying the solution of the race problem."[105] But Mueller also complained that Schulze quoted synodical writers such as C. F. W. Walther and W. H. T. Dau. Mueller stated, "Fairness demands that quotations should not be applied to conditions which the writers did not have in mind."[106] As a critic of Mueller pointed out, if this were true, all of J. T. Mueller's theological works and sermon helps might as well be thrown away.[107] Mueller also made the very serious accusation that Schulze "twisted" Scripture. As Schulze wrote in a letter, he should have been defrocked if everything Mueller wrote was true.[108]

Mueller's main criticism of *My Neighbor of Another Color* was that it promoted the social gospel. Mueller accused Schulze of confusing social equality with spiritual equality. He particularly objected to Schulze's cautious approval of interracial marriage. Mueller objected to the idea that "Christian love must manifest itself in full social equality and miscegenation."[109] He viewed racial segregation as *adiaphoron*, a matter of theological indifference. Mueller concluded, "As soon as a church…tampers with the social and economic conditions prevailing in the state, it will soon get itself into serious trouble and in the end it will neglect the spiritual Gospel of Christ, which to proclaim is its crown and glory."[110]

---

[104] Andrew Schulze to H. Nau, 25 November 1942 (copy), Andrew Schulze Papers, CHI, St. Louis MO.

[105] Mueller, "A Review and Opinion on My Neighbor of Another Color," 5

[106] Ibid., 3–4.

[107] "An Examination of Dr. J. T. Mueller's 'A Review and Opinion on Pastor's Schulze Book, *My Neighbor of Another Color*,'" Andrew Schulze Papers, CHI, St. Louis MO.

[108] Andrew Schulze to Rev. Albert F. Jess, 10 December 1942 (copy), Andrew Schulze Papers, CHI, St. Louis MO.

[109] Mueller, "A Review and Opinion on My Neighbor of Another Color," 12

[110] Ibid., 12.

J. T. Mueller was not alone in his views. Mueller's views about social action reflected the prevailing attitudes in the Missouri Synod. G. M. Kramer, a white Lutheran pastor and leader of black Lutheran ministry in the South, also spoke out against social change. He gave a negative review of Schulze's book at a pastoral conference in New Orleans.[111] Kramer's views on black ministry were featured in a 1940 article in the *Lutheran Witness*. Kramer recalled when there were external pressures to do no mission work among black Americans. But he concluded, "Now danger looms from another direction. Now comes the invitation 'to join' in general Negro uplift work. Race betterment associations, urban leagues, interracial committees, bid for our support. It is tempting to join, for without a doubt some of these agencies accomplish much good. But it is not the work that the Lord has assigned to His Church.... Our work must remain on the spiritual plane only and always."[112]

Though this was a difficult period for Schulze, a few colleagues wrote letters of encouragement to Schulze after reading Mueller's review. Paul Amt, a pastor in Fort Wayne, Indiana, who was also an early advocate of integration in the church, wrote to Schulze with a comparison to Martin Luther. Amt wrote, "I suppose you've been doing some Reformation ruminating these days.... Have the courage to stand your ground, like Luther at Worms, wherever you have the opportunity. You can be certain that God's Word is on your side. Hence the cause cannot possibly suffer defeat."[113] Schulze's *My Neighbor of Another Color* can be viewed as the "Ninety-Five Theses" of his career. The publication of *My Neighbor of Another Color* was the defining event of his ministry that henceforth boldly committed him to racial reform in the church.

After Schulze received J. T. Mueller's review, he tried twice to meet with him. Mueller declined Schulze's invitations. But months later, in the fall of 1943, Mueller met with Schulze and apologized. Mueller said that he was withdrawing his review and that he was now in agreement with

---

[111] Schulze, *Race against Time*, 98–99.

[112] G. M. Kramer, "Our Negro Mission—a Doxology," *The Lutheran Witness* 59 (23 July 1940): 262–63.

[113] Paul Amt to Andrew Schulze, 4 November 1942, Andrew Schulze Papers, CHI, St. Louis MO.

Schulze.[114] But around the same time, the *Concordia Theological Monthly* published "The Spiritual, Not the Social Gospel in the Church (With Special Reference to the Race Relations Problem)" by J. T. Mueller. The article included no mention of Schulze or his book, but Mueller repeated many of the arguments that he made in his review of Schulze's book.[115] It seems that Mueller regretted the personal attacks that he made against Schulze but still retained a traditional Lutheran suspicion of anything resembling social action by the church.

Lutherans had a long history of being wary of political and social action. They were little influenced by the late nineteenth-century Social Gospel Movement. The Social Gospel Movement developed in response to social problems that arose with the industrialization and urbanization of America.[116] At the time, Lutheranism had a primarily rural base and was further isolated by its immigrant character. But the main reasons for Lutheranism's distance from the Social Gospel Movement were theological. Many of those who advocated for the social gospel were liberal in terms of their theology. As Fred W Meuser explained in *The Lutherans in North America*, "Nowhere in Lutheranism was there any inclination to substitute sociology for theology or to accept social progress in lieu of spiritual change. Lutherans recoiled instinctively from the secularization of Christianity by the more extreme advocates of social Christianity.... Many, fearing for the integrity of the Christian faith, even doubted that social matters were a

---

[114] Schulze, *Race against Time*, 100–101.

[115] John Theodore Mueller, "The Spiritual, Not the Social Gospel in the Church (With Special Reference to the Race Relations Problem)," *Concordia Theological Monthly* 14 (October 1943): 682–93. Also see John Theodore Mueller, "Orthodoxy, Too, Has Its Social Gospel," in the Theological Observer of the *Concordia Theological Monthly* 15 (June 1944): 420–22. Mueller's title quoted an article published in *Christian Century*. Despite the title, Mueller maintained that the "'social gospel' is no gospel at all. It has nothing to do with the real Gospel. In fact, it is the Modernist substitute for the Christian Gospel."

[116] See Robert T. Handy, ed., *The Social Gospel in America* (New York: Oxford University Press, 1966); Aaron I. Abell, *The Urban Impact on American Protestantism, 1865–1900* (Cambridge: Harvard University Press, 1943); and Henry F. May, *Protestant Churches and Industrial America* (New York: Harper & Bros., 1949).

legitimate Christian concern."[117] Social gospelers were concerned with the corruption of society while Lutherans remained concerned with the corruption of individual human hearts.

Lutherans did develop a fairly large network of social service agencies, but these were often directed at taking care of the needy within their own circles. As Eugene Fevold explained, "Traditionally the Lutheran church has manifested social concern in its inner mission activity, concentrating on the alleviation of distress and the care of the ill, the poor, orphans, the aged, and the like."[118] But these traditional methods of social outreach were different from the social activism of other Christians. Many Lutherans believed that the church should not be so focused on the temporal realm and remain concentrated on things eternal. This question over the appropriate role of the church in society was not limited to Lutherans, but was debated by various Christian denominations, both black and white. But Lutherans were especially cautious with regard to becoming involved in social action. However, during the middle decades of the twentieth century, social action became less controversial among Lutherans, and Andrew Schulze came to embrace it fully.

Andrew Schulze was part of an awakening Lutheran social consciousness that was emerging in the middle decades of the twentieth century. Lutheran attitudes toward social action began to change during the

---

[117] Fred W. Meuser, "Facing the Twentieth Century, 1900–1930," in *The Lutherans in North America*, rev. ed., ed. E. Clifford Nelson (Philadelphia: Fortress Press, 1980) 386.

[118] Eugene Fevold, "Coming of Age, 1875–1900" in *The Lutherans in North America*, rev. ed., ed. E. Clifford Nelson (Philadelphia: Fortress Press, 1980) 355. Also see F. Dean Lueking, *A Century of Caring, 1868–1968: The Welfare Ministry among Missouri Synod Lutherans* (St. Louis: The Board of Social Ministry of The Lutheran Church—Missouri Synod, 1968). Walter Rauschenbusch, one of the foremost advocates of the Social Gospel Movement, was particularly critical of Lutherans. See R. L. Moellering, "Rauschenbusch in Retrospect," *Concordia Theological Monthly* 27 (August 1956): 613–33. "Rauschenbusch observed in 1912 that the Lutherans maintained many excellent charities, but revealed no interest in social progress generally" (Norman A. Graebner, "Lutherans and Politics" in *The Lutheran Church in North American Life*, ed. John E. Groh and Robert H. Smith [St. Louis: Clayton Publishing House, 1979] 20).

decade of the Great Depression.[119] As Christa Klein concluded, "Further enticement for Lutherans to formulate their own social ethic came with Hitler's rise to power and the advent of World War II, Protestant Neo-Orthodoxy, the new scholarship in Luther's thought, and the civil rights movement."[120] But at the time Schulze published *My Neighbor of Another Color*, Schulze was still cautious on the issue of social action. He pointed out to critics that he was not interested in changing society, but in changing the church.[121]

While change within the church remained Schulze's lifelong priority, he became much more supportive of efforts to change society. In his 1972 memoirs, Schulze stated that he now was embarrassed by his first book. As he concluded, "Though the book recognized many of the racial injustices of our society and called upon the church to remove the color bar present in the church itself, it did not in a direct manner see it to be the church's responsibility to lead the way in working toward the elimination of racial injustices outside the fellowship of the church, that is, in society in general."[122]

However, *My Neighbor of Another Color* did make a substantial impact on attitudes about race relations among Lutherans in America. The controversy that surrounded Schulze's first book generated increased attention for Schulze and for the racial issue. There was another printing of the book in 1944. *My Neighbor of Another Color* became the topic of discussion at many pastoral conferences. Schulze received many letters

---

[119] See Lloyd Svendsbye's "The History of a Developing Social Responsibility among Lutherans in America from 1930 to 1960, With Reference to the American Lutheran Church, the Augustana Lutheran Church, the Evangelical Lutheran Church, and the United Lutheran Church in America" (Th.D. diss., Union Theological Seminary, 1966). Also see John E. Groh and Robert H. Smith, eds., *The Lutheran Church in North American Life* (St. Louis: Clayton Publishing House, 1979).

[120] Christa R. Klein, "Lutheranism," in *The Encyclopedia of American Religious Experience: Studies of Traditions and Movements*, ed. Charles H. Lippy and Peter W. Williams (New York: Scribner, 1988) 448. Also see Christa R. Klein, with Christian D. von Dehsen, *Politics and Policy: The Genesis and Theology of Social Statements in the Lutheran Church of America* (Minneapolis: Fortress Press, 1989).

[121] Andrew Schulze to G. M. Kramer, 12 September 1941 (copy), Andrew Schulze Papers, CHI, St. Louis MO.

[122] Schulze, *Race against Time*, 102.

commenting on the book, most encouraging his stand.[123] It was publication of *My Neighbor of Another Color* that helped to transform Schulze from a very successful pastor and leader within the Synodical Conference's program of black missions to a spokesperson for race relations among Lutherans all over America.

In the late 1930s and early 1940s, Schulze began to publish his views in a variety of Lutheran publications. *The Walther League Messenger*, the publication of the Missouri Synod's youth organization, was one of the first periodicals that featured Schulze's articles. In one article in *The Walther League Messenger*, he described the faith and accomplishments of Dr. George Washington Carver, the black American scientist who developed many applications for agricultural goods.[124] Another article, "A People You Can Love," Schulze wrote in the spirit of opening up youth to the idea of developing relationships with their fellow black Americans. In it, he concluded, "If according to human standards they appear to you to be an unlovely people—remember then that God loved you when you were as an unclean thing and when your righteousnesses were as filthy rags (Isaiah 64:6)—and you will see in Negroes a people you can love."[125] But Schulze was disappointed that this particular article was only published in the foreign edition of *The Walther League Messenger*.[126]

Schulze also contributed to *American Lutheran*, a publication of the American Lutheran Publicity Bureau (ALPB). The American Lutheran Publicity Bureau began in 1914 by a group of clergy and laymen in New

---

[123] Andrew Schulze Papers, CHI, St. Louis MO. See correspondence on *My Neighbor of Another Color*.

[124] Andrew Schulze, "God, What Is A Peanut?" *The Walther League Messenger* 47 (November 1938): 166–67, 195.

[125] Andrew Schulze, "A People You Can Love," *The Walther League Messenger*, foreign ed. 48 (December 1939): 200–201.

[126] "The article was intended for consumption by people in the U.S.A.... At best it was naïveté on the part of the *Messenger* office to have thought that people in Canada, or in Central and South America, would be edified by something intended to help readers in the United States.... Or was the publication of the article in the 'foreign' edition the result of fear on the part of *Messenger* office personnel that unfavorable repercussions from prejudiced readers would be the result of publishing the article in the 'domestic' edition?" (Schulze, *Race against Time*, 107–108).

York City interested in developing public relations for their church. A regular monthly publication began in 1918 under the editorship of the Rev. Paul Lindemann. Alan Graebner described the emergence of ALPB's periodical as "the only non-censored, Synod-wide publication concerned with many facets of practical church work, the *American Lutheran* was a prominent rostrum for more acculturated spokesmen to urge ideas not yet accepted by those still thinking along lines traditional in the German Lutheran community."[127] Even after the Missouri Synod became more Americanized, the *American Lutheran* continued to be a progressive influence.

American Lutheran began promoting liturgical renewal, a broader movement in the Christian Church, that flourished during the 1930s, initiated by Virgil Michel from the Catholic monastery in Collegeville, Minnesota. Though the liturgical movement drew on the early history of Christianity, it had contemporary implications. Michel and others who promoted liturgical renewal also promoted a vision of an active Christian community acting upon its social responsibilities.[128] While Lutherans were eventually influenced by the liturgical movement, Andrew Schulze was a part of a small minority of Missouri Synod pastors who were immediately receptive to its influences. Schulze was able to read positive Lutheran attitudes about the liturgical movement on the pages of *American Lutheran*.

Schulze contributed articles to *American Lutheran* on the racial situation in the church, society, and the world.[129] He continued to write strongly against racial discrimination in the church, stating, "It gives offense

---

[127] Graebner, "The Acculturation of an Immigrant Lutheran Church," 227.

[128] "'The fostering of the liturgical life brings about the realization of participation in the Corpus Christi Mysticum, and therefore must be the destroyer of individualism'.... [Those supporting the liturgical movement] regretted the infrequency of Communion celebrations, the non-observance of church festivals, ignorance of the Psalter and of the pericopes" (David L. Scheidt, "The 'High Church Movement' in American Lutheranism," *Lutheran Quarterly* 9 [November 1957]: 344).

[129] Andrew Schulze, "Racial Segregation in Society in General" *American Lutheran* 27 (July 1944): 9–10, 16. Andrew Schulze, "Racial Segregation in the Church," *American Lutheran* 27 (October 1944): 9, 22–23, 25. Andrew Schulze, "A Transition Period," *American Lutheran* 29 (May 1946): 6–8, 26.

in the very house of God."[130] However, Schulze's writings were also giving more attention to world-shaping events and their implications for race relations. In the midst of World War II, Schulze wrote connecting the struggle in Europe to the struggle at home: "Racial segregation is in open opposition to the democratic ideology that our soldiers, sailors, and marines are told at every turn they are fighting to uphold."[131]

The idea of "Double Victory," against fascism abroad and racism at home, was a common hope for black Americans during World War II.[132] Still, Schulze was among the first white Americans who made the connection between what was happening in Europe and what was happening in America. Before World War II began, Schulze was reproached for comments he made during a radio broadcast on the Missouri Synod's radio station KFUO. Schulze was invited as an occasional guest on KFUO. After a May 1939 broadcast, Schulze was informed by the station's director that the "Radio Committee did not appreciate the comparison between the discrimination against Jews in Germany and the treatment of Negroes in America."[133]

Schulze's position was even more unusual within the context of Missouri Synod Lutheranism. The official magazine of the Missouri Synod, *The Lutheran Witness*, prior to the beginnings of World War II in 1939, "reflected a 'starry-eyed approval of the Nazi regime'" and did not seriously criticize Nazism until 1945.[134] In the early and middle 1930s, the popular Missouri Synod radio preacher, Walter A. Maier, had also spoken favorably about Adolf Hitler. In 1937 Maier turned against all European

---

[130] Schulze, "Racial Segregation in the Church," 9.

[131] Schulze, "Racial Segregation in Society in General" 10.

[132] *The Pittsburgh Courier*, one of the most respected black newspapers in America, did the most to promote the idea of "Double Victory."

[133] H. H. Hohenstein to Andrew Schulze, 17 May 1939, Andrew Schulze Papers, CHI, St. Louis MO.

[134] E. Clifford Nelson, "The New Shape of Lutheranism," in *The Lutherans in North America*, ed. E. Clifford Nelson, 473. "This caused an LCMS scholar [John G. Mager] to raise the question 'Can the church...abandon its role as a light and as a conscience to the world and still remain a church?'" (Nelson, "The New Shape of Lutheranism," 473).

totalitarianism and became especially known for his anti-communism.[135] The Missouri Synod's conservative German base made it more prone than other Lutherans to sympathize with Germany during World War II. But Ronald Webster also found similar misperceptions among other American Lutherans as well as other Americans. Webster concluded, "American Lutherans did not really manage to penetrate the smoke screen of propaganda…to interpret…the true picture of the racist and anti-Christian policies of the most vicious regime in modern memory…like everyone else outside of Germany in the 1930s, they did very little to press for action against the revolutionary whirlwind of Nazi ideological incursions and racist crimes."[136]

Schulze's participation in fighting the Germans in World War I demonstrated that he could see Germany as the enemy. It was ironic, then, that someone accused Schulze of un-American activities during World War II. A visitor to St. Philip's accused Schulze of delivering a sermon in which "he stated that the Axis was justified in its stand and because of past grievances the colored people were not bound to cooperate with the white people in aiding our war effort." The Federal Bureau of Investigation looked into the charge but found no one else who would corroborate it. The informant admitted that she may have misunderstood the meaning of the sermon, and the case was quickly closed.[137]

Americans were becoming more aware of racial issues during World War II. The Swedish sociologist Gunnar Mydral wrote and published *An American Dilemma: The Negro Problem and Modern Democracy* during the war. Mydral described America's dilemma as the conflict between its "high national and Christian precepts" and the manifestations of racial prejudice found throughout American life.[138] Mydral's *An American Dilemma* received a great deal of attention in the academic community.

---

[135] See Maier, *A Man Spoke, A World Listened.*

[136] Ronald Webster, "American Lutheran Opinion Makers and the Crisis of German Protestantism under Hitler," *Essays and Reports of the Lutheran Historical Conference* 17 (1999): 218.

[137] "Andrew Schulze," FBI file 14-863, Federal Bureau of Investigation, Washington DC.

[138] Gunnar Myrdal, with the assistance of Richard Sterner and Arnold Rose, *An American Dilemma: The Negro Problem and Modern Democracy* (New York: Harper &

Many ordinary Americans awakened to the dangers of poor race relations after a race riot in Detroit during World War II. War industries demanded a greater supply of labor and African Americans migrated in greater number to the industrial cities of the North. While this solved many industrial problems, it also led to greater social tensions between blacks and whites. These tensions exploded in Detroit during the summer of 1943: "A two-day free-for-all between ten thousand whites and their black victims, fighting hand-to-hand in the streets of downtown—sealed Detroit's image for a generation."[139]

The well-respected St. Louis Seminary professor, Richard R. Caemmerer, wrote his thoughts about the Detroit race riot in his "We Look at the World" column of the *Lutheran Witness*. Caemmerer, then "cautious in his approach to social problems…nonetheless recognized that they should not be ignored."[140] He argued that the church did have a role to play in improving American race relations. As Caemmerer wrote, "The Christian Church is in the business of changing human nature….The Christian Church is in the business of implanting the Spirit into human hearts."[141] Schulze wrote to Caemmerer praising his article and asking him to write more on the subject. However, *The Lutheran Witness* again displayed a more typical Missouri Synod attitude the following month when Rev. L. A. Wisler was quoted as saying, "The race problem is not one for the Church to solve."[142]

Included in his letter to Caemmerer was a concern that Schulze would continue to observe. Schulze noted that the more liberal denominations were making a stand against racism while conservative denominations, such as the Missouri Synod, were all too silent. Schulze said, "The farther they are removed from the truly Christian Gospel the closer they move toward

---

Bros., 1944) lxxi. Myrdal pointed out that "the moral struggle goes on within people and not only between them" (Myrdal, *An American Dilemma*, lxxi).

[139] Tamar Jacoby, *Someone Else's House: America's Unfinished Struggle for Integration* (New York: Basic Books, 1998) 235.

[140] Moellering, "The Missouri Synod and Social Problems," 149.

[141] R[ichard] R. C[aemmerer], "We Look at the World," *The Lutheran Witness* 62 (6 July 1943): 231.

[142] Stephen M. Tuhy, "Slovak Lutherans Meet in Convention," *The Lutheran Witness* 62 (3 August 1943): 262–63.

honesty in looking into the problems of race prejudice and seeking solutions." Schulze believed that this was extremely unfortunate as it was the pure Gospel that had the power to change people's lives.[143]

The Detroit riot of 1943 opened up an opportunity for Andrew Schulze to play a role, not only in the church, but also in society. The shock of the riot in Detroit led to the creation of interracial commissions in cities all across America.[144] The mayor of St. Louis, William Dee Becker, fearful of the possibility of a similar race riot in St. Louis, discussed the idea of creating a Mayor's Commission on Race Relations. The city's newspapers praised the idea of a commission on race relations. *The St. Louis Star Times* recalled the bloody race riot that took place in 1917 in its neighbor city across the Mississippi, East St. Louis, and warned that St. Louis was not immune from such problems.[145] A couple of months after the Detroit race riot and the death of Mayor Becker, the new mayor of St. Louis, Aloys P. Kaufmann, appointed seventy-two individuals to the Mayor's Commission

---

[143] Andrew Schulze to Prof. R. R. Caemmerer, 14 July 1943 (copy), Andrew Schulze Papers, CHI, St. Louis MO.

[144] "The race riot that erupted in Detroit on June 20, 1943, transmitted shock waves throughout the nation.... The depth of the panic generated by the specter of racial violence in 1943 was best revealed by the creation of a new urban institution. At least thirty-one cities created municipal interracial commissions between the summer of 1943 and 1944" (Arnold R. Hirsh, *Making the Second Ghetto: Race and Housing in Chicago, 1940–1960* [Chicago: The University of Chicago Press, 1998] 42).

[145] "St. Louis Needs This Committee," *St. Louis Star Times* (15 July 1943): 14. For more on the race riot in East St. Louis, see Elliott Rudwick, *Race Riot at East St. Louis, July 2, 1917* (Carbondale: Southern Illinois University Press, 1964). "St. Louis was experiencing the typical black phenomenon of Northern urban centers. Since World War I, blacks from the deep South had been migrating in huge waves.... The black population of St. Louis had jumped from 43,960 in 1910 to 69,854 in 1920. By the beginning of World War II, black St. Louisans numbered 125,000 and jumped quickly to 180,000 by 1945. The ghetto prepared for them sprawled inexorably westward from its early base within a small half-circle surrounding the downtown area on St. Louis's eastern border, the Mississippi River. Across that river stood East St. Louis, Illinois, scene of one the many race riots of 1917–1919, and a grim reminder of what might lie ahead" (Donald K. Kemper, "Catholic Integration in St. Louis, 1935–1947," *Missouri Historical Review* 73 [October 1978]: 2).

on Race Relations.[146] Andrew Schulze was one of the members of the newly formed Mayor's Commission on Race Relations, indicating that he was also seen as a leader in the St. Louis community.

The purpose of the Mayor's Commission on Race Relations was "the promotion of good will between white and colored citizens of the City of St. Louis and to that end to inquire into their mutual and respective problems in the fields of housing, health and sanitation, employment, education and recreation in the City, and to make reports and recommendations of practical measures for improvement."[147] The Mayor's Commission broke up into various committees and Schulze became a part of the Education Committee.[148] Though formed with good intentions, the Mayor's Commission did not achieve many lasting accomplishments. As the chairman of the commission, Edwin Meissner wrote, "Although we have made progress, we all agree that we have not accomplished all that we had hoped to achieve."[149] Nonetheless, Schulze's service on the commission was appreciated. Chairman Meissner wrote Schulze in 1947 upon his departure for Chicago, "I shall always remember your example and endeavor in my way to emulate the same."[150]

During this same period, Schulze also led in the formation of the St. Louis Lutheran Society for Better Race Relations. A few years earlier, a Lutheran social worker had suggested to Schulze the idea of starting a race relations study group.[151] But the idea took root in 1943, probably inspired by the immediate context of the times. As Schulze explained in an announcement about a society meeting, "The world is all astir about race

---

[146] Patricia L. Adams, "Fighting For Democracy in St. Louis: Civil Rights During World War II," *Missouri Historical Review* 80 (October 1985): 67.

[147] "Purpose and Activities of St. Louis Race Relations Commission," Fannie Cook Papers, box 9, folder 1, Missouri Historical Society, St. Louis MO.

[148] "St. Louis Race Relations Commission, Executive and Committee Personnel," Fannie Cook Papers, box 9, folder 2, Missouri Historical Society, St. Louis MO.

[149] Edwin Meissner, 27 December 1945, Fannie Cook Papers, box 9, folder 14, Missouri Historical Society, St. Louis MO.

[150] Edwin Meissner to Andrew Schulze, 1 August 1947, Andrew Schulze Papers, CHI, St. Louis MO.

[151] "St. Philip, Distinguished Negro Church, Has Built Well the Walls of Its Zion," *The St. Louis Lutheran* 1 (19 May 1946): 9.

these days. The Church should be."[152] Schulze had the example of the Mayor's Commission before him. The St. Louis chapter of the NAACP was also active during the World War II years. It tried unsuccessfully to end discrimination at lunch counters in downtown St. Louis. Additionally, the Fellowship of Reconciliation, a Christian pacifist group that began during World War I, had sponsored a three-day race relations institute on nonviolent, direct action in St. Louis during the spring of 1943.[153] Members of the Fellowship of Reconciliation were active in starting the Congress of Racial Equality (CORE) in Chicago in 1942. CORE and the National Association of the Advancement of Colored People (NAACP) were later joined by the Southern Christian Leadership Conference (SCLC) and the Student Nonviolent Coordinating Committee (SNCC) to make up the four major organizations of the emerging civil rights movement.[154]

The purpose of the St. Louis Lutheran Society for Better Race Relations was "to foster better race relations, especially within the Lutheran Church; to this end to meet for mutual study; and when opportunity presents itself, to take action that will help eliminate racial discrimination, especially in the Church."[155] The St. Louis Lutheran Society for Better Race Relations was interracial in membership, numbering about sixty persons in its first years. While Lutheran in its focus, it also saw itself in its wider Christian context. The society recognized that there was secular and Catholic leadership in the area of race relations and therefore was dedicated to the discussion of race relations from the evangelical Christian point of

---

[152] Andrew Schulze, Announcement for the St. Louis Lutheran Society for Better Race Relations, 3 January 1944, Andrew Schulze Papers, CHI, St. Louis MO.

[153] Adams, "Fighting for Democracy in St. Louis," 66–75.

[154] See August Meier and Elliott Rudwick, *CORE: A Study in the Civil Rights Movement, 1942–1968* (New York: Oxford University Press, 1973); Adam Fairclough, *To Redeem the Soul of America: The Southern Christian Leadership Conference and Martin Luther King, Jr.* (Athens: University of Georgia Press, 1987); and Clayborne Carson, *In Struggle: SNCC and the Black Awakening of the 1960s* (Cambridge: Harvard University Press, 1981).

[155] Pamphlet for the St. Louis Society for Better Race Relations, Andrew Schluze Papers, CHI, St. Louis MO.

view.[156] In 1945 the St. Louis Society began publishing a monthly news bulletin, *Lutheran Race Relations Bulletin*, later known as *Focus*, which continued for five years. The editorial staff of *Lutheran Race Relations Bulletin* included four persons: Andrew Schulze; Rev. Otto H. Theiss, executive secretary of the Walther League; Miss Esther Feddersen; and Prof. Alfred M. Rehwinkel.[157]

In 1946 the St. Louis Lutheran Society for Better Race Relations hosted its first Lutheran Race Relations Institute at St. Matthew's Lutheran Church in St. Louis. News about the institute was featured in the local Lutheran newspaper, *The St. Louis Lutheran*: "Six hundred persons, among them visitors from seven states and 16 cities and representing church officials, pastors, teachers and persons from all walks of life participated."[158] The institute was a three-day event, featuring speakers such as Marmaduke N. Carter, Henry Nau, Alfred M. Rehwinkel, and Clemonce Sabourin. Schulze later recalled that "an embryonic Lutheran ecumenicity was also involved: the Rev. Ervin E. Krebs, the executive secretary of Negro mission work of the American Lutheran Church, was invited and attended this institute structured within the Missouri Synod."[159]

The 1946 institute recognized that Lutherans did have obligations to improve race relations in society as well as the church. Participants of the institute passed a resolution that stated that "we as individual Christians shall by every good means seek to understand what is Christian in race relations; that we shall endeavor in love to help bring the same viewpoint to others, that we shall uphold the efforts of them that endeavor to eliminate racial discrimination from within the local congregation and the Church at large, that we shall—God helping us—work towards the Christian ideal of race relations also in all phases of civic life." Those who supported the Lutheran Race Relations Institute felt that it was vital that the church be involved in improving race relations. As O. H. Theiss, executive secretary of

---

[156] [Andrew Schulze], "Resolution Relative to a Christian Racial Understanding," 2–4.

[157]"An Editorial Staff of Four Persons," *Focus: Lutheran Race Relations Bulletin* 1 (August 1945): 6.

[158] "Lutheran Better Race Relations Institute Attracts Six Hundred," *St. Louis Lutheran* 1(2 June 1946): 1–2.

[159] Schulze, *Race against Time*, 121.

the Walther League explained, "Prejudice must be cured by repentance, not simply by enlightenment."[160] Another Lutheran Race Relations Institute was organized in St. Louis in 1947. Andrew Schulze was the guiding force behind these institutes. In the following years, institutes were organized in Chicago and Valparaiso, Indiana.

One of Schulze's key supporters during his years in St. Louis was Concordia Seminary professor, Alfred M. Rehwinkel. Rehwinkel had advised Schulze on the writing of his book, *My Neighbor of Another Color*, and during the controversy that followed its publication.[161] Rehwinkel was also crucial during the beginning of the St. Louis Lutheran Society for Better Race Relations and for his assistance in supporting the first Race Relations Institute. Rehwinkel served as the society's first president and also became a part of the Mayor's Commission on Race Relations in 1946. Rehwinkel was a unique and colorful member of the St. Louis seminary faculty. Rehwinkel "stood almost alone for many years in his insistence on making Christian orthodoxy relevant to contemporary problems."[162]

During the late 1960s, Rehwinkel changed his position on race relations and stood against some of the progress of the civil rights movement. Rehwinkel "never was known for being in step with the spirit of the times, but perhaps nowhere was he more consistently anachronous than in the area of race relations."[163] Still, Schulze remembered Rehwinkel fondly in his memoirs, "although, ironically in the 1960's [sic] he seemingly became an advocate of racial segregation, I shall not forget his friendship, and hope

---

[160] "Lutheran Better Race Relations Institute Attracts Six Hundred," 2.

[161] Schulze, *Race against Time*, 137. Rehwinkel and others counseled Schulze to remain silent during the controversy to "produce the best psychological effect" (Andrew Schulze to Clemonce Sabourin, 21 October 1942 [copy], Andrew Schulze Papers, CHI, St. Louis MO).

[162] Moellering, "The Missouri Synod and Social Problems," 540.

[163] Ronald W. Stelzer, *Salt, Light and Signs of the Times: An Intimate Look at the Life and Times of Alfred (Rip) Rehwinkel* (New Haven MO: Lutheran News, Inc., 1993) 228. Rehwinkel was also involved in the America First Movement prior to America's entrance into World War II. "At the mass rally for American First on 3 May 1941 at the Saint Louis Arena, Rip shared the speakers platform with Col. Charles Lindbergh, America's foremost hero and a persuasive articulator of isolationism before the nuclear age" (Stelzer, *Salt, Light and Signs of the Times*, 128).

to remain grateful to God and him for the assistance he gave in earlier years."[164]

When the St. Louis Lutheran Society for Better Race Relations began, racial justice was still a controversial issue at Missouri Synod seminaries. The society wanted to meet at the campus of Concordia Seminary. But after a couple of meetings at the seminary, the Board of Control of Concordia Seminary, St. Louis passed a policy stating, "Meetings of church groups discussing and advocating controversial matters are not to be held at the Seminary."[165] The society solved the problem by hosting their gathering in the home of the Rehwinkels. As a postscript on a notice for an upcoming meeting explained, "For the benefit of those who may not know, Prof. Rehwinkel's residence is on the campus of Concordia Seminary."[166] A few months later, the situation was resolved and the society was once again meeting in the main buildings of Concordia Seminary.[167]

Schulze was very interested in getting the next generation of pastors involved in racial issues. The Schulzes were frequent hosts, and seminary students were often their guests. Schulze used these opportunities to discuss the status of race relations in the church: "The dinner and after-dinner conversations afforded a golden opportunity to discuss the subject in an effort to prepare them for effective work at my own church and to help get them ready for the places of leadership they were to hold in the church."[168] In the next decades, Schulze took advantage of many opportunities to lecture and preach throughout the country. Through personal contacts and correspondence, Andrew Schulze was developing a network of individuals, many of them young pastors, who shared his interest in racial justice in the church. Some of the students and young pastors who became involved with Schulze in St. Louis included Walter Heyne, George Hans Liebenow, Martin Marty, Jaroslav Pelikan, and William Schiebel.

---

[164] Schulze, *Race against Time*, 138.

[165] Rev. W. Maschoff to Andrew Schulze, Andrew Schulze Papers, CHI, St. Louis MO.

[166] Andrew Schulze, notice, 3 March 1944, Andrew Schulze Papers, CHI, St. Louis MO.

[167] Andrew Schulze, notice, 8 November 1944, Andrew Schulze Papers, CHI, St. Louis MO.

[168] Schulze, *Race against Time*, 136.

Concordia Seminary's student newspaper, *The Seminarian*, featured a lengthy article promoting racial integration in 1943, but included an editorial disclaimer that stated that further study and additional articles should follow.[169] *The Seminarian* took a bolder stand in 1946 when it dedicated an entire issue to racial matters. Included in the issue was an article, "Race, as a Negro Views It," by Jeff Johnson, a black seminary student who had broken the racial barrier at Concordia Seminary. Alfred M. Rehwinkel and Richard Caemmerer also contributed articles with their perspective on racial matters.[170] During this period, Concordia Seminary, St. Louis began developing a much greater sensitivity to racial issues than its sister seminary in Springfield.

Even though Springfield's Concordia Theological Seminary had accepted black students in the late nineteenth century, it turned away black students as late as the 1940s.[171] Andrew Schulze became especially involved with the case of Samuel Hoard, a member of his congregation in St. Louis. In 1946 Hoard applied for admission to study for the ministry at Springfield and, as was customary, was recommended for study by his pastor. Schulze knew Hoard well and had a very personal interest in his desire to become a Lutheran pastor. In the summer of 1946, Schulze received a letter from Concordia's president, G. Christian Barth, which stated the decision of the faculty, "In view of our very large enrollment and furthermore in view of the fact that we have Immanuel College at Greensboro, North Carolina, for the training of colored men for the ministry, we cannot receive Mr. Hoard as one of our students."[172] As Sam Hoard recalled, Concordia Theological Seminary fell "behind the times." After all, by 1946, Jackie Robinson was on his way to play for the Dodgers, becoming the first black baseball player in the Major Leagues.[173]

---

[169] "Facing the Issue in the Negro Question!" *The Seminarian* 34 (17 November 1943): 4–6.

[170] Ross P. Scherer, ed., *The Seminarian* 37 (27 March 1946): 1–10.

[171] Schulze, *Race against Time*, 21–22.

[172] G. Christian Barth to Andrew Schulze, 8 August 1946, Andrew Schulze Papers, CHI, St. Louis MO.

[173] Samuel Hoard, interview by author, 20 July 2000, telephone. Concordia Theological Seminary's G. Christian Barth made the same decision in 1947 in the

Hoard had no desire to attend the Missouri Synod's segregated seminary in Greensboro, North Carolina. While Concordia Seminary in St. Louis demonstrated that it would be willing to accept black students, as the "classical" seminary, it had stricter admission requirements. In order to attend Concordia Seminary in St. Louis, Hoard would be required to study two years at one of the church's preparatory colleges, in order to develop a working knowledge of classical languages such as Greek and Latin. Andrew Schulze wrote to a member of the faculty at Concordia College in Fort Wayne, Indiana, to try and secure admission for Hoard. As he explained in his letter, "The difficulty that this decision of our faculty at Springfield imposes is not one of my congregation merely, but of our entire Negro church and mission field." Schulze drew on his own personal knowledge of Springfield stating, "There is...no justification for the closing of the doors of our northern institutions to Negro students. Especially is this the case in Springfield, where all the schools of the city have been mixed throughout its history, where the tomb of Abraham Lincoln is to be found."[174]

But the admission of a black student to Concordia College, Fort Wayne also proved to be a difficult task. There was resistance on the part of some at the college, and the synod's president, John Behnken, was consulted about the situation. Behnken responded by noting that the Synodical Conference had recently agreed to opening of its colleges and seminaries to black students, but that the decision was not binding on the Missouri Synod. Behnken offered no solid advice, concluding, "If you say yes it isn't right and if you say no it isn't right." Above all, he regretted "that this issue is forced upon us" and "that there has been agitation" in the matter. Behnken sent a carbon copy of the letter to Schulze, who, by this time, had long been considered an "agitator" by many in the church.[175]

In the end, the board of Concordia, Fort Wayne decided to admit Hoard as a student but made arrangements for him to live off-campus.

---

case of another prospective black student, Lindsey Robinson (G. Christian Barth to Andrew Schulze, 2 July 1947, Andrew Schulze Papers, CHI, St. Louis MO).

[174] Andrew Schulze to Prof. E. E. Foelber, 13 August 1946 (copy), Andrew Schulze Papers, CHI, St. Louis MO.

[175] J. W. Behnken to Prof. Erwin Schnedler, 3 September 1946 (copy), Andrew Schulze Papers, CHI, St. Louis MO.

Hoard was eager to live with other seminary students, and shortly after the year began, a vacancy opened in one of the dorm rooms. Hoard made a request to the board to move to campus, but they stalled making a decision for months. Another early supporter of integration, Paul Amt, lobbied on Hoard's behalf. As Hoard described in his autobiography, *Almost a Layman*, Pastor Amt "let it be known that if I did not return after Christmas as a bona fide dormitory student, he and his family would be leaving the city. He pointed out that he could not effectively serve as their so-called 'Negro missionary' if, on the one hand, he was being told by Lutheran congregations to win converts, and on the other hand, people from these same congregations were refusing to treat fairly the only black Lutheran who was already in their midst."[176] Hoard graduated from Concordia College, Fort Wayne and then went on to graduate from Concordia Seminary, St. Louis. Over the course of his career, he served congregations in New Jersey, New York, Kansas, and Florida and also served for many years as a military chaplain in the United States Army.

Though small in numbers, black Lutheran pastors played a critical role in forcing the Lutheran Church to deal with racial issues.[177] It was Clemonce Sabourin who played a crucial role in helping to bring about the first stage of integration for Lutherans associated with the Synodical Conference. In 1944 Clemonce Sabourin became the pastor of Mount Zion Lutheran Church in Harlem. That summer, Sabourin was accompanied to New York by Andrew Schulze, and a few others, who had all been at the meeting of the General Conference held in Philadelphia.[178] Schulze later recalled what a wonderful opportunity it was to see the place where

---

[176] Samuel Hoard, *Almost a Layman* (Orlando FL: Drake's Publishing, 1981) 18. Amt was quick to write Schulze about the decision: "By this time (when you read this) no doubt Sam has gotten in touch with you to tell you about his 'best' Christmas present—the Board's decision last night to admit him as a full-time dormitory student" (Paul Amt to Andrew Schulze, 20 December 1946, Andrew Schulze Papers, CHI, St. Louis MO).

[177] In the early 1940s, there were about thirty black Lutheran pastors associated with the work of the Synodical Conference (List of pastors present and absent from the 6th Meeting of the General Conference, August 1941, Andrew Schulze Papers, CHI, St. Louis MO).

[178] Clemonce Sabourin, Oral History Collection, 74–75.

Sabourin conducted his ministry. Schulze also enjoyed the chance to see some of the sights of Harlem and New York City and to see a Broadway performance of the famous actor Paul Robeson in *Othello*.[179]

Sabourin had the opportunity to name his congregation and named it "Mount Zion Lutheran Church" after his home congregation in New Orleans.[180] Mount Zion Lutheran Church was located not too far from Adam Clayton Powell's well-known Abyssinian Baptist Church. Mount Zion Lutheran Church was a mission effort begun by the Atlantic District in what was once property of St. Matthew Lutheran Church, the oldest Lutheran church in North America, founded in 1664 by Dutch immigrants. Because of the changing neighborhood, St. Matthew Lutheran Church moved to Sherman Avenue in the 1940s.[181] Under Sabourin, Mount Zion Lutheran Church and School became one of the most successful outreach efforts of the Atlantic District.

In 1944 the Missouri Synod, the largest member of the Synodical Conference, requested that the Synodical Conference organize the structure of its black mission congregations so that they would be more financially sound. For decades the general conference of workers in black mission congregations had been struggling to find a way to structure black ministry in such a way that black pastors and teachers would have greater influence in how ministry would be conducted. An Augmented Survey Committee was formed to propose a reorganization of the Synodical Conference's black congregations. Two places on the committee were reserved for representatives of the General Conference. The General Conference elected to have Andrew Schulze and Clemonce Sabourin as its representatives. Sabourin suspected that Missouri Synod's president, John Behnken, went along with the choice, even though he opposed "agitators," because he and

---

[179] Andrew Schulze, "Hotel Theresa—Harlem," *The Vanguard* 7 (October 1960): 2.

[180] Clemonce Sabourin, Oral History Collection, 78.

[181] "This church had stood...to the 1940s, almost a visible symbol of what Jesus meant when he said the gates of hell shall not prevail against my church...but what the gates of hell couldn't do was done by Negroes who moved into the neighborhood" (ibid., 73).

Schulze were both from the Missouri Synod rather than another synod associated with the Synodical Conference.[182]

The idea of creating a separate structure for black Lutheran congregations was one suggested method of reorganization. In committee meetings, Sabourin spoke out against a separate structure and suggested that black congregations should be integrated into the synodical districts in which they were located. Sabourin was met with the response that black Lutherans did not want such integration. In order to counter that response, Sabourin went ahead and surveyed the opinions of workers of the General Conference without the knowledge of the Survey Committee. Though they were close friends, Sabourin did not involve Schulze in any way in this process. As he explained in a letter, "Realizing that my method of securing the information I wanted might endanger my position on the Committee, I did not consult Schulze.... I felt that what I did was necessary, but I also felt it necessary that one of our representatives...remain in the good graces of the other Committee members."[183]

Sabourin wrote out his ideas in a twenty-page paper titled "Cards on the Table" and sent it to workers of the General Conference. In "Cards on the Table," Sabourin reacted strongly against the idea of a separate structure for black Lutherans. As he expressed, "To invite people who are daily fighting against segregation into a segregated Church is utter folly. It would be pouring water on the wheel of those who contend that the organized Church is the last strong-hold of racial prejudice... And that is exactly what we would be doing if we established a Negro Lutheran Church, District, or Synod."[184]

Sabourin then put the issue in a comparative context. He gave the example of the Boy Scouts of America, a secular organization, that had succeeded at integration even in the South. He also gave the example of the Catholic Church. As he explained, because an integrated Church was the official vision of the Catholic Church, "Many Negroes do not turn against

---

[182] Ibid., 109.

[183] Clemonce Sabourin to Paul D. Lehman, 19 November 1945 (copy), Clemonce Sabourin Papers, in the possession of William Carr.

[184] Clemonce Sabourin, "Cards on the Table," July 1945, Clemonce Sabourin Papers, in the possession of William Carr, 3.

the Church when an individual layman or priest discriminates against them…. Further, the Catholic Church officially, not only does not segregate the Negroes, but it also takes an active part in the general fight against segregation and discrimination." Sabourin noted that the success of the Catholic Church among African Americans was all the more remarkable as many blacks had "mental reservations" about Catholicism due to the fact that traditional African-American denominations were Protestant.[185]

Sabourin thought that Lutheranism had great possibilities among black Americans if it removed its discriminatory policies. He noted that there was some dissatisfaction with traditional African-American churches and that some black Americans were "searching for a true expression of Biblical Christianity in teaching and in practice." He told of one Baptist pastor who acknowledged that "the level of education among Negroes throughout the country is constantly rising. But our Church, as a whole, has not kept pace with this movement."[186]

Sabourin acknowledged that he met a few black churchworkers who held the position, "white Lutherans don't want to be bothered with us. So I don't want to be bothered with them."[187] But explained that such segregationist attitudes were not an expression of true Christianity. Sabourin also attacked the idea that integrated churches may mean the loss of some white members of the church. As he expressed, "I am convinced that the Church has lost more souls by failing to practice what it preaches than it will ever lose by living up to Christian principles." Sabourin stood against a separate structure for black Lutherans for primarily spiritual reasons, believing it to be a "physical denial of spiritual unity."[188]

The Survey Committee also needed to make a recommendation regarding Immanuel, the black Lutheran seminary in Greensboro. Because the number of students at Immanuel was small, there was a push to close it. Sabourin concluded, "When the entrance of Negro ministerial students into our regular institutions becomes a general thing, the theological department at Immanuel Lutheran College should be discontinued, but not before

---

[185] Ibid., 4–5.
[186] Ibid., 6.
[187] Ibid., 7.
[188] Ibid., 9.

then!" Sabourin thought that eventually the facilities at Immanuel should be used for some kind of Lutheran educational institution such as a high school or junior college.[189]

Sabourin was very pleased with the response to "Cards on the Table" from the workers of the General Conference. Very few pastors who wrote to Sabourin objected to his position.[190] When the official plan for integration was presented at the 1946 meeting of the General Conference, some black pastors did voice concern over the proposal. Some were worried about "the fragmentation of black leadership and the isolation that might occur" with integration. But the General Conference voted to proceed with the plan.[191]

Sabourin offered his correspondence to the Survey Committee as proof that black churchworkers did want integration. The committee eventually decided to go forward with the idea of administrative integration, recognizing that it would take place in some districts more quickly than in others.[192] The "Brief Report" issued by the Survey Committee reflected some paternalistic attitudes. For example, it conveyed the idea that the time had come "to place greater confidence in our Negro Missions and their workers and to grant them a greater measure of rights and privileges."[193] But

---

[189] Ibid., 19–20.

[190] P. D. Lehman was one pastor who disagreed with Sabourin: "We were offered a plan of organization whereby we would in time become completely autonomous. Does 'Normal Integration' offer us more than this? In my opinion, it offers us much less. Think it over! Admitting for the sake of argument that 'Normal Integration' is the ideal situation, there still remains the simple fact that our people, white and colored, are not ready for it. I refuse to get excited over a problem the solution of which cannot be looked for and expected for a lifetime yet" (P. D. Lehman to Clemonce Sabourin, 5 November 1945, Clemonce Sabourin Papers, in the possession of William Carr).

[191] Johnson, *Black Christians*, 199. Johnson noted that the proposal passed by just one vote. But as there was a large percentage of white workers in the General Conference, it is difficult to determine how close the vote was among black churchworkers.

[192] Clemonce Sabourin, Oral History Collection, 113.

[193] "A Brief Report of the Survey Committee Appointed by the Synodical Conference to Carry out the Proposed Reorganization of Negro Missions," Clemonce Sabourin Papers, in the possession of William Carr. Members of the

the era in which paternalistic attitudes toward black ministry held sway was beginning to come to an end. Richard Dickinson concluded, "The era came to an end, not because of decisions at the top but because men had decided that they would no longer permit themselves to be treated as children."[194] Attached to the "Brief Report" was a minority position offered by Clemonce Sabourin and Andrew Schulze. The minority opinion mainly concerned the need to keep Immanuel Lutheran College open at this time, but also noted other objections. As Sabourin and Schulze expressed, "While the original Survey Committee report calls attention to some difficulties, it does not, in the opinion of the undersigned, point to still other underlying or basic difficulties. These basic difficulties are part and parcel of the difficulties…found hampering our Negro mission work in its every phase."[195]

There were also political and practical concerns involved with restructuring the Synodical Conference's program of black mission work. Since the Missouri Synod was the largest member of the Synodical Conference, it would gain the vast majority of black congregations as they merged into their geographical districts. There were also some fears that the fellowship of the Synodical Conference would be weakened as its efforts in black ministry was the main practical work holding the conference together.[196] Nonetheless, the Synodical Conference decided in 1946 to support the idea of administrative integration and also decided that the black Lutheran seminary in Greensboro should remain open. The concept of administrative integration was accepted by the Missouri Synod at its national convention in 1947.[197]

---

committee included Clemonce Sabourin, Andrew Schulze, E. L. Wilson, G. W. Wittmer, Carl Buenger, Wm. Lochner, and Chairman F. C. Streufert.

[194] Richard Dickinson, *Roses and Thorns*, 98.

[195] "Survey Committee Minority Report on Immanuel College," Clemonce Sabourin Papers, in the possession of William Carr.

[196] Clemonce Sabourin, "Cards on the Table," 12–13. The Synodical Conference did break up in 1961 when the Wisconsin Synod formally suspended relations with the Missouri Synod. See Mark Braun, "Changes within the Evangelical Synodical Conference of North America which led to the Exit of the Wisconsin Evangelical Lutheran Synod" (Ph.D. diss., Concordia Seminary, St. Louis, 2000).

[197] Johnson, *Black Christians*, 198–99.

The 1947 convention also marked the hundredth anniversary of the founding of the German Evangelical Lutheran Synod of Missouri, Ohio, and Other States. The convention was held in Chicago, the same location at which the synod was originally founded. At that convention, the synod also officially adopted a new name, "The Lutheran Church—Missouri Synod." It was this historic convention that also marks the first step toward integration in the Lutheran Church—Missouri Synod. The synod was still years away from promoting integration at the local level, in the local congregation.[198] However, administrative integration was a step in the right direction, a theoretical acknowledgement that all Lutheran congregations, whether white or black, were equal. Once the resolution to integrate was passed, it was up to the individual districts to act on the decision. By 1950 all districts of the Missouri Synod accepted black congregations, except for the Southern District. The Southern District, which included Alabama, Mississippi, Louisiana, and northwest Florida, did not integrate until 1961.[199]

During this period, other Christians were pushing for a change in the racial status quo. In 1946 the Federal Council of Churches, a Protestant organization considered too liberal for the Missouri Synod, began calling for "a non-segregated church in a non-segregated society." However, Schulze was more influenced by the fight for integration among American Catholics. While the top hierarchy of the Roman Catholic Church took an early stand against discrimination, compared to most Protestants, Catholic practice varied considerably from location to location.[200] Some Catholics in the St.

---

[198] "The 1954 Supreme Court Brown vs. Board of Education decision was the most immediate encouragement for the Missouri Synod to begin the second stage of its policy of integration—integration within the local congregation" (ibid., 201).

[199] See Richard O. Ziehr, *The Struggle for Unity: A Personal Look at The Integration of the Lutheran Church in the South* (Milton FL: CJH Enterprises, 1999).

[200] "Roman Catholicism was at war with racism long before Protestants became aware of its evils and began fighting the same. It knows it must either eliminate racism or abandon its claim to universality" ([Andrew Schulze], "The Kingdom—And Race," *Lutheran Race Relations Bulletin* 1 [September 1945]: 4). Similarly Schulze concluded, "If the Lutheran boast concerning pure doctrine is not to return to mock them that make it, they must assume the responsibility that accompanies the grace they claim to possess. They must be in the vanguard to demonstrate their faith in a life of love, in love towards races, that is toward people"

Louis area, led by a few Jesuit priests, began advocating the cause of racial justice during the 1930s and challenged the segregationist policies of the Archbishop John J. Glennon. Schulze was especially impressed with the Rev. Fr. Claude H. Heithaus, a Jesuit priest who was an early advocate of integration in St. Louis.[201] The fact that Schulze was interested in and open to developments in the Catholic Church was quite significant for a Lutheran in the years before Vatican II.

A major step toward Catholic integration in St. Louis occurred at the end of August 1947. The new Archbishop of St. Louis, Joseph E. Ritter, sent a directive that there was to be no discrimination in Catholic schools. When some Catholic parishioners moved toward legal action over Ritter's new integrationist policies, the archbishop threatened excommunication. The controversy ended quickly and integration was quickly achieved in St. Louis Catholic schools.[202]

Lutherans were opposed to such a dictatorial approach in church matters. As Schulze commented in the *Lutheran Race Relations Bulletin*, "There is power in the evangelical approach that far outshines that of the decree of an archbishop, or the threat of papal excommunication. The Gospel of the love of God for man in Christ Jesus has in it the power to change the hearts of men so that they will want to do the will of God." However, Schulze was not unimpressed by the Archbishop's stand: "Though the tactics dictated by the Pope and faithfully followed by the archbishop in

---

([Andrew Schluze], "Much Given—Much Required," *Lutheran Race Relations Bulletin* 2 [April 1946]: 2).

[201] "Father Heithaus was instrumental in opening the doors of St. Louis University when he made an eloquent plea before a large number of students asking them to be truly 'catholic' in their attitude towards Negroes. Soon after Father Heithaus made his plea before the students, Negro students were admitted to the University. He was removed from the St. Louis scene soon thereafter.... God speed the day when there shall arise from the Lutheran Church men of the Father Heithaus who will stir the consciences of evangelical Christians to throw off the disgrace of racism" ([Andrew Schulze], "Remember Him," *Focus: Lutheran Race Relations Bulletin* 4 [March–April 1948]: 7).

[202] Kemper, "Catholic Integration in St. Louis," 1–22. For more on Catholic integration, see John T. McGreevy, *Parish Boundaries: The Catholic Encounter with Race in the Twentieth-Century Urban North* (Chicago: The University of Chicago Press, 1996.)

St. Louis will be deplored by evangelical Christians, the courage that moved him to defy racism and to open the parish schools of his archdiocese for all, is to be commended and patterned after."[203]

In August 1947 Andrew Schulze ended his ministry in St. Louis to become the Director of Negro Missions for the Northern Illinois District. Schulze's ministry flourished at St. Philip's, and he enjoyed the faithful support of a strong congregation as he began his effort to improve race relations throughout the synod. After almost twenty years in St. Louis, Schulze felt called to new opportunities and challenges that he found in his new ministry on the South Side of Chicago.

---

[203] [Andrew Schulze], "Roman Catholic Schools in St. Louis—Open," *Lutheran Race Relations Bulletin* 3 (October–November 1947): 5.

Chapter 4

Chicago, 1947–1954

Like St. Louis, Chicago was another important city in the history of American Lutheranism. Today, Chicago serves as the headquarters for the largest Lutheran church body in America, the Evangelical Lutheran Church in America (ELCA). Though Chicago could not claim that position in the 1950s, it was both geographically and numerically the center of Lutheranism in America. Chicago was near the very center of the Lutheran population in America, and it was also the city with the greatest number of Lutherans and Lutheran congregations in America.[1] Additionally, Chicago was home to a significant number of Lutheran educational institutions. It was calculated that over half of the Lutherans in America lived within a 500–mile radius of Chicago and that Lutheran church members in Chicago outnumbered church members of any other Protestant denomination.[2]

---

[1] Erik W. Modean, "As the Center of Lutheranism, Chicago Needs Downtown Church," news release from the News Bureau of the National Lutheran Council, 8 December 1953, Evangelical Lutheran Church in America (ELCA) Archives, National Lutheran Counicl Papers, Chicago IL. "There are 195 Lutheran congregations with a total baptized membership of 153,968 in Chicago, against 137 congregations with 136,265 members in Minneapolis-St. Paul, 160 congregations with 123,404 members in New York, and 85 congregations with a combined membership of 61,027 in Philadelphia" (Modean, "As the Center of Lutheranism,").

[2] Modean, "As the Center of Lutheranism." Around the time of the famous 1893 World's Fair in Chicago, there were 115 Lutheran churches in "Chicagoland." As one observer pointed out, Chicago was "not only the greatest Lutheran city in America, but in the world, in that it has more Lutheran churches than in Berlin, Copenhagen, Stockholm, or Christiania.... In 1893 there may have been more Lutherans in Chicago than any other denomination of Protestants, but it would be hard to imagine a 'denomination' less united. Six different languages and twelve

Chicago was also a place of significance for Missouri Synod Lutherans in particular.[3] In 1847 the Missouri Synod was formally organized by representatives of fourteen congregations at St. Paul's Lutheran Church in Chicago. One of the Missouri Synod's colleges was located in River Forest, a suburb of Chicago. Though much of the Missouri Synod's official operations were located in St. Louis, prior to the 1950s, the presidents of the Missouri Synod had other places for their residences and home offices. President Friedrich Pfotenhauer served in Chicago from 1911–1935. President John W. Behnken also spent part of his tenure in Oak Park, a suburb of Chicago, from 1935–1951.[4] From 1947–1954 Chicago was also the home of Andrew and Margaret Schulze and a place of significant conflict over the nature of black Lutheran ministry.

By the time Andrew Schulze moved to the South Side of Chicago, the South Side had already surpassed Harlem as "the capital of black America." As Nicholas Lemann explained in *The Promised Land: The Great Black Migration and How It Changed America*, the South Side:

> was (and still is) the largest contiguous settlement of African-Americans. It was home to the heavyweight boxing champion of the world (and the most famous black man in America), Joe Louis; the only black member of Congress, William Dawson; the most prominent black newspaper, the *Defender*; the largest black congregation, J. H. Jackson's Olivet Baptist Church…. In the mid-1930s Elijah Muhammad (born Elijah Poole on a Georgia farm) moved his organization, the Lost-Found Nation of Islam, better know as the Black Muslims, from Detroit to the South Side…. By

---

different synods—this was the Lutheran Church in Chicago in 1893" (Robert Wiederaenders, "History of Lutheranism in the Chicago Area" in *Chicago Lutheran Planning Study* [National Lutheran Council, 1965] 2:31. Chicago Historical Society, Chicago IL .

[3] Statistics from 1942 showed that 72 of the 190 Lutheran congregations in the Chicago area belonged to the Missouri Synod (*Chicago Lutheran Planning Study*, 2:57).

[4] "Synodical Information" in *The Lutheran Annual* (St. Louis: Concordia Publishing House, 1999) 41.

the 1940s, Chicago supplanted Harlem as the center of black nationalism in the United States.[5]

African Americans had been a part of Chicago since its very beginnings, but it was the Great Migration that transformed black Chicago into the "Black Metropolis" or "Bronzeville."[6]

Allan Spear's study of Black Chicago found that white indifference to blacks turned to white hostility as more and more black Americans moved to the city between 1890 and 1910. With America's involvement in World War I, an ever greater number of black Americans began migrating to Chicago. The industrial demands of World War I set off the Great Migration of blacks from the South to urban centers in the North and West. Chicago was one of the most popular destinations, in part due to its location. Chicago was a very accessible Northern city for blacks from Mississippi, Louisiana, and Alabama as it marked the end of the Illinois Central Railroad.[7] Additionally, Chicago served as a symbol of the opportunities in Northern cities: "The Chicago *Defender*, the most widely read newspaper in the black South, afforded thousands of prospective

---

[5] Nicholas Lemann, *The Promised Land: The Great Migration and How It Changed America* (New York: Alfred A. Knopf, 1991) 64.

[6] See St. Clair Drake and Horace R. Cayton, *Black Metropolis: A Study of Negro Life in a Northern City*, vol. 1 and 2, rev. ed. (New York: Harper & Row, 1962). Martin Marty thought the study, originally published in 1945, was comparable to the more well-known Gunnar Mydral's *An American Dilemma*. "The Works Progress Administration of the New Deal and the Julius Rosenwald Fund, which meant Sears, Roebuck and Company earnings, subsidized an equally important but localized study. St. Clair Drake and Horace Cayton published the most extensive study yet of a metropolitan black community, including its churches" (*Modern American Religion, Under God, Indivisible, 1941–1960* [Chicago: The University of Chicago Press, 1996] 3:70.

[7] Allan H. Spear, *Black Chicago: The Making of a Negro Ghetto, 1890–1920* (Chicago: University of Chicago Press, 1967) 7–8, 129. Spear attempted "to show how, in a thirty year period, a relatively fluid pattern of race relations gave way to a rigid pattern of discrimination and segregation." "Most observers—both Negro and white—agreed that the status of Negroes in Chicago was deteriorating, and some saw parallels between developments in Chicago and the hardening of Jim Crow patterns of the South" (Spear, *Black Chicago*, xi, 48).

migrants glimpses of an exciting city with a vibrant and assertive black community."[8]

Even before the onset of the Great Migration, Chicago's physical ghetto had already formed, a large, almost all-black enclave on the South Side and a smaller, almost all-black enclave on the West Side.[9] Even though black Americans were restricted to a segregated existence as they moved to cities throughout America, many white Americans were threatened by their new presence. In the year following the end of World War I, race riots broke out in two dozen American cities. Chicago's riot was the worst. The Chicago Riot of 1919 was a series of brutal confrontations between black and white citizens that resulted in dozens of deaths and hundreds of injuries.[10] The Chicago Riot of 1919 added further impetus for the development of the self-sufficient black community of Bronzeville. By the end of World War II, Bronzeville was "a city within a city," a narrow strip of land, seven miles long and one and a half miles wide, with more than 300,000 black residents.[11]

At the center of Bronzeville was the crossing of Forty-seventh Street and South Parkway. Bronzeville's major community institutions were located within a half-mile radius of this intersection. These institutions included Provident Hospital, the George Cleveland Hall Library, the YMCA, the Hotel Grand, the largest black Catholic church in the country, and the largest Protestant church in the country.[12] Andrew Schulze's ministry in Chicago was eventually centered just to the northeast of Bronzeville's center at Christ the King Lutheran Church at Thirty-seventh Street and Lake Park.

Schulze originally came to Chicago under the auspices of the Mission Board of the Northern Illinois District of the Missouri Synod. By doing so,

---

[8] James R. Grossman, *Land of Hope: Chicago, Black Southerners, and the Great Migration* (Chicago: University of Chicago Press, 1989) 4.

[9] Spear, *Black Chicago*, 11.

[10] Arnold R. Hirsch, *Making the Second Ghetto: Race & Housing in Chicago, 1940–1960* (Chicago: The University of Chicago Press, 1998) 1. See William M. Tuttle, Jr., *Race Riot: Chicago in the Red Summer of 1919* (New York: Atheneum, 1970).

[11] Drake and Cayton, *Black Metropolis*, 1:12.

[12] Drake and Cayton, *Black Metropolis*, 2:380.

he again placed himself under the authority of a mission board and gave up some of the independence he enjoyed as pastor of St. Philip's. Before accepting the call to Chicago, he had a frank discussion with the Northern Illinois District Mission Board about his views about race relations in the church. Schulze later recalled that though there were disagreements, "The chairman of the board said what seemed to be the consensus, that it would be my privilege to speak on the matters of race as my conscience dictated."[13]

Shortly after Schulze arrived, he began receiving invitations to preach and speak at local congregations. Though a very strong person, Schulze was very warm and soft-spoken in his relations with other people. His sermons and speeches contained only mild injunctions; he continually stressed to others the need to be evangelical with regard to improving race relations. As he recalled, his Chicago remarks included something to this effect, "I am sure that, as you pray for and give toward the work I am doing, if and when a Negro attends your church as a direct result of the Lutheran Hour or of my work on the South Side, you will freely and cordially welcome him."[14]

Soon Schulze was asked by the district to "desist from 'disturbing' congregations by preaching about or alluding to what [he] believed was a Christian response to the question of racial integration." This marked the first of many conflicts that Schulze had with the district during his years in Chicago.[15] When the Northern Illinois District called Schulze, he already had a reputation as an activist regarding racial issues in the church. Yet Schulze also had a record of building up self-supporting black congregations. By calling Schulze, the Mission Board of the Northern Illinois District demonstrated that they wanted an effective program of black Lutheran ministry. However, the mission board was soon caught in a dilemma as they also wanted black Lutheran ministry to remain removed from white Lutheran congregations. The mission board was interested in having Schulze establish "Negro congregations." But Schulze saw his calling to both "establish new congregations where geography dictated, and to help prepare already established Lutheran congregations to accept the challenge

---

[13] Schulze, *Race against Time*, 47.
[14] Ibid., 48.
[15] Ibid., 48.

presented by the racial change that was or would be taking place in their communities."[16]

Andrew and Margaret Schulze moved to Chicago in August 1947. In September 1947 Schulze gave a broad outline of his vision for ministry in Chicago to the Northern Illinois District Mission Board. Schulze discussed a twenty-year plan during which ten new churches might be erected. At the same time, Schulze wanted to identify the Lutheran churches that might already border the Black Belt. He wanted to work closely with the only well-established black Lutheran congregation in Chicago, St. Philip's and its pastor, Marmaduke N. Carter. Members of St. Philip's had already given Schulze names of potential parishioners. Additionally, Schulze was interested in making contacts with other Lutheran pastors who would be willing to serve in inner-city Chicago in the future.[17]

Schulze's plan also included making significant contacts with the Chicago community. He wanted to develop relations with the Chicago *Defender*, the National Association for the Advancement of Colored People, the Urban League, and the Mayor's Race Relations Committee. He also wanted to stay well-informed on the work of other denominations in the Chicago area. Schulze hoped to learn more about traditional African-American churches in Chicago from the faculty of the University of Chicago's Divinity School. He also planned to "keep an eye on the activity of the Roman Catholic church in the Negro area."[18] Schulze was firmly convinced that "we can learn something from Roman Catholicism in the matter of transition parishes."[19]

---

[16] Ibid., 52.

[17] Minutes of the Regular Meeting of the Mission Board, 15 September 1947, Archives of the Northern Illinois District of the Lutheran Church—Missouri Synod, Chicago IL.

[18] Ibid.

[19] [Andrew Schulze], "Transition Parish," *Lutheran Race Relations Bulletin* 3 (December 1947): 7. "Rome can create a transition parish by means of its claim to universality and the application of Papal fiat. Protestant churches, and Lutherans especially can do it by the process of truly courageous evangelical preaching which makes the proper application of Christian faith to Christian life" ([Schulze], "Transition Parish," 8).

There were several large Catholic parishes in Chicago that served black parishioners, including St. Monica's, St. Elizabeth, St. Anselm's, Corpus Christi, and Holy Angels. Holy Angels was the largest and was located on Oakwood Boulevard, not far from a struggling black Lutheran mission that Schulze was called to stabilize.[20] As John McGreevy pointed out in his study of racial transition in Catholicism, "For Catholics in city neighborhoods... the stakes remained high.... No other denomination possessed such numbers in the northern cities; no other organization faced such financial risk."[21] In contrast, Lutherans were less experienced with urban settings. However, the middle decades of the twentieth century did see growing urbanization and suburbanization among Lutherans. As was true for other Protestant denominations, "these years marked the beginning of a new understanding of the church's role in the inner city, something which Roman Catholics had been engaged in for several years."[22]

Besides providing all the distractions of a bustling urban center, Chicago was a thriving religious center. Schulze's work on the South Side was set amid several competing religious traditions. At the time of St. Clair Drake and Horace Cayton's study of Chicago, the South Side was home to some 500 churches and 200,000 members of 30 different denominations.[23] Milton Sernett noted that "Chicago offered migrants a far greater choice in religious affiliation than did the South where most African Americans were either Baptists or Methodists.... Newcomers could shop around for a church in which they felt comfortable."[24] Besides the Catholic parishes and the

---

[20] For more on black Catholicism in Chicago, see Steven M. Avella, *This Confident Church: Catholic Leadership and Life in Chicago, 1940–1965* (Notre Dame: University of Notre Dame Press, 1992).

[21] John T. McGreevy, *Parish Boundaries: The Catholic Encounter with Race in the Twentieth Century Urban North* (Chicago: The University of Chicago Press, 1996) 84–85.

[22] E. Clifford Nelson, "The New Shape of Lutheranism, 1930–Present" in *The Lutherans in North America*, rev. ed., ed. E. Clifford Nelson (Philadelphia: Fortress Press, 1980) 486.

[23] Martin Marty, *Modern American Religion*, 3:71.

[24] Milton C. Sernett, "When Chicago Was Canaan" in *Bound for the Promised Land: African American Religion and the Great Migration* (Durham NC: Duke University Press, 1997) 161.

plethora of storefront churches, there were also several large Baptist and Methodist churches. Olivet Baptist Church was not only one of the largest black Baptists churches in the country, it was one of the largest Protestant churches in the country. Olivet, always well known on the South Side, became well known nationally during the civil rights movement as its pastor served as a main critic and competitor of Martin Luther King, Jr.[25]

There were also those religious movements that were not a part of the Christian tradition. Elijah Muhammad's growing black Muslim movement, the Nation of Islam, was based on the South Side of Chicago. His most famous disciple, Malcolm X, served as a powerful symbol for many African Americans in the nation's inner-cities during the 1960s. Muhammad's palatial home was located in North Kenwood, the neighborhood just to the south of where Schulze's ministry was centered.[26]

When Schulze first began serving the Northern Illinois District Mission Board, it was clear that his work on the South Side was not work he could do alone. There was talk from the beginning about providing not only office support, but also finding another pastor to work with Schulze. But his work in Chicago was always under-financed and under-staffed. During his tenure in Chicago, the number of blacks migrating to the city continued to increase. Taken in that context, Schulze's position in Chicago was "pretty absurd.... The rate of influx of blacks from the South at that time was simply beyond realistic reach.... It was something like a thousand newcomers a week."[27] The mission board never came through with the support Schulze needed to enable his work.

---

[25] "John H. Jackson, the pastor of the magnificent yellow-brick Olivet Baptist Church...is probably best known now for having been the leading enemy of Martin Luther King within the black Baptist church; when the city of Chicago changed the name of South Parkway, the boulevard on which Olivet stands, to King Drive after King's death, Jackson changed the address of the church to Thirty-first Street so he wouldn't have to have King's name on his letterhead" (Lemann, *The Promised Land*, 47).

[26] James R. Ralph, Jr., *Northern Protest: Martin Luther King Jr., Chicago, and the Civil Rights Movement* (Cambridge: Harvard University Press, 1993) 76.

[27] Karl E. Lutze, interview by James W. Albers, 20 July 1981 and 26 October 1981, Oral History Collection, Archives of Cooperative Lutheranism, ELCA Archives, Chicago IL, 2.

For the first two years that Andrew and Margaret were in Chicago, their home and their work was of a somewhat transitory nature. The housing originally provided by the Northern Illinois District Mission Board was quite inadequate. They first resided in a small three-room apartment on East Sixty-first Street. Living conditions were not good during this period on the South Side of Chicago. It was left to Andrew and Margaret to find better living arrangements for themselves. As Schulze recalled, "To find and rent an apartment fit for human habitation in that part of over-crowded Chicago was like searching for the proverbial needle in the haystack."[28] During their years in Chicago, the Schulze sons were all away for their studies. All three of them were following in their father's footsteps, on their way to become Lutheran pastors. When all the Schulze sons were home during their vacation periods, the apartment was especially crowded.

Schulze began his work in Chicago by shoring up a struggling Lutheran mission that began in 1941 as the result of a community canvass by Verna Schultz, an employee of the Northern Illinois District.[29] A Lutheran storefront church and school were in operation when Schulze arrived. The district had been renting a space at 3802 Cottage Grove Avenue. The storefront mission and school took the name of the Ida B. Wells Lutheran Mission. The Lutheran mission was located nearby Chicago's first public housing project, the Ida B. Wells Homes, constructed in the late 1930s.[30] The Ida B. Wells Homes covered forty-seven acres between Thirty-seventh and Thirty-ninth streets and provided housing for over 1,600 black families. The homes and the mission were named for the activist Ida B. Wells, who was well-known for her crusade against lynching. However, Wells's "interests also led her into the women's suffrage movement, women's club activities, social settlement work, and progressive

---

[28] Schulze, *Race against Time*, 49–50.

[29] "Christ the King Lutheran School, An Anniversary Celebration," 4 June 1994, files of Christ the King Lutheran Church, Christ the King Lutheran Church, Chicago IL.

[30] Hirsch, *Making the Second Ghetto*, 10. "The construction of the Ida B. Wells public housing project destroyed nearly as many apartments as it supplied. When the project finally opened in 1941, 17,544 applications were received for its 1,662 units" (Hirsch, *Making the Second Ghetto*, 18).

politics.... She was the only Chicago Negro to sign the call for the conference that led to the establishment of the NAACP in 1909."[31]

The storefront location of the Ida B. Wells Lutheran Mission had several disadvantages. Besides the high rent charged for the use of the facilities, the congregation also had to deal with rats running around during their regular Sunday service.[32] This was not a problem limited to this particular location. Because of the overcrowded nature of South Side neighborhoods, "building inspections and garbage collection...fell 'far below the minimum mandatory to healthful sanitation'.... Rats continued to flourish in Chicago, and by the summer of 1953 the city's rat control officer estimated that there were as many rats as humans in the city."[33] Additionally, Schulze also had strong feelings that Lutheran congregations should not be based in storefront locations.

Shortly after he arrived in Chicago, Schulze began to lobby the Northern Illinois District to construct a church building for the congregation. In the meantime, Schulze also found another location, also on Cottage Avenue, in which the small mission could worship. The district rented a space at Sims Funeral Parlor until a church home was built and dedicated in 1949.[34] For a time, the mission school also had a different location, but eventually the school was shut down.[35] The closing of the school was meant to be on a short-term, temporary basis, but it was not until 1973 that a Lutheran school was reestablished as a part of this congregation.

In 1948 the Northern Illinois District Mission Board purchased a lot on Thirty-seventh and Lake Park Boulevard for the Ida B. Wells Mission. However, Schulze and the board continued to have disagreements. He opposed another proposal of the mission board to start another black Lutheran congregation near an already established white Lutheran church.

---

[31] Spear, *Black Chicago*, 59–60.

[32] Schulze, *Race against Time*, 54.

[33] Hirsch, *Making the Second Ghetto*, 25.

[34] The use of the Funeral Parlor was a better solution than the rat-infested storefront. However, Schulze recalled that there were times when caskets were still in view during worship services and that this was not appropriate for worshipping He who came that people "might have life and have it more abundantly" (John 10:11) (Schulze, *Race against Time*, 55).

[35] Ibid., 54–55.

In September 1948, one year after Schulze arrived in Chicago, he read an essay to the board on his thoughts about how black Lutheran ministry should proceed in Chicago. The board responded by reemphasizing its willingness "to do all in our power to help our (colored) brother to obtain and maintain his chapel and school in which he and his can worship as a colored congregation, but that it would not be wise at this time to compel 'white' congregations to take into membership colored Lutherans since in most sectors of our District this may still cause much harm."[36]

Even though the Mission Board of the Northern Illinois District did not seem to be listening to Schulze, other Lutherans were. Besides his work for the district, Schulze continued as an unofficial advisor for racial concerns among Lutherans. Especially after the publication of *My Neighbor of Another Color*, Lutherans from all over wrote to Schulze, asking his opinion on racial matters.[37] Several white Lutheran pastors consulted with him as they began their ministries among black Americans. This was how Andrew Schulze first got to know Karl Lutze, a pastor who began serving in an African-American community in Tulsa, Oklahoma, in the late 1940s. As Lutze recalled, Schulze was considered "*the* mentor" among white pastors serving in positions of black ministry.[38] During the 1960s, Lutze became Schulze's successor as the Executive Secretary of the Lutheran Human Relations Association.

Just as Schulze worked to create the St. Louis Lutheran Society for Better Race Relations, he now worked to create a similar society in Chicago. In 1948 First St. Paul's Lutheran Church in Chicago, the same church in which the Missouri Synod was originally organized in 1847, hosted the Lutheran Race Relations Institute. A group of Chicago Lutherans came together to sponsor the institute, but attendance was less than expected. Nonetheless, larger possibilities were being discussed for the future. The *Lutheran Race Relations Bulletin* reported that plans to organize a Lutheran Society for Better Race Relations in Chicago were underway. It also stated

---

[36] Minutes of the Regular Meeting of the Mission Board of the Northern Illinois District, 15 September 1948, Archives of the Northern Illinois District of the Lutheran Church—Missouri Synod, Chicago IL.

[37] Andrew Schulze Papers, Concordia Historical Institute (CHI), St. Louis MO.

[38] Lutze, Oral History Collection, 4.

that three such organizations already existed, in St. Louis, Missouri; Houston, Texas; and Chattanooga, Tennessee. There was also talk about the formation of other Lutheran race relations organizations in cities with substantial Lutheran populations.[39]

In 1946, the year before Schulze moved to Chicago, Schulze was elected as a member of the Synodical Conference's missionary board. He was elected at the same convention that voted for the integration of black congregations into their local synodical district. The election of Schulze to the missionary board reflected that some members of the Synodical Conference did want the board to become more sensitive to racial matters. As Schulze later pointed out, most members of the Missionary Board had little intimate contact with black Americans. The three main executive secretaries of the missionary board during the twentieth century— Christopher F. Drewes, Louis A. Wisler, and Karl Kurth—all lived in white neighborhoods and were members of white congregations.[40] It was not until just before the Synodical Conference's missionary board was dismantled, in the early 1960s, that a black pastor, Joseph Lavalis, became a part of the missionary board.[41]

Schulze's service on the missionary board, 1946–1952, coincided closely with his years in Chicago. Through his formal involvement with the missionary board, he tried to persuade it to make changes in its handling of black Lutheran ministry. One issue of concern was Lutheran publications and the way they handled or ignored racial matters.[42] This had been one of Schulze's concerns for some time and was part of the motivation behind the development of the *Lutheran Race Relations Bulletin*. As an early issue of the *Bulletin* expressed, "This Bulletin will be ready to bow out of the picture as soon as other regular line Lutheran periodicals, intended to reach both the clergy and the laity (such as the *Concordia Theological Monthly* and the

---

[39] "Third Lutheran Race Relations Convention and Institute Held in Chicago," *Lutheran Race Relations Bulletin* 4 (May 1948): 5.

[40] Schulze, *Race against Time*, 72.

[41] Jeff G. Johnson, *Black Christians: The Untold Lutheran Story* (St. Louis: Concordia Publishing House, 1991) 201.

[42] For a good overview of Lutheran publications and race relations, see George Hans Liebenow, "Attitudes and Policies of the Lutheran Church Toward the Negro" (Bachelor's Thesis, Concordia Seminary, St. Louis, 1957).

Lutheran Witness), are prepared for and committed to a proper discussion of this problem now confronting the world, nation, and the Church."[43]

Shortly after Schulze arrived in Chicago, he became concerned about a tract on black Lutheran ministry that the missionary board was planning to publish. Dr. John H. C. Fritz, dean of students at Concordia Seminary in St. Louis, prepared the tract. The Missouri Synod had long looked to its seminary faculty as standard-bearers for the church's stance on contemporary theological issues. But as Schulze pointed out, Fritz was not a person who had much experience in the area of race relations.[44] The tract was intended to encourage white Lutherans to be more accepting of their fellow black Lutherans. As it stated in one section, "No Christian in a white congregation should object to have a Negro, or a person of any other color, to sit along side of him in church and worship God together with him, no more than a rich man should object to worship God along side of a poor man."[45]

However, there were many other problems with the publication. The draft of the tract was originally titled in a very patronizing manner as "Our Friend, The Negro." The draft also included sentences that stressed "the social problem of the Negro is not the direct concern of the Church." These statements were removed along with other glaring problems in the text, and it was published under the title "The Lutheran Church and The Negro."[46] But Schulze was still not satisfied with the final result. He believed that the tract was "in the final analysis...paternalistic and left loopholes for the segregationist to vindicate himself." Though Schulze dissented, the board voted to print the tract.[47]

Another major area of concern and conflict during these years was the development of "Jim Crow" churches. Schulze was upset that some black Lutheran missions were being started in "changing communities" in various

---

[43] *Lutheran Race Relations Bulletin* 2 (November 1946): 1.

[44] Schulze, *Race against Time*, 73.

[45] This statement is found both in the original draft and the final publication. "Our Friend, The Negro" and "The Lutheran Church and The Negro," Andrew Schulze Papers, CHI, St. Louis MO.

[46] "Our Friend, The Negro" and "The Lutheran Church and The Negro," Andrew Schulze Papers, CHI, St. Louis MO.

[47] Schulze, *Race against Time*, 73–74.

cities so that local white Lutheran churches could direct interested blacks to the services of black Lutheran missions. Schulze had hoped that by the late 1940s, the era of black Lutheran missions was over. As he wrote to Clemonce Sabourin, "I am trying presently to avoid the Board's establishing a separate mission among the 14,000 Negroes of Milwaukee who are surrounded by about eight large Lutheran churches. Pray that I may be able to throw the monkey-wrench into the works to forestall the establishment of such a mission in the year of our Lord 1949."[48] Once again, Schulze voted against the majority of the mission board and a newly sponsored black Lutheran mission was begun in Milwaukee. The Synodical Conference's program of black Lutheran ministry was still operating within the mindset and the framework of segregation.

Schulze became so frustrated with his experiences on the mission board that he considered resigning. At one point, he wrote a long letter of resignation that explained some of his frustrations with the board. As Schulze stated, "There has been at the Board meetings of the past two and one half years almost no discussion of the matter that at this time should be discussed most thoroughly to the end that God's way and will may be ascertained. I am referring to the acceptance by established congregations of members of minority racial groups living in their respective communities."[49] But Schulze never sent the letter. He was counseled by friends and supporters to remain on the board. In particular, O. H. Theiss, executive secretary of the Walther League, advised Schulze that he would be "more influential inside than outside the power structure."[50]

By 1950 Schulze became more settled in his ministry in Chicago. Andrew and Margaret had moved into a better housing situation, living in a house at 6952 S. Calumet Avenue, located in a "changing neighborhood." The home was a good distance to the south of the Ida B. Wells Mission. At the time when Andrew and Margaret decided on the home in late 1948, Schulze planned to spread his time between different locations on the South

---

[48] Andrew Schulze to Clemonce Sabourin, 7 January 7 1949 (copy), Andrew Schulze Papers, CHI, St. Louis MO.

[49] Andrew Schulze to Pastor Schlueter, (draft), Andrew Schulze Papers, CHI, St. Louis MO.

[50] Schulze, *Race against Time*, 77.

Side of Chicago. During the first part of his years in Chicago, he was also active in Princeton Park, an area on the far South Side of Chicago. This was a more affluent black neighborhood and Schulze believed that it had the potential for the development of a new black Lutheran congregation.

But Schulze eventually became more committed to his work with the Ida B. Wells Mission. In 1949 the mission took on a new name, The Lutheran Church of Christ the King and constructed a new church building with funds from the Northern Illinois District, the Lutheran Women's Missionary League, and the Church Extension Fund.[51] Christ the King was situated at Thirty-seventh Street and Lake Park in the neighborhood known as Oakland. In the fall of 1950, the small congregation, with a little over 200 baptized members, called Andrew Schulze to be their first pastor. Schulze consulted with the Northern Illinois District about his new call. He chose to accept the call, with the understanding that he would also continue in his role as an advisor to the district's program of black Lutheran ministry in Chicago.[52]

Schulze's work in the Princeton Park area helped to lay the groundwork for Resurrection Evangelical Lutheran Church, officially organized in 1952. Resurrection, located at 9417 South Lafayette, joined St. Philip's and Christ the King as the third black Lutheran congregation in Chicago affiliated with the Missouri Synod. Reverend Moses S. Dickinson was called and installed as Resurrection's first pastor. Dickinson had previously been pastor in Charlotte, North Carolina, and brought ten years of pastoral experience with him.[53] Moses served Resurrection for the rest of his ministry, providing a model of local community leadership and pastoral service for many people in the Chicago area and for the larger Lutheran community. As Karl Lutze recalled, "There was an attitude prevalent among pastors generally that the black pastors just weren't qualified.... Moses was set to challenge that impression.... His work became paradigmatic for

---

[51] Andrew Schulze, "Brick Walls, A Roof and A Floor," in the "Northern Illinois Messenger," local supplement to the *Lutheran Witness* 68 (31 May 1949).

[52] Minutes of Special Committee Meeting, 18 September 1950, Archives of the Northern Illinois District of the Lutheran Church—Missouri Synod, Chicago IL.

[53] Program for the Dedicatory Services, 17 February 1952, Church files, archives of the Northern Illinois District of the Lutheran Church—Missouri Synod, Chicago IL.

almost all, and an inspiration for almost all black pastors."[54] From the days when Marmaduke N. Carter first began as pastor of St. Philip's, Chicago became a place for the emergence of leadership within the black Lutheran community. In the late 1960s and early 1970s, Chicago served as the center of the movement to form the Association of Black Lutheran Clergymen.

Schulze continued to ask the Northern Illinois District to do more among Chicago's African-American community. At a meeting of the mission board in 1951, Schulze "pleaded that the Chicago Negro Mission field be worked with even greater vigor." [55] He pointed out that there was no program of Lutheran outreach to Chicago's black community on the West Side. A couple of years later, an established congregation, Immanuel Lutheran Church, under the pastoral leadership of Ralph Luther Moellering, began to reach out to its immediate community on the West Side.[56] But Lutherans were generally slow to adjust to the rapidly changing racial situation in Chicago during the years following World War II.

One of Schulze's main concerns was the lack of leadership that he saw in the church in the area of race relations. He recalled a conversation that he had during these years with Rev. Karl Kurth, the executive secretary of the Synodical Conference's missionary board. Kurth stated that he agreed with Schulze about the issue of integration, but Kurth advised, "Don't do anything about it. It's coming." Schulze believed that similar views were

---

[54] Lutze, Oral History Collection, 8.

[55] Minutes of the Northern Illinois Mission Board, 18 April 1951, Archives of the Northern Illinois District of the Lutheran Church—Missouri Synod, Chicago IL.

[56] See Ralph L. Moellering, "Lutheran Progress in Human Relations And the Story of First Immanuel Lutheran Church of Chicago," *Proceedings* of the Lutheran Human Relations Association of America, Summer Institute, 9–11 July 1954. "At its centennial in 1960, this congregation on the near west side, which had grown to three thousand in the late nineteenth century and was now back to three hundred.... With Ralph Moellering this became the first Chicago LCMS congregation to accept African Americans and other minorities into a previously white fold. During the Chicago civil rights movement, with Donald Becker as pastor, this congregation opened its doors to a Martin Luther King rally by a painful, racially divided margin of one vote" (Richard Luecke, "Themes of Lutheran Urban Ministry, 1945–1985," *Churches, Cities, and Human Community: Urban Ministry in the United States, 1945–1985*, ed. Clifford J. Green (Grand Rapids: William B. Eerdmans Publishing Company, 1966) 142.

found within "the power structure of the Missouri Synod in general."[57] Schulze was disheartened by these attitudes as he believed this was a time for vigorous, not passive, leadership in the church. So he continued his work outside of the official structures of the church.

The organizations Schulze began, the St. Louis and Chicago Societies for Better Race Relations, continued to sponsor summer race relations institutes. In 1950 O. P. Kretzmann, the president of Valparaiso University and long-time friend to Andrew Schulze, invited the societies to host their institutes on Valparaiso's campus in Valparaiso, Indiana, about one hour east of Chicago. Beginning in the summer of 1950, annual institutes were held at Valparaiso until the 1970s. Valparaiso was affiliated with the Missouri Synod, but was not a synodically owned institution as were many Missouri Synod schools. Valparaiso was a Lutheran institution independent from the official structures of the church, but it also served a large Lutheran constituency. From the 1950s through the 1970s, the campus and resources of Valparaiso University were made available to the cause of promoting better race relations in both church and society.

On 18–19 July 1950 a group of Lutherans gathered on the campus of Valparaiso University for mutual fellowship and inspiration as they heard speakers on contemporary racial issues. While race relations in the church remained the central concern of the institute, topics for discussion also included societal issues such as equal employment and housing and education without discrimination. Both Lutherans and non-Lutherans, both community leaders and leaders within the church, were featured speakers. Beginning in 1950, the essays delivered at the annual summer institutes were published together and distributed to those who wished copies. For the 1950 institute, both Andrew Schulze and Clemonce Sabourin served as main speakers.

Schulze spoke on "The Ultimate in Christian Race Relations— Communicant Integration." Schulze defined communicant integration as "the complete elimination of the color line in the local parish." The primary example of this was welcoming all who profess the same faith to Holy

---

[57] Schulze, *Race against Time*, 79.

Communion, "the high point in Christian fellowship."[58] Lutherans, as members of a church that valued both Word and Sacrament, needed to break down the barriers of race that obstructed Christian unity. Schulze knew all too well that there were many black Lutherans being denied equal fellowship in the larger Lutheran community. Schulze explained, "Unfortunately most churches—including the Lutheran Church—have allowed the world to set the pattern in the matters of social living." But as Schulze pointed out, "Not the world, but the church has been called to exercise leadership in moral and spiritual matters."[59]

While Alfred Rehwinkel had been Schulze's primary supporter at Concordia Seminary during his years in St. Louis, in the 1950s, Schulze gained two new supporters at Concordia Seminary, St. Louis. It was helpful to have seminary professors lend their talents as well as their stature to the cause of improving race relations in the church. Besides influencing seminary students, seminary professors were generally held in high regard by the church at large. Both Rev. Dr. Arthur Carl Piepkorn and Rev. Dr. Martin Scharlemann joined the St. Louis faculty in the early 1950s and soon became involved with the work of Andrew Schulze. Piepkorn and Scharlemann may have been sensitive to racial matters due to their experiences as military chaplains during World War II. But their commitment to racial justice was not only based on practical experiences alone, it was also a part of their theological outlook.

Arthur Carl Piepkorn was a rising star among Lutheran theologians. Piepkorn was committed to a very historical and liturgical vision of the church. He was the featured speaker of the 1952 institute, delivering a long address to begin the three-day institute. Piepkorn borrowed his title from the famous words that Martin Luther stated at Worms before Emperor Charles V in 1521, "Here I Stand." Like Luther before him, Piepkorn based his stand on racial issues on the word of God. Piepkorn explained that segregation had no basis in scripture or in the historic creeds and confessions of the church: "There is on the other hand a repeated, a

---

[58] Andrew Schulze, "The Ultimate in Christian Race Relations—Communicant Integration," *Proceedings* of the Lutheran Race Relations Institute, 18–19 July 1950, 22.

[59] Ibid., 26.

reiterated, a Catholic and Scriptural emphasis upon the equality of individuals under sin and grace, upon the unity and divine character of the Church, and upon a redeeming and unifying Saviour in Whom there is neither Jew nor Greek, but in Whom all are one." Piepkorn also stressed that though Missouri Synod had a congregational polity, congregations were not wholly free, but bound by their relationship to God and to one another.[60]

Beginning in 1952, the sponsors of the annual institute began referring to the gathering as the Human Relations Institute rather than the Race Relations Institute. The switch in wording reflected the sponsors desire to be broad and inclusive in their efforts. In 1952 the group of about seventy-five individuals who attended the annual institute also discussed the development of an organization that would work on a year-round basis to promote improved race relations in church and society. The idea was to merge local Lutheran race relations societies into a national organization. Plans were in the works to create the Lutheran Human Relations Association of America.[61]

Though these efforts to improve race relations in the church were mainly initiated by members of the Missouri Synod, and especially directed at the Missouri Synod, they also involved individuals from other Lutheran synods. Even in the early years of the institutes, speakers included Lutherans from other synodical backgrounds. Though the movement for greater Lutheran cooperation and Lutheran unity had been gaining momentum since the early part of the twentieth century, the Missouri Synod remained cautious when it came to its relationship with other synods. The official stance of the Missouri Synod opposed "unionism," or fellowship with other

---

[60] Arthur Carl Piepkorn, "Here I Stand," *Proceedings* of the Lutheran Human Relations Institute, 28–30 July 1952, 8–9. "The individual congregation is not wholly autonomous. Its autonomy extends only to those things concerning which God has not pronounced. Where its sovereign Head has spoken, the Church has no scope for dispensation or contrary legislation. The autonomy of the individual congregation is further limited by the mere existence of other congregations. No individual congregation is the Church; it is only a part of the Church" (Piepkorn, "Here I Stand," 28).

[61] Andrew Schulze to Clemonce Sabourin, 8 August 1952 (copy), Andrew Schulze Papers, CHI, St. Louis MO.

Christians with whom it did not share complete doctrinal agreement. Missourians believed that the practice of unionism would weaken the synod's witness to the truths it held so dear. But within the synod, there was some debate over what exactly constituted unionism. The Missouri Synod did cooperate with other Lutherans in limited ways.[62]

Race relations were also a concern for other Lutheran church bodies, especially in the years following World War II. Besides Missouri, two of the other large Lutheran synods in America were the United Lutheran Church in America (ULCA) and the American Lutheran Church (ALC). Both the ULCA and the ALC had a history of involvement with black Lutherans. The United Lutheran Church in America had its roots on the East Coast, dating back to the colonial period. The United Lutheran Church in America had a considerable number of black members as they were the church body connected to the Lutheran churches in the Virgin Islands, formerly the Danish West Indies. As early as the 1870s, black Lutherans from the Danish West Indies began migrating to New York City where they formed new congregations. Beginning in the 1930s, the ULCA donated money to the Synodical Conference and the American Lutheran Church for their efforts in black Lutheran ministry, but the ULCA made no independent efforts at mission work among black Americans.[63]

The American Lutheran Church, largely based in the Midwest, had a spotty record of black Lutheran ministry. The ALC had a history of black Lutheran missions going back to the 1880s, but these efforts were

---

[62] See Frederick K. Wentz, *Lutherans in Concert: The Story of the National Lutheran Council, 1918–1966* (Minneapolis: Augsburg Publishing House, 1968). Though the Missouri Synod was not a member of the National Lutheran Council, it did cooperate with other Lutherans in specific areas such as immigration services and the 1953 production of the "Martin Luther" film. Martin Luther continued to be an inspiring figure for Schulze and others. As Schulze responded to the film in a letter to a friend, "I saw the Martin Luther film today. It is superb and just the thing for the times in which we are living" (Andrew Schulze to Wallie Heyne, 16 September 1953 [copy], Andrew Schulze Papers, CHI, St. Louis MO).

[63] Johnson, *Black Christians*, 173, 189. As late as the 1930s, the ULCA had more black members than the Synodical Conference. "The majority (though not all) of their black members were in the Virgin Islands; but they were, nevertheless, members of an American Lutheran body, not part of a foreign mission field" (Johnson, *Black Christians*, 189).

concentrated in just two cities, Washington DC and Baltimore, Maryland. The American Lutheran Church also had black Lutheran mission efforts in Alabama and Mississippi dating from the early part of the twentieth century. But by the 1930s, the ALC had grown frustrated with these limited efforts in the South. The Synodical Conference had gained six times as many black members as the ALC in approximately the same number of years.[64] In response to this situation and the changing racial dynamics of the post-World War II era, the ALC first handed its black Lutheran missions in the South over to the National Lutheran Council. Later, some of its black congregations were handed over to the Missouri Synod.

As Milton Sernett pointed out in his study of the American Lutheran Church's experiences in black Lutheran ministry, "Once again the church, weather-vane like, had moved with the ever-shifting winds of social history."[65] The ALC was attempting to respond to the integrationist spirit of the times. As it had no white congregations in Alabama or Mississippi, it wanted to end treating black congregations as "a separate and almost foreign mission field."[66] But the local black congregations involved in the transfer from the ALC to the Missouri Synod were not involved in the decision-making process. There was some local resentment as to how the situation was handled.[67]

In looking at the wider Lutheran context in America, it was clear that the Missouri Synod, and others in the Synodical Conference, did play the leading role in the development of black Lutheranism in America.[68] Some suggest that this gave the Missouri Synod a larger obligation to develop

---

[64] Ibid., 186, 188.

[65] Milton C. Sernett, "A Question of Earnestness: American Lutheran Missions and Theological Education in Alabama's 'Black Belt,' *Essays and Reports of the Lutheran Historical Conference* 9 (1982): 104.

[66] Ibid., 104.

[67] Nelson W. Trout, interview by Norman E. Minich, 19–20 August, 1982, Oral History Collection, Archives of Cooperative Lutheranism, Lutheran Council in the USA, ELCA Archives, Chicago IL, 66–68.

[68] Though both of today's major Lutheran church bodies include very small percentages of black members, the Lutheran Church—Missouri Synod (LCMS) still has a larger proportion of black Lutherans than the larger Evangelical Lutheran Church in America (ELCA).

improved race relations in church and society. Missouri Synod Lutherans owed a greater debt to their fellow black Lutherans after years of unequal and paternalistic treatment.[69] But some Missourians had also been fortunate to have more contact and interaction with black Lutherans, and more contact and interaction often led to greater understanding.[70] Though the Missouri Synod was regarded as the most conservative and insular synod among the larger Lutheran synods in America, some members of the Missouri Synod did have experience and sensitivities in the area of race relations.

Black Lutheran ministry also came under the responsibilities of the National Lutheran Council, an organization for cooperative Lutheran efforts formed in the midst of World War I. The National Lutheran Council included the United Lutheran Church in America, the American Lutheran Church, and several other Lutheran synods, but not the Missouri Synod. In the early 1950s, the American Lutheran Church turned over about a dozen black mission congregations to the oversight of the National Lutheran Council.[71] Just a couple of years before, members of the National Lutheran Council realized that increasing numbers of their northern urban congregations were in neighborhoods with a changing racial composition.[72] In response, the National Lutheran Council worked to develop consulting services to help local congregations better serve their changing neighborhoods and to help church bodies plan new mission efforts in black communities.[73]

The Missionary Board of the Synodical Conference was also at work in these years to develop guidelines for its congregations regarding the integration of non-white members into its congregations. In 1952 the missionary board issued "Guidelines on the Integration of Negroes" and sent the document to every district president and district mission board of the Synodical Conference. The 1950 convention of the Synodical Conference had requested that the missionary board study the issue of

---

[69] Lutze, Oral History Collection, 17.

[70] Trout, Oral History Collection, 68.

[71] Wentz, *Lutherans in Concert*, 123.

[72] Johnson, *Black Christians*, 190.

[73] Wentz, *Lutherans in Concert*, 123.

integration and offer guidelines to its congregations as to how integration should proceed.[74] The development of the "Guidelines" began in earnest in 1951 when the executive secretary of the missionary board, Karl Kurth, sent an inquiry about integration to various people involved in black Lutheran ministry.

Kurth received a variety of responses to his inquiry. Some responses were not that favorable to the idea of integration. Albert Dominick, a black Lutheran pastor in Mobile, Alabama, wrote that integration was "not what the Negro wants. He simply wants equal opportunity. He wants the privilege of becoming a member of a white congregation if he so desires; but by and large, he desires to have his own church." The Rev. Geo. Lillegard of the Norwegian Synod suggested that black Lutherans be encouraged "to organize their own congregation and seek to bring in more of their fellow-negroes. (This was the way in which German and Scandinavian churches were built up.)" Others thought that more time was necessary before integration could take place. Seminary professor J. T. Mueller stressed that the matter "should not be forced as the race relations committees now force matters…. Negro congregations should not feel offended if Caucasian churches are not ready to receive them, but wait patiently." But others pushed that integration should take place wherever possible. Clemonce Sabourin suggested that congregations invite black visitors and treat them just as they would invite and treat white visitors. Andrew Schulze stressed that existing examples of integration by Lutheran congregations as well as congregations from other denominations be held up as models for how integration can happen.[75]

Schulze was not impressed with the end result of all the inquiries. He scrawled his judgment on the front cover of his copy of the "Guidelines." Schulze wrote that it was "a wishy-washy middle of the road, equivocating,

---

[74] Letter and "Guidelines" from Karl Kurth, 2 June 1952, papers of the Synodical Conference Missionary Board, Domestic Negro Missions, box 17, CHI, St. Louis MO.

[75] A. Dominick to the Missionary Board—Synodical Conference, 15 August 1951; Geo. O. Lillegard to Rev. Karl Kurth, 23 August 1951; J. T. Mueller to Dr. Kurth, 31 July 1951; Clemonce Sabourin to Dr. Kurth, 5 September 1951; Andrew Schulze to Pastor Kurth, 8 August 1951, papers of the Synodical Conference Missionary Board, Domestic Negro Missions, box 17, CHI, St. Louis MO.

principle-denying statement."[76] The "Guidelines" explained that the segregation of congregations resulted not from "ill-will and prejudice," but from "the general consensus that people belonging to this and that race or nationality preferred to band together and form a separate organization." It also included statements such as, "The congregation has the right to sell its church building and move to another section of the city. However, such a move should not be made hastily and determinately by a congregation without a thorough appraisal of its functional potentialities." The "Guidelines" ended with anonymous excerpts from the letters that Kurth received, some giving a greater emphasis to the need for integration than others.[77]

Schulze continued to be frustrated with the official response of the church to race relations. He had made his position clear in an article, "All One Body, We" published in the April 1952 edition of *The Cresset*. Schulze wrote, "There are no two sides to the question. Christ's answer is clear and emphatic.... God in His holy word doesn't give a congregation the power to choose its brethren in faith nor give it the privilege of deciding who is to be included in His fellowship." [78] Maintaining peace within the congregation was no excuse for avoiding integration. Schulze compared that peace with the peace that the priest and the Levite had as they passed the injured man by in the parable of the Good Samaritan.

Though Schulze believed that the congregational polity of the Missouri Synod was a good reflection of the Christian freedom found in the New Testament, he was also disturbed about how the autonomy of the congregation was being misused to avoid integration. He was offended by the fact that some congregations voted as to whether to accept people of a different racial background. However, members of the Missouri Synod were also known for their respect and deference toward the clergy and their church officials. Occasionally, Schulze was reminded that the president of

---

[76] Andrew Schulze's copy of the "Guidelines," Andrew Schulze Papers, CHI, St. Louis MO.

[77] "Guidelines for the Integration of Negroes,"papers of the Synodical Conference Missionary Board, Domestic Negro Missions, box No. 17, CHI, St. Louis MO.

[78] Andrew Schulze, "All One Body, We," *The Cresset* 15 (April 1952): 12.

synod, John Behnken, did not agree with his stand, as if to prove his "unorthodoxy." But as Schulze saw it, Lutheranism was about following the orthodoxy of the Word of God, not the will of the congregation or the position of church leaders.[79]

In the spring of 1953, in honor of his work in the area of race relations, Andrew Schulze was awarded an honorary doctorate of laws from Valparaiso University. His honorary doctorate soon opened a new opportunity for him on the campus of Valparaiso University. During the annual institute held at Valparaiso, Indiana, on 24–26 July 1953, attendees voted the Lutheran Human Relations Association of America (LHRAA) into existence.[80] At the time, it was still a venture of faith, but foundations were being laid for a larger effort to improve race relations in both church and society. The initial officers of the organization included Andrew Schulze, Walter Heyne, John C. Ballard, Martin E. Nees, Gertrude Fiehler, Moses S. Dickinson, G. Hans Liebenow, and Paul Simon.[81] Paul Simon, a lawyer who later served for many years as a distinguished senator for the state of Illinois, made the arrangements for the legal work necessary to incorporate the organization.[82]

Over the next few months, funds were gathered to enable the creation of a full-time position for the executive secretary of the Lutheran Human Relations Association of America. The position was to be funded jointly between the LHRAA and Valparaiso University. In return, the executive secretary was also required to teach theology courses at Valparaiso. Because of his previous leadership in race relations and now with an honorary doctorate to his name, Andrew Schulze was the natural choice for the first executive secretary of the Lutheran Human Relations Association of America. The offer to head the LHRAA and become a faculty member at Valparaiso was a recognition of the previous contributions and achievements of Andrew Schulze.

Publication of the *Lutheran Race Relations Bulletin* or *Focus* ended in 1950. Now with the formation of the Lutheran Human Relation

---

[79] Schulze, *Race against Time*, 52.

[80] *Proceedings* of the Lutheran Human Relations Institute, 24–26 July 1953, 2.

[81] Schulze, *Race against Time*, 123.

[82] Paul Simon to Andrew Schulze, n.d., Andrew Schulze Papers, CHI, St. Louis MO.

Association, a new newsletter was launched. Schulze named it "The Vanguard" and titled his feature column, "That The Church May Lead." The first issue came out in January–February 1954. Schulze explained that there were six purposes for the new organization: to develop the annual institutes; to assist local human relations societies; to gather and disseminate human relations information; to encourage the publication of relevant articles in church periodicals; to assist pastors and congregations in the process of integration; and to work with officers of the church at large.[83]

While this was a time of great change in Schulze's life, it was also a momentous time for the nation. On 17 May 1954, the United States Supreme Court ruled in the case of *Brown v. Board of Education* that the practice of "separate but equal" was inherently unequal. The *Brown* decision laid the framework for the emerging civil rights movement and brought dramatic changes to American society. Schulze also hoped that it would bring dramatic changes to the church. He wrote a short article on the Supreme Court's decision for the *Lutheran Witness*. In his article, Schulze quoted a memorandum issued by the National Lutheran Council, "The Church has trailed the conscience of the courts too long. Here is a chance to remedy the weakness of our witness."[84]

In response to the *Brown v. Board of Education* decision, Dr. Oswald Hoffmann and Dr. Arthur Miller pushed President Behnken to call an informal and private meeting for various Missouri Synod church officials. The main purpose of the meeting was "to explore the new situation created by the recent decision of the United States Supreme Court on the subject of the segregation of negroes."[85] At the time, Oswald Hoffmann was the head of the Missouri Synod's public relations office, located in New York City. Hoffmann explained that there was tremendous pressure for the public relations department to have a statement on this matter from the synod. Arthur Miller was on the synod's Board for Parish Education and was

---

[83] Andrew Schulze, "That the Church May Lead," *The Vanguard* 1 (January–February 1954): 1, 4.

[84] Andrew Schulze, "Segregation—in Public Schools...in the Church," *The Lutheran Witness* 73 (20 July 1954): 10.

[85] "Minutes of the Special Meeting on the Implication of the Supreme Court Ruling in the Matter of Segregation of Education," 25 June 1954, John W. Behnken Papers, CHI, St. Louis MO, 1.

particularly interested in how the decision would affect the synod's large system of parochial schools. The meeting was called specifically for representatives of the synod who served in districts below the Mason-Dixon line. It was agreed that the meeting would not be publicized in anyway as "it would embarrass some Districts."[86]

Representatives from the southern districts of the Missouri Synod attended the meeting, along with several church officials. The meeting began with a legal analysis of the Supreme Court decision. Then followed analysis from theological and practical points of view. Dr. Martin Scharlemann, professor at Concordia Seminary, St. Louis, provided a theological response to the decision. Scharlemann concluded, "It took a secular court to say in unmistakable language what we should have been urging for many decades."[87] Karl Lutze recalled that President Behnken was not even present for the entire meeting. Once, when he was present, he raised a question about whether white Christians were really obligated to fraternize with their fellow black Christians. Lutze quickly responded to counter Behnken's point.[88] The fact that the meeting took place, and these issues were being discussed, was a step forward for the church. But progress was made in spite of President Behnken, not because of him.

Others, including Karl Lutze, spoke on the practical aspects of the situation. Martin L. Koehneke presented a paper on the issue of Sunday school and parochial school education. It was predicted that the decision would bring new interest in private and parochial schools in the South. It was noted that "the public schools are our schools also. We would do ourselves and the public schools a dis-service if we seized upon this occasion to provide an out for such parents who want to resist the Supreme Court decision."[89] Andrew Schulze was not involved in any way with the meeting. This was probably because his position on the matter was already quite well known, and it was not a position that was particularly welcomed among representatives from the South.

---

[86] Ibid., 1–12, 12.

[87] Martin Scharlemann, "The Supreme Court Decides," attached to the "Minutes of the Special Meeting," CHI, St. Louis MO, 1.

[88] Lutze, Oral History Collection, 28–29.

[89] "Minutes of the Special Meeting," 9.

On 16 June 1954 Schulze wrote to his old friend O. P. Kretzmann to inform him that he received a peaceful dismissal from his congregation and accepted the position offered to him by Valparaiso University and the Lutheran Human Relations Association of America. Valparaiso University was a prominent Lutheran institution that had a national reputation among Lutherans. The position with the Lutheran Human Relations Association and Valparaiso University provided Schulze with a national platform and freed him from the oversight and the restraints of the Northern Illinois District. Schulze was excited by his new opportunities for ministry and the spirit of change in the nation. He prayed that God would grant him "wisdom and understanding to do His will in 'such a time as this.'"[90]

Some of those who had worked with Schulze at the Northern Illinois District were pleased to see him go. As the president of the Northern Illinois District wrote to Karl Kurth regarding Schulze's departure for Valparaiso, "I need not tell you that our Mission Board feels greatly relieved." The district president also made a request regarding Schulze's replacement, "May I stress most emphatically that we do not want a radical race relations man, but a man who has a heart for these people and has only one objective to save their souls."[91]

The district president's letter also noted that "it appears as though Schulze does not want a negro pastor as his successor. Why, I do not know."[92] Schulze explained his thoughts privately in a letter to his sons. Eventually, the Rev. William Griffin was called as pastor of Christ the King Lutheran Church. Schulze described his successor as "a very fine man from Montgomery, Alabama. The only difficultly involved—and this does not reflect on him—is expressed by Wallie Heyne in a recent letter to me: 'Looks like Jim Crow is now firmly entrenched in Chicago Missouri Synod Lutheranism...four Negro churches with four Negro pastors.'"[93] But the dynamics of race were changing. The Rev. Dr. Martin Marty served as an

---

[90] Andrew Schulze to Rev. O. P. Kretzmann, 16 June 1954 (copy), Andrew Schulze Papers, CHI, St. Louis MO.

[91] A. H. Werfelmann to Rev. Karl Kurth, papers of the Synodical Conference Missionary Board, Domestic Negro Missions, box 17, CHI, St. Louis MO.

[92] Ibid.

[93] Andrew Schulze to the boys, 4 April 1956, Schulze family papers, in the possession of Raymond Schulze.

interim pastor for Christ the King during part of its vacancy. Marty recalled that right during the time when he was serving Christ the King, the mood of the times had changed. Previously, it had been more prestigious for a black congregation to have a white pastor, but now it was more prestigious for a black congregation to have a black pastor.[94]

William Griffin came to Chicago from Montgomery, Alabama. He left Montgomery in the midst of a year-long bus boycott that had begun in December 1955. The Montgomery Bus Boycott marked the beginning of the civil rights movement and launched Martin Luther King, Jr. to national prominence. Because of his strict Missouri Synod training, Griffin was hesitant about participating in such a civic matter. But he and his congregation did participate in the boycott. Griffin was comforted in his decision to participate by recalling a theological discussion he had years earlier with Andrew Schulze at a meeting of the General Conference.[95] Little did Griffin know then that he would follow Schulze in Chicago and continue his civil rights activism in the North.[96] As for Schulze, he now responded to a new calling, to demonstrate his leadership through the Lutheran Human Relations Association and Valparaiso University during the years of the civil rights movement.

---

[94] Martin Marty, interview by author, 24 January 2000.

[95] William Griffin, interview by author, 27 January 2000.

[96] For a time during the 1960s, Griffin chaired the Kenwood-Oakland Community Organization that included a young Chicago seminary student, Jesse Jackson (Luecke, *Churches, Cities, and Human Community*, 141). For more on Chicago's place in the civil rights movement, see Ralph, *Northern Protest.*

Chapter 5

Valparaiso, 1954–1968

In the early 1920s, Valparaiso University, a private, regional university located in Valparaiso, Indiana, experienced a severe financial crisis. The university was offered for sale and attracted the attention of the local Ku Klux Klan. During the 1920s, the Ku Klux Klan achieved widespread popularity in the Midwest, particularly in the state of Indiana. The Ku Klux Klan of the 1920s was different from the more vicious and violent Klan that emerged decades later in reaction to the civil rights movement, but it still was an organization exclusivist in nature.[1] The Klan of the 1920s was especially known for its anti-Catholicism and anti-Semitism. The homogeneity of the region's population contributed to Klan's success in Indiana and elsewhere in the Midwest.[2] Valparaiso University and local Klan officials did actually reach an agreement on terms of sale for the university, but the national Klan headquarters did not approve the purchase.[3] Two

---

[1] "While the Klans of the Reconstruction and civil rights eras were driven primarily by the single issue of white supremacy in the South, the Klan of the 1920s espoused…a more complex creed of racism, nativism, Americanism; the defense of traditional moral and family values; and support for Prohibition" (Leonard Moore, *Citizen Klansmen: The Ku Klux Klan in Indiana, 1921–1928* [Chapel Hill: University of North Carolina Press, 1991] 3).

[2] Along with the study by Moore, see Richard K. Tucker, *The Dragon and The Cross: The Rise and Fall of the Ku Klux Klan in Middle America* (Hamden CT: Archon Books, 1991) and Kenneth Jackson, *The Ku Klux Klan in the City, 1915–1930* (New York: Oxford University Press, 1967).

[3] John Strietelmeier, *Valparaiso's First Century: A Centennial History of Valparaiso University* (Valparaiso IN: Valparaiso University, 1959) 74.

years later, in 1925, the Lutheran University Association bought Valparaiso University, marking Valparaiso's beginnings as a Lutheran institution.

The Lutheran University Association was headed by the Rev. John C. Baur of Fort Wayne, Indiana. Just a few years earlier, Baur headed the American Luther League, a largely lay organization that fought local Klan attempts to close parochial schools. The American Luther League allied with representatives from other denominations to insure the failure of the Klan's legislative attempts to limit religious education in the area. Baur and his new organization, the Lutheran University Association, now turned to a new challenge, to sponsor a Lutheran university primarily dedicated to lay education.[4]

Valparaiso was sponsored by Missouri Synod Lutherans, but was different from the other Missouri Synod institutions of higher education. From the beginning, the ownership and operation of the institution were independent of the synod. Valparaiso's emphasis on lay education also set it apart from the other synodical institutions of higher education that were primarily dedicated to educating churchworkers. Valparaiso had a unique status among Missouri Synod institutions of being "in the Church but not of it."[5]

In the spring of 1940, just fifteen years after the university's establishment as a Lutheran institution, the university elected the Rev. Dr. Otto Paul Kretzmann as its president. Kretzmann left his post as executive secretary of the Walther League, the synod's youth organization, to accept the position as Valparaiso's president. Kretzmann served as president of Valparaiso University from 1940 to 1968 and did much to establish the university as one of the premier Lutheran institutions in the country. The dedication of the campus's majestic and imposing Chapel of the Resurrection in 1959 was symbolic of the university's expansion and its new stature.

President O. P. Kretzmann had a long association with Andrew Schulze, dating back to their days at Springfield's Concordia Theological Seminary. Kretzmann had also dealt with Lutheran racial prejudice in his

---

[4] Ibid., 82.
[5] Ibid., 126.

position with the Walther League.[6] It was Kretzmann who was behind the invitation for the Lutheran Race Relations Institutes to meet on the campus of Valparaiso University beginning in 1950. Kretzmann also brought his vision and support to the creation of the Lutheran Human Relations Association of America (LHRAA) in 1953. Throughout his tenure at Valparaiso, Kretzmann continued to be a strong and consistent supporter to Andrew Schulze and the Lutheran Human Relations Association. While Schulze was the natural leader for the Lutheran Human Relations Association, O. P. Kretzmann put his support and financial backing behind the push to make Schulze the executive secretary of the organization. Kretzmann had Schulze's leadership in mind when he was engineering the University's support of the organization.[7]

The position of executive secretary was funded as a half-time position. It was made full-time with the addition of a part-time teaching load of theology classes at the University. Valparaiso provided office space, financial assistance, and the campus setting for the Lutheran Human Relations Association. A generation after its potential sale to the Ku Klux Klan, Valparaiso University became home to the Lutheran Human Relations Association, an organization that promoted progressive attitudes toward race relations. Kretzmann repeatedly expressed his belief that the Lutheran Human Relations Association did more for the university than the university did for the Lutheran Human Relations Association.[8]

Andrew Schulze was installed in his new position on 10 July 1954. After thirty years as a parish pastor, mainly in large urban centers, he spent the rest of his career in this small-town, university setting. Andrew and Mar-

---

[6] O. P. Kretzmann, "Education without Discrimination," *Proceedings* of the Lutheran Race Relations Institute, 18–19 July 1950. For more on Kretzmann and Kretzmann's presidency, see Richard Baepler, "Otto Paul Kretzmann (1901–1975)" *Concordia Historical Institute Quarterly* 73, (Fall 2000) 132–46. Richard Baepler, "O. P. Kretzmann's Valparaiso University Presidency," *Concordia Historical Institute Quarterly* 73 (Winter 2000) 194–211.

[7] Oral History from Karl Lutze, interview by James W. Albers, 20 July, 1981 and 26 October 1981, Archives of Cooperative Lutheranism, Lutheran Council in the USA, ELCA Archives, Chicago IL, 6.

[8] Andrew Schulze, *Race against Time* (Valparaiso: Lutheran Human Relations Association, 1972) 132.

garet lived in a home not far from the university campus. He began his academic career, teaching courses in New Testament theology. Schulze gained much from his teaching experiences. He was forever grateful for the opportunity to teach the New Testament courses as he felt that they enriched his own theological growth.[9] Later, Schulze also taught a sociology course on the church and racial issues. Schulze influenced numerous students in the classroom, but he also continued to influence wider developments concerning race relations and the church. As executive secretary of the LHRAA, Schulze's work included organizing the annual summer institutes, writing and editing the organization's newsletter, organizing efforts to lobby the church on racial matters. Schulze recalled that his new calling at Valparaiso was like starting two new careers at the same time.[10]

While the Supreme Court's *Brown v. Board of Education* decision marked a watershed for the nation with regard to race relations, it also galvanized resistance from those who wanted no change in the racial status quo. Some Americans showed an understanding of the significance of the need to improve race relations, while other Americans showed skepticism, ambiguity, and opposition to efforts to improve race relations. A similar dynamic existed with the church. Within Lutheran circles, some opposed the new Lutheran Human Relations Association and the values for which it stood. Some of the first sentiments against the work of the Lutheran Human Relations Association came from the Northern Illinois District, the district where Andrew Schulze had recently served.

In the spring of 1955 A. T. Kretzmann presented a conference paper on race relations at the Northern Illinois District Pastoral Conference held in Park Ridge, Illinois. A. T. Kretzmann's paper viewed the practice of segregation and integration as *adiaphoria*, a matter of theological indifference. The paper attempted to separate racial attitudes from racial practices. While the United States Supreme Court had declared that segregation was inherently unequal, this paper made the argument that "segregation, wholly or in part, is not in itself sinful." After decades of segregated practices within the church, this paper was quick to warn against the dangers of coerced integration. As the paper concluded, "We are not against segregation or

---

[9] Lutze, Oral History Collection, 2.

[10] Schulze, *Race against Time*, 124.

integration, but we are most strongly opposed to all legalistic attitudes and loveless actions used in support of either segregation or desegregation." [11]

Included in A. T. Kretzmann's paper were specific references to Andrew Schulze and *The Vanguard*, the publication of the Lutheran Human Relations Association. As the paper stated, "It is being maintained, especially in the periodical 'Vanguard' in our circles, that the Church should lead in the solving of purely social problems. That is not the business of the Church. In such purely social problems there should be no interference on the part of the Church."[12] Some Lutherans continued to view race relations as a social rather than theological issue, as though there was a complete separation between social and theological matters.

But the leaders of the Lutheran Human Relations Association believed that the church had an important role to play in society. When a Missouri Synod organization, the Lutheran Women's Missionary League (LWML), planned to hold their convention in the segregated city of New Orleans during the summer of 1955, members of the Lutheran Human Relations Association lobbied against the planned conference. In the spring of 1955, members of the Lutheran Human Relations Association sent telegrams and letters to the leaders of the Missouri Synod and the Lutheran Women's Missionary League to call off plans for the summer convention. Arguments against the planned convention stressed not only that the church should live up to its principles but that the church also should act as a witness to society. Coming after the 1954 Supreme Court decision, a segregated convention would serve as an example of the church not measuring up to society. Letters also stressed the responsibility the LWML had because of its history of supporting mission projects among people of different racial and ethnic backgrounds.[13]

---

[11] A. T. Kretzmann, "Race Relations," conference paper, based on race relations theses by Pastor Gerhard Huebener, read to the Northern Illinois District Pastoral Conference, 19–20 April 1955, Park Ridge, Illinois, Synodical Conference Missionary Board Papers, Domestic Negro Missions, box 17, Concordia Historical Institute (CHI), St. Louis MO, 1, 10.

[12] Ibid., 1, 3.

[13] See letters by Andrew Schulze, Clemonce Sabourin, Anna Engelbrecht, and Paul Simon, among others, Andrew Schulze Papers, CHI, St. Louis MO.

Considerable work had already gone into planning the summer convention in New Orleans, and it was too late to make plans to hold a convention in another city. The president of the Lutheran Women's Missionary League, Mrs. Arthur Preisinger, recalled that the decision to cancel the conference was the "most difficult decision that had to be made during my term as president."[14] Nonetheless, the convention was cancelled and a statement was released that explained, "Local customs of segregation make it impossible for the New Orleans Zone fully to entertain the International Lutheran Women's Missionary League in a manner characteristic of this organization."[15] After the controversy was over, President John W. Behnken wrote a letter of concern about the matter to Andrew Schulze. He expressed sympathy for those in New Orleans and "regretted that some of the letters breathed a spirit which should not be found among our church members...one or the other even contained a threat of boycotting the convention."[16] President Behnken continued to seem content with the status quo with regards to race relations.

But the Missouri Synod did take an historic step in 1956 at its national convention held in St. Paul, Minnesota. Beginning with the convention in 1956, through the early 1970s, the Lutheran Human Relations Association worked to get several resolutions passed at national conventions of the Missouri Synod, typically held once every three years.[17] Resolutions concerning race relations were drawn up by members of the Lutheran Human Relations Association and then put forward by supporting congregations. This was done to be in accordance with the by-laws of the convention; individual congregations could propose resolutions, but not church-related organizations.

---

[14] Ruth Fritz Meyer, *Women on a Mission: The Role of Women in the Church from Bible Times up to and including a History of the Lutheran Women's Missionary League during its First Twenty-Five Years* (St. Louis: Concordia Publishing House, 1967) 180.

[15] Press Release, Department of Public Relations, The Lutheran Church—Missouri Synod, 6 May 1955, Andrew Schulze Papers, CHI, St. Louis MO.

[16] John W. Behnken to Andrew Schulze, 10 May 1955, Andrew Schulze Papers, CHI, St. Louis MO.

[17] *Human Relations: Resolutions of the Lutheran Church—Missouri Synod* (St. Louis: Lutheran Church—Missouri Synod and the Lutheran Human Relations Association, 1969).

In 1956 the Lutheran Human Relations Association was a fairly new organization with a limited budget, so it did not have a booth of its own at the synod's convention. Dr. Henry F. Wind, executive director of the Missouri Synod's Department of Social Welfare and advisory member of LHRAA, offered to share his booth with the LHRAA. Both Dr. Wind and Dr. Martin Scharlemann, Professor at Concordia Seminary, St. Louis, provided advice on getting resolutions concerning race relations passed through the convention. Part of the original overtures to the convention included an emphasis on a confession and repentance for sins of racial prejudice. However, "for strategic reasons, those who met at the LHRAA booth thought it well not to press the matter about confession and repentance, and to concentrate on…the directive re discrimination in society in general."[18]

Martin Scharlemann suggested that Schulze include a scripture reference as a part of the resolutions. Schulze chose Micah 6:8, "He has showed you, O man, what is good. And what does the Lord require of you? To act justly and to love mercy and to walk humbly with your God." In many ways the passage was a motto for Andrew Schulze's life. Among other resolutions, the Missouri Synod's convention resolved with near unanimity that "since Christians are constrained to do justice and love mercy, we acknowledge our responsibility as a church to provide guidance for our members to work in the capacity of Christian citizens for the elimination of discrimination, wherever it may exist in community, city, state, nation, and world."[19] It must have been a bittersweet experience for Andrew Schulze.

---

[18] Schulze, *Race against Time*, 89.

[19] The resolution caused a "heated argument…until finally it was discovered that the whole argument was caused by a mis-placed comma, because as we had drawn up the resolution we had said we would work toward integration in the home community, state, nation, and world…[someone placed a comma after home]…all of this heat was generated by the fact that nobody has any right to come into my home and tell me what to do. Nobody has any right to say that my daughter should marry a Negro" (Clemonce Sabourin, interview by Karl Lutze, 21–22 April, 1983, Oral History Collection, Archives of Cooperative Lutheranism, Lutheran Council in the USA, ELCA Archives, St. Louis MO, 118). The controversy was resolved as the words "the home" were dropped from the resolution (Andrew Schulze, *Race against Time*, 90).

His church body did take a stand for racial equality, but the church had followed rather than led society.[20]

Once the resolutions passed, Schulze recalled that the national news media focused on the resolutions more than did the Missouri Synod's own publications.[21] He stressed the importance of the resolution in an article published months later in the *Lutheran Witness*. Schulze stressed that "the Missouri Synod is not living in a vacuum, but in a very real world and is related to the world by the commandment of love." He explained that the church had a unique role in society, a responsibility to show moral leadership. He concluded that the church now needed to put these resolutions into action. "In the area of race relations we have a long way to go truly to be the church as Christ would have us to be, but...we are, by His grace, on the way."[22]

Schulze expressed his views on a regular basis through his column, "That The Church May Lead" in *The Vanguard*, the newsletter published by the LHRAA. *The Vanguard* came out on a bi-monthly to monthly basis during the 1950s and 1960s. Another regular columnist of *The Vanguard* during its early years was the Rev. Dr. Martin Scharlemann, Professor of Concordia Seminary, St. Louis. Scharlemann's own experiences as a military chaplain in World War II helped to awaken his racial consciousness.[23]

---

[20] While some other Lutheran bodies had made statements against racial prejudice prior to 1954, the strongest statements embracing racial equality followed after the Supreme Court decision. For an overview of some of the statements by other Lutheran church bodies regarding race relations, see Lloyd Svendsbye, "The History of a Developing Social Responsibility among Lutherans in America from 1930 to 1960, with Reference to the American Lutheran Church, the Augustana Lutheran Church, the Evangelical Lutheran Church, and the United Lutheran Church in America" (Th.D. dissertation, Union Theological Seminary, 1966). A collection of statements on race relations by various Lutheran bodies can be found in Alf M. Kraabel, *Grace and Race in the Lutheran Church* (Chicago: National Lutheran Council, 1957).

[21] Schulze, *Race against Time*, 91–92.

[22] Andrew Schulze, "Synod's Witness on the Race Issue," *The Lutheran Witness* 75 (4 December 1956): 15.

[23] Martin Scharlemann, interview by Edith Rehbein, 9–10 August 1980, Oral History Collection, Archives of Cooperative Lutheranism, Lutheran Council in the USA, ELCA Archives, Chicago IL, 10.

Scharlemann's column, "A Look Around" surveyed race relations in Lutheran churches and institutions around the country. Scharlemann responded to the recent resolutions passed by the Missouri Synod stating that they "invite the Church 'to be the Church,' and not a social club, a cultural pocket, or even a network of lecture halls where great truths are nobly uttered and promptly ignored."[24]

The Vanguard not only commented on racial issues within the church, but also provided perspective on racial issues in society. For example, Schulze's column in *The Vanguard* in January 1956 focused on the tragic case of Emmett Till, a fourteen-year-old black boy who was killed on a visit to his relatives in the South in the summer of 1955. Till's white murderers, who later confessed to the press, were found "not guilty" by an all white jury.[25] Schulze believed that events such as this called for the church to be vocal and active in the world. As he expressed, "the Christian Church and the Christian citizen must find something to do about it and a time to speak out."[26]

Others, too, believed that it was time for fundamental changes in race relations. Schulze's years of active leadership in the Lutheran Human Relations Association coincided with the major events of the civil rights movement. With the Supreme Court decision of 1954, the federal government had taken a stand supporting the principle and practice of integration. Local movements throughout the country tested the nation's commitment to equality in various ways for over the next dozen years. The first successful stand-off of the civil rights movement began on 1 December 1955, when Rosa Parks was arrested for not giving up her bus seat for a white man in Montgomery, Alabama.[27] A year-long bus boycott by

---

[24] Martin Scharlemann, "A Look Around," *The Vanguard* 3 (October 1956): 2.

[25] See Stephen J. Whitfield, *A Death in the Delta: The Story of Emmett Till* (New York: Free Press, 1988).

[26] Andrew Schulze, "That the Church May Lead," *The Vanguard* 3 (January 1956): 2.

[27] Contemporary observers and later historians have stressed the important role that Parks's character played in rallying all sides of Montgomery's black community to the cause. Rev. Robert Graetz, a boycott participant, described Parks as "about the meekest and mildest person that I have ever met.... If someone else had been arrested instead, perhaps the whole course of history might be different. But then,

Montgomery's black community followed under the leadership of a young
Baptist preacher, the Rev. Dr. Martin Luther King, Jr.

Schulze paid considerable attention to the events in Montgomery.
When the opportunity presented itself, Andrew and Margaret went to
Chicago in April 1956, to hear Martin Luther King, Jr. speak about the
boycott. King was invited to speak at the Rockefeller Chapel at the
University of Chicago. Schulze wrote about the experience to his sons,
"Mother and I went to Chicago on Friday to hear Martin Luther King, the
courageous leader of the Montgomery bus boycott. His appearance at
Rockefeller Chapel was under the auspices of the 'Religious Liberals'
(Unitarians and Universalists). (It's strange, isn't it, that these fellows must
lead in areas of this kind.)"[28] Schulze continued to be concerned that there
was not more leadership in race relations from white Christian
conservatives.

The civil rights activities in the South were largely generated through
the black Christian community. Though greatly outnumbered by Baptist
and Methodist participants, Lutherans were also involved with the local
struggle in Montgomery. Rosa Parks was Methodist, but she had contacts
with one of Montgomery's black Lutheran churches. Parks worked with a
NAACP Youth Council which met at Trinity Lutheran Church. Trinity
Lutheran Church was one of the black mission churches sponsored by the
American Lutheran Church. In 1955 the black pastor of Trinity, Nelson
Trout, left for a new position and just missed the chance to be involved with
the bus boycott. Trout later reflected that "maybe I missed my destiny,
because I should have been there at that time."[29] But Trout did have the
opportunity to meet Martin Luther King, Jr. and others who rose to
national prominence beginning with the Montgomery Bus Boycott. Once

---

God has a way of arranging for His people to be at the right place at the right time"
(Robert S. Graetz, "The Montgomery Bus Boycott—My Part in It," *Proceedings* of
the Lutheran Human Relations Association of America, Summer Institute, 13–15
July 1956, 25).

[28] Letter from Andrew Schulze to the boys, 26 April 1956, Schulze family papers,
in the possession of Raymond Schulze.

[29] Nelson W. Trout, interview by Norman E. Minich, 19–20 August 1982, Oral
History Collection, Archives of Cooperative Lutheranism, Lutheran Council in the
USA, ELCA Archives, Chicago IL, 21.

Trout "felt enough at ease to ask as a Lutheran how King, a Negro Baptist, had acquired the name Martin Luther. King looked searchingly at Trout for some time, then smiled and parried with a question of his own: "how did a Negro like Trout come to be a Lutheran?"[30]

In 1955 the Rev. Robert Graetz, a white pastor, was assigned as the new pastor of Trinity Lutheran Church. Graetz became the only white minister who was actively involved in the Montgomery Bus Boycott. Because Graetz was white, he and his family received additional attention for their involvement. The Graetzes received many negative comments by phone and through the mail. There were two attempts to bomb the Graetz home during the boycott. But the significant attention Graetz received from the national press did provide him and his family with some protection.[31] The Graetzes also felt the support of their church body, the American Lutheran Church, particularly its Board of American Missions.[32]

At the Lutheran Human Relations Association's Summer Institute in 1956, Robert Graetz presented an essay, "The Montgomery Bus

---

[30] Taylor Branch, *Parting the Waters: America in the King Years, 1954–1963* (New York: Simon & Schuster Inc., 1988) 125. Martin Luther King Jr. was originally named Mike King Jr. after his father, Mike King Sr. In 1934 Mike King Sr. traveled to Europe and the to sites of the Protestant Reformation and shortly thereafter changed his name and his son's name to Martin Luther King. "After the boycott, the mantle of fame fell ever more personally on King [Jr.], who told *Time* that he and his father had chosen to call themselves after Martin Luther, the founding Protestant, and that 'perhaps we've earned our right to the name.' It was a proud but tentative 'perhaps'" (Branch, *Parting the Waters*, 203).

[31] "The symbolic importance of a white minister risking his own safety by supporting a black-led movement was not lost on the media. The black magazine *Jet* published a photograph of him, and Graetz was the subject of stories in the *New York Times* and religious journals" (Michael B. Freidland, *Lift up Your Voice Like a Trumpet: White Clergy and the Civil Rights and Antiwar Movements, 1954–1973* [Chapel Hill: The University of North Carolina Press, 1998] 29).

[32] Robert S. Graetz, *Montgomery: A White Preacher's Memoirs* (Minneapolis: Fortress Press, 1991) 64, 59. The "Theological Observer" of the *Concordia Theological Monthly* reprinted a story from the *Minneapolis Tribune* on Graetz and the Bus Boycott. It quoted an American Lutheran Church official who described racial integration as "the Christian way" (*Concordia Theological Monthly* 27 [April 1956]: 305). Taylor Branch's coverage of the Montgomery Bus Boycott gives significant attention to Graetz, (Branch, *Parting the Waters*, 124–205).

Boycott—My Part in It." Though in the midst of the boycott, Graetz was confident about the outcome. Reflecting on the efforts of Montgomery's black community, Graetz concluded, "We might say that they have already won their struggle. For it is basically a struggle for human dignity; and that they have already found."[33] Graetz also observed that black and white churches seemed to be going in opposite directions. He expressed disappointment that white churches were not playing any kind of supportive role in the struggle and seemed interested in maintaining the status quo in race relations.

Another speaker at the Summer Institute in 1956 was the Illinois state politician Paul Simon. Simon stated that he was happy about the resolutions passed at the recent Missouri Synod convention, but stressed that Christian action was also needed.[34] Simon was a close observer of race relations and traveled to Montgomery to observe what was happening there with the bus boycott. A year after the successful conclusion of the bus boycott, community activists in Montgomery organized an Institute on Non-Violence and Social Change. Paul Simon, Bob Graetz, and Martin Luther King, Jr. signed a copy of the institute's program and sent it with their greetings to Andrew Schulze.[35] Schulze had made some contact with Martin Luther King, Jr., as he had tried to get King to be a speaker at the Summer Institute in 1956, but he declined due to other commitments.[36]

After the first few years of getting the Lutheran Human Relations Association established, Andrew Schulze broadened his vision and his contacts. In 1957 he was invited to participate in a conference on Native American issues. Soon after, the Lutheran Human Relations Association began giving attention to Native American issues. Native American concerns were discussed occasionally in *The Vanguard* and at the summer institutes. Native American issues became a long-standing concern of the

---

[33] Robert S. Graetz, "The Montgomery Bus Boycott—My Part in It," 30.

[34] Paul Simon, "Mountain Peaks to Climb," *Proceedings* of the Lutheran Human Relations Association of America, Summer Institute, 13–15 July 1956, 46–51.

[35] Program from the Second Annual Institute on Non-Violence and Social Change, 5–8 December 1957, Andrew Schulze Papers, CHI, St. Louis MO.

[36] "Institute Notes," *The Vanguard* 3 (June 1956): 2.

Lutheran Human Relations Association.[37] The LHRAA promoted a resolution that passed at the Missouri Synod convention in 1959 and encouraged ministry among "neglected groups" such as Asian, Jewish, Hispanic, and Native Americans, as well as "anonymous 'lost' men and women in the slums and on the skid rows of our cities."[38] While relations between black and white Americans remained the main focus of the LHRAA, the LHRAA branched out to discuss the specific concerns of other disadvantaged groups within American society.

In 1959 the Lutheran Human Relations Association of America added another part-time administrator to its office at Valparaiso University, the Rev. Karl Lutze. Karl Lutze eventually succeeded Schulze as the executive secretary of the LHRAA, but through the mid-1960s, Lutze and Schulze worked together as close partners. Lutze was also a white pastor who had experience working with an integrated congregation in Tulsa, Oklahoma. Lutze was originally assigned the position of field secretary, with the task of advising the various local chapters of the Lutheran Human Relations Association. During the height of its activity, the Lutheran Human Relations Association had over fifty local chapters throughout the United States.[39] Even though the LHRAA had a national network of chapters, it was

---

[37] Karl Lutze, who followed Andrew as executive secretary of the LHRAA, also served in a leadership role of an organization called the Lutheran Church and Indian People (LUCHIP). A few Lutheran Indians were involved with the American Indian Movement (AIM) that began during the late 1960s. The Rev. Paul Boe, a pastor of the American Lutheran Church (ALC), played an important role during the crisis at the 1972 commemoration of the massacre at Wounded Knee, South Dakota (Lutze, Oral History Collection, 91–99).

[38] *Human Relations: Resolutions of the Lutheran Church—Missouri Synod* (Lutheran Church—Missouri Synod and the Lutheran Human Relations Association, 1969) 8.

[39] "Naturally the St. Louis and Chicago ones were the models, and we never could get more models like those two operatives, because those two had started around Andrew Schulze. Well where do you find some more Andrew Schulzes around with which to start chapters?... What we would do is try to find—that was Andrew's style—to find someone like Andrew Schulze who could pull people together. So he would very often find an individual whom he could fire up with information and zeal and commitment, and this person then would gather a group of people around him or her, and that's the way the thing would develop" (Lutze, Oral History Collection, 15).

relatively limited in terms of the size of its membership. The LHRAA never had more than a couple thousand members out of some nine million American Lutherans.

Schulze continued to be behind the planning and organizing of the LHRAA's annual summer institutes. The institutes attracted an increased number and variety of speakers and participants. Every year throughout the 1950s and 1960s, hundreds of people took part in the annual institutes. Several people recalled that during those years, the program and the camaraderie of the institutes served as a powerful inspirational and motivational force, encouraging people to work toward better race relations in their own congregations and communities. Beginning in 1958, the institutes often focused on particular issues or themes. The 1958 institute was mainly devoted to the issue of interracial marriage from biological, sociological, and theological perspectives.

A feature speaker at the 1958 institute was Dr. Louis P. Lochner. Lochner's banquet address introduced a new topic, "The Impact of Race Relations in Our Land on Other Nations for the Weal or the Woe of Church and State." Louis Lochner was a Pulitzer-prize winning journalist who served as a reporter in Germany during World War II. Lochner had recently traveled throughout the world with a group of individuals who were assigned to evaluate the United Nations Department of Public Information. Lochner came from a family with deep roots in the Missouri Synod. His father, John Frederick Carl Lochner, was one of the first pastors sent to America by Rev. Wilhelm Loehe and was one of the first organizers of the Missouri Synod. Lochner explained that he first became aware of racial issues in 1905 when his brother was called to serve as a professor at Immanuel Lutheran College, the black Lutheran seminary in Greensboro, North Carolina.[40]

---

[40] As Lochner explained, "It seemed unbelievable to me that, as his letters revealed, he and his white colleagues were socially ostracized by a large element of the white population of the city for no other reason than that they were associating with Negroes. I was shocked to read in one of his letters, 'Many white people here insist that the Negro has no soul'" (Louis Lochner, "The Impact of Race Relations in Our Land on Other Nations for the Weal or Woe of Church and State," *Proceedings* of the Lutheran Human Relations Association of America, Summer Institute, 25–27 July 1958, 40).

Lochner began his address with references to the crisis that occurred when there was an attempt to integrate gradually the high school in Little Rock, Arkansas, in 1957. The crisis had been temporarily resolved only after President Eisenhower authorized federal troops to protect the nine black students who attended the previously all-white high school. Lochner concluded, "It staggers the imagination…to realize what tremendous damage to our prestige abroad, to our moral leadership in the world, to other nations' faith in our sincerity has been done by the events in Little Rock."[41] Lochner explained how the Soviet Union used the incident as anti-American propaganda and how the incident was perceived elsewhere in the world. He also spoke of Ghana, the newly independent nation in West Africa, and suggested its importance for race relations throughout the world. In conclusion, Lochner referred to all that he had witnessed in Germany and warned of the potential consequences of racism. Lochner's address expressed an urgency that Americans and Christians everywhere work to combat the evils of racism.

The international implications of American race relations later served as the theme of future summer institutes. The Summer Institute in 1959 took the theme "The Nations Are Waiting." Speakers included Dr. Marguerite Cartwright, former delegate to the United Nations, and the Rev. Alvaro Carino, missionary to the Philippines. Institute speakers such as Cartwright and Carino stressed that American racial prejudice damaged the position of the nation and the church abroad. Also included in the Summer Institute in 1959 was an address by the Rev. Alf M. Kraabel of the National Lutheran Council titled "My Neighbor Is A Jew."[42] This was the first time that the summer institutes dealt so directly with the issue of prejudice against Jews. The LHRAA occasionally continued to devote some significant attention to Christian-Jewish relations as there were some prominent Jewish leaders active in the civil rights movement.

While Schulze was interested in improving race relations in American society and in the world, his primary focus always remained on improving

---

[41] Ibid., 41.

[42] *Proceedings* of the Lutheran Human Relations Association of America, 24–26 July 1959. This was a significant development as Lutherans had a history of Jewish prejudice that stretched back to Martin Luther himself.

race relations within the church. He often expressed his hope that the church might practice what it preached. As one of the primary writers and editors of *The Vanguard*, Schulze's approach usually concentrated on positive examples of racial progress within local Lutheran congregations. By highlighting the Lutheran congregations that were successful at integrating their memberships, he hoped that other congregations would be encouraged by their examples. But the congregations that were actively integrating their membership were exceptions to the rule. Schulze estimated out of all the Missouri Synod congregations in the country, less than a dozen congregations were actively trying to integrate their membership during the years just after the *Brown v. Board of Education* decision.[43]

Schulze also used *The Vanguard* to give witness to the continuing examples of Lutheran prejudice. The July 1957 *Vanguard* included stories of how black families in Chicago were affected by a Lutheran school that did not admit black children and a Lutheran cemetery that did not sell burial plots to black Lutheran families. It also featured a picture of St. Mark's Lutheran Church in Detroit with the caption that while St. Mark's stayed in city, twenty-two Lutheran churches moved out. Schulze concluded, "Why Mention It? The prophet Amos was not willing to remain silent; he cried out against the social abuses of Israel."[44]

In the January 1959 *Vanguard*, Schulze's column posed the question, "Can a Church Paper Remain Silent?" He criticized the official periodical of the Missouri Synod, *The Lutheran Witness*, for its lack of attention to the issues of race and social action. He encouraged readers to turn to *The Christian Century* for its coverage of race relations.[45] Some people resonated to the idea that more should be expected from church periodicals. As one

---

[43] Andrew Schulze to the Rev. Vernon Schreiber, 4 September 1956 (copy), Andrew Schulze Papers, CHI, St. Louis MO.

[44] *The Vanguard* 4 (July 1957): 1.

[45] [Andrew Schulze], "Can a Church Paper Remain Silent?" *The Vanguard* 6 (January 1959): 1, 4. [Andrew Schulze], "The Christian Century Speaks Out" *The Vanguard* 6 (January 1959): 3. During these crucial years in American race relations, the editorial staff of *The Christian Century* included Kyle Haselden, a native white Southerner, who was particularly concerned about the shameful record of white denominations with regards to race relations. See Kyle Haselden, *The Racial Problem in Christian Perspective* (New York: Harper, 1959).

contributor to the LHRAA wrote, "I have long wondered how the 'Witness,' the LLL [Lutheran Layman's League] paper and so many of our leaders can seem so oblivious toward the number one moral issue facing our country today. People who can find time to discuss the moral propriety of everything from church suppers to pre-martial kissing seemingly can find no time for this far more fundamental issue."[46] The Missouri Synod convention in 1959 again passed resolutions generated by the LHRAA, one of which urged "the editors of the Lutheran Witness and other official publications and literature to give frequent expression to the stand which our church has taken on racial discrimination."[47]

In January 1960 *The Lutheran Witness* did give new attention to racial issues with the article "Is the Church Retarding Integration?" But the message of the article was disappointing to Schulze and others who wanted the periodical to take a bold stand on race relations. The article began by stating, "There is no one easy answer to such charges and questions."[48] Most of the article was based on an interview with Rosa Young, the black Lutheran schoolteacher who had done so much to establish Lutheranism in Alabama. Young took the position that while unity in the church was desirable, Alabama was not ready for integration and that the situation should not be forced. The author of the article, Elmer A. Kettner, summarized Young's views stating, "This pioneer Lutheran is more concerned that her people shall hear the Gospel than that they hear it in the presence of whites, more concerned that white and colored pastors and teachers be trained than that they be trained together."[49]

Included in the next *Lutheran Witness* were several letters to the editors, most of which criticized the content of the article on integration. Of all the letters, Andrew Schulze's was the longest, but he was by no means alone in his stand. He stated his high regard for Rosa Young but also stated that she "has been thoroughly conditioned for her viewpoint by the pattern of

---

[46] Arnold W. Buehler to the Rev. Andrew Schulze, 9 February 1959, Andrew Schulze Papers, CHI, St. Louis MO.

[47] *Human Relations: Resolutions of the Lutheran Church—Missouri Synod* (Lutheran Church—Missouri Synod and the Lutheran Human Relations Association, 1969) 7.

[48] Elmer A. Kettner, "Is the Church Retarding Integration?" *The Lutheran Witness* 79 (12 January 1960): 6.

[49] Ibid., 7.

segregation in which she has been working." Schulze's letter objected to the idea that "preaching the Gospel" was a sufficient solution to the problem, as he explained, "One's witness to Christ must be a total witness."[50] John Strietelmeier, a Valparaiso colleague and active member of the Lutheran Human Relations Association, also wrote a forceful argument. The Rev. Donald Becker of Chicago, Illinois, pointed out that the church had a double standard with how it treated the sins of racial discrimination. The church did not treat other social sins with similar patience. As he explained, "We don't 'wait until the husbands are ready' before we tell them they must be faithful to their wives."[51]

But there were other strong reactions to the article. One writer concluded, "Any magazine as pro-integration as your Jan. 12 issue is unfit to be seen in any decent home. God separated the races. Keep it that way." A Southern pastor wrote that the content of the article was excellent, though the title of the article was misleading. The pastor complained that "playing up integration" was hurting the church's work in the South. He also expressed some frustration with Northern attitudes toward the situation: "It's much easier to expound one's views behind an editorial desk in northern areas, but it is our own Southern workers, whom the church has sent to do mission work, who must deal at first hand with these problems."[52] Complaints that race relations were local affairs, not national priorities, were common during the years of the civil rights movement.

In 1961 Concordia Theological Seminary in Springfield, Illinois, awarded Rosa J. Young an honorary degree. Some members of the Lutheran Human Relations Association were concerned that she was being awarded the degree as an endorsement of her statements in the article in *The Lutheran Witness*. The honorary degree was being presented not just as recognition of Young's past service to the church, but for her present leadership.[53] For many involved with the LHRAA, Young was far too

---

[50] "Letters to the Editors," *The Lutheran Witness* 79 (9 February 1960): 22.

[51] Ibid., 28, 31.

[52] Ibid., 31.

[53] Martin W. Mueller, "Rosa Jinsey Young," *The Lutheran Witness* 80 (13 June 1961): 3.

accommodating to the segregationist point of view.[54] No doubt, Young was influenced by her segregationist environment. But she was not merely conditioned by her environment; she did seek to change it in her own way. As Jeff Johnson described her, Young was "determined, patient, persistent, and pushy in that uniquely southern manner that was always cloaked in polite, good manners. She was committed to one thing throughout her life: lifting up black people in rural Alabama."[55] Still, in the early 1960s, Rosa Young's segregationist perspective seemed out of step with the times.

The official magazine of the Missouri Synod did begin to give increasing attention to race relations and other social issues during the decade of the 1960s. Dr. Martin W. Mueller served as the editor of *The Lutheran Witness* from 1960–1975 and gave more attention to contemporary issues.[56] Others who were interested in social issues, such as Pulitzer-prize winning journalist Louis Lochner, also served on the committee that advised *The Lutheran Witness* during these years.[57] Andrew Schulze was quick to recognize the change. In November 1961 he commended the magazine's recent response to a letter to the editor that stated, "There will be more pictures of whites and Negroes....What's more, The Witness will not be bought off, intimidated, or cajoled. Nor will it duck its head when tough issues call for clear and forthright witness to the truth." Schulze concluded that expressions such as this helped the LHRAA with "its accepted goal—self-elimination."[58]

Besides Schulze's interest in church-related publications, he had also been long interested in the racial situation in church-related institutions of higher education. He knew of examples dating back to the 1920s of black students being denied admission to Lutheran institutions. But the situation

---

[54] Clem Sabourin to Andrew Schulze, 19 June 1961; Andrew Schulze to Clem Sabourin, 23 June 1961 (copy), Andrew Schulze Papers, CHI, St. Louis MO.

[55] Jeff G. Johnson, *Black Christians: The Untold Lutheran Story* (St. Louis: Concordia Publishing House, 1991) 167.

[56] Leland Stevens, "Trends in the Missouri Synod as Reflected in The Lutheran Witness, 1960–Early 1990s," *Concordia Historical Institute Quarterly* 69 (Winter 1996): 165–82.

[57] Press release, LHRAA papers, Valparaiso University Archives, Valparaiso IN.

[58] Andrew Schulze to the editor of the *Lutheran Witness*, 16 November 1961 (copy), Andrew Schulze Papers, CHI, St. Louis MO.

had changed in the few years since *Brown v. Board of Education*. In 1958 the Lutheran Human Relations Association worked with the National Lutheran Council (NLC) to conduct a survey of Lutheran colleges and seminaries. They sent questionnaires to the institutions regarding their racial policies and practices. While the number of minority students at Lutheran institutions was limited, Schulze concluded that the responses to the questionnaires reflected that Lutheran institutions were not only willing, but desired to enroll minority students.[59]

However, Schulze and others associated with the Lutheran Human Relations Association were concerned about the two institutions begun on a segregated basis by the Synodical Conference. Immanuel Lutheran College in Greensboro, North Carolina, and Alabama Lutheran Academy and College in Selma continued to serve all-black student bodies. The Synodical Conference's two historically black institutions had been a subject of discussion for some time. There were concerns that the two institutions were not of the same quality as other Lutheran institutions of higher education. Schulze and others wanted to close the schools at Greensboro and Selma and to integrate the other Lutheran institutions to prepare the churchworkers of the future.[60]

Schulze believed that those who wanted to maintain the schools in Greensboro and Selma were still thinking in the segregated past. A discussion of the past was bound up with the discussion of the future regarding what to do about these schools and Lutheran race relations in general. In a letter sent out recommending the closure of the schools in Greensboro and Selma, Schulze addressed some of the objections to that proposal. One reaction to the criticism of this segregated system of education was an attitude which defended the "church fathers" of the past who founded these schools.[61] As Karl Lutze once pointed out, it was difficult

---

[59] Andrew Schulze, "Lutheran Schools of Higher Learning—A Survey Report," 25 August 1958, Andrew Schulze Papers, CHI, St. Louis MO.

[60] See Clemonce Sabourin, "A Statement about Race and Professional Church Workers," presented at Selma, AL, 3 April 1959 at an open hearing meeting of a study commission appointed by the Evangelical Synodical Conference, Andrew Schulze Papers, CHI, St. Louis MO.

[61] Andrew Schulze to "Concerned Friends," 9 February 1959 (copy), Andrew Schulze Papers, CHI, St. Louis MO.

to criticize the past record of the church "because everything the church had done had had a sanctity about it." Missouri Synod Lutherans, in particular, had a spirit of deference and tradition that "wouldn't begin to question the motives or the style of any of other faithful fathers in the past. And while this stance was intended to be one of humility and submitting to one's elders in respect and deference and reverence, it was really a type of arrogance, as if we could do no wrong."[62]

Andrew Schulze and his colleagues did not see the past or present church hierarchy as being particularly sacrosanct. They were willing to challenge church leaders concerning the schools at Greensboro and Selma and on other issues. In some of their personal correspondence, they joked about the paternalistic nature of the Missouri Synod's leaders, referring to them as the "Great White Fathers." Clemonce Sabourin showed his frustration with the continual reelection of the Missouri Synod's president, John W. Behnken, referring to him as "John the Permanent."[63] But relations between the leaders of the Lutheran Human Relations Association and the Missouri Synod hierarchy did improve in the years after the LHRAA first began in 1953. President Behnken never embraced the organization, but others in Missouri Synod officialdom did begin to ask the LHRAA for advice on certain matters.[64] Still, the LHRAA did not fully get its way concerning the black Lutheran institutions in Greensboro and Selma.

Before the Synodical Conference began to come apart in the early 1960s, a study committee recommended the closure of Immanuel Lutheran College. For decades, Immanuel had served as the only Lutheran seminary for the training of black Lutheran pastors. It had struggled over the years

---

[62] Lutze, Oral History Collection, 41.

[63] Rev. Walter Heyne to Andrew Schulze, 22 February 1955; Rev. Clemonce Sabourin to Andrew Schulze, 2 March 1959, Andrew Schulze Papers, CHI, St. Louis MO.

[64] On Behnken, see Lutze, Oral History Collection, 24–25. Andrew wrote a memo to O. P. Kretzmann, noting that officials in the Missouri Synod were no longer giving the LHRAA the "silent treatment," but asking for their advice and consultation (Andrew Schulze to President Kretzmann, 13 January 1958 (copy of memorandum), Andrew Schulze Papers, CHI, St. Louis MO.

with a small student body and limited resources.[65] For years, there were complaints that Immanuel provided an inferior education compared with other Lutheran seminaries. The Synodical Conference had previously considered the closing of Immanuel, but finally resolved that it be closed in the summer of 1961. Many of those involved with the LHRAA and who wanted to move with the integrationist spirit of the times were pleased with the closure of Immanuel Lutheran College. However, many of Immanuel's alumni believed that the seminary did produce quality graduates and regretted the decision to close it. Many alumni believed that the seminary served as an important institution for black Lutherans and that Immanuel's closure contributed to the continuing shortage of black Lutheran pastors.[66]

The other historically black Lutheran institution of higher education was Alabama Lutheran Academy and College in Selma, Alabama. The same Synodical Conference committee that recommended the closure of Immanuel also recommended that Alabama Lutheran be retained and expanded. Shortly after the Synodical Conference made this recommendation, it transferred the ownership and oversight of Alabama Lutheran directly to the Missouri Synod. The Missouri Synod began to explore possibilities to rebuild and expand Alabama Lutheran. But the debate over what to do with Alabama Lutheran continued.

The Board of Directors of the Lutheran Human Relations Association issued "A Statement" and "An Open Letter" to challenge the plans to re-invest in Alabama Lutheran Academy and College. The leadership of the LHRAA viewed the plans to re-invest in Alabama Lutheran as a compromise with the forces of segregation. "An Open Letter" stressed that "the Church can accommodate to local customs and mores only when these are morally

---

[65] The Synodical Conference committee concluded, "Both institutions stand as dismal monuments to the neglect, lack of vision, and stepchild approach of the supporting synods in the area of Negro education" (George J. Gude, "Training of African-American Church Workers in the LCSM/Synodical Conference," *Concordia Historical Institute Quarterly* 68 [Fall 1995]: 112).

[66] See Richard Dickinson, *Roses and Thorns: The Centennial Edition of Black Lutheran Mission and Ministry in The Lutheran Church—Missouri Synod* (St. Louis: Concordia Publishing House, 1977) 117. Also see Robert H. King, *Pastor Jenkin's Said "Hang on to Matthew 6:33:" Autobiography of Robert H. King* (St. Louis: Concordia Publishing House, 1999) 106.

neutral.... The Church's witness must be clear and unequivocal."[67] The leadership of the Lutheran Human Relations Association made theological, ethical, and practical arguments against retaining a school of higher education in Selma. It argued that more and more black pastors were being called to minister in integrated settings and therefore needed an integrated educational experience. Instead of investing more in Alabama, the LHRAA had visions of starting a new integrated Lutheran institution in the South in a more racially progressive city such as Atlanta, Georgia.[68]

The LHRAA's "Open Letter" generated some strong responses, one from Walter H. Ellwanger, president of Alabama Lutheran Academy and College, and one from Rosa J. Young, the pioneer of black Lutheran missions in Alabama. Ellwanger wrote that "moving the school to an area already integrated, with the prime motive of integrating the South, would be a surrender to the 'principalities' of evil rather than a victory for the Gospel." Ellwanger pointed out that the school was already making a statement in the South with its integrated faculty. Ellwanger believed that the school needed to concentrate on its work in spreading the Gospel and then integration would eventually follow.[69] Rosa J. Young also wrote "An Answer to the 'Open Letter.'" Young's response reflected the fact that she did not see integration as a top priority for her people. As she expressed, "Integration is not the salvation of the world."[70] The Missouri Synod eventually proceeded with its plans to rebuild and remodel Alabama Lutheran. More recently, in 1989, the Missouri Synod made the decision to

---

[67] "An Open Letter" to the board of directors of synod, to the "Commission of Five" (evaluating the Selma expansion project), to presidents of districts of synod from the Board of Directors of the Lutheran Human Relations Association, Clemonce Saborin, president, 11 January 1961, Andrew Schulze Papers, CHI, St. Louis MO.

[68] "A Statement" by the Board of Directors of the Lutheran Human Relations Association of America, RE: The Rebuilding of Alabama Lutheran Academy and College, Selma, Alabama, Andrew Schulze Papers, CHI, St. Louis MO.

[69] Walter Ellwanger to the Lutheran Human Relations Association, The Rev. Clemonce Sabourin, president, 24 February 1961, papers of the Synodical Conference Missionary Board, supplement 5, box 23, CHI, St. Louis MO.

[70] Rosa J. Young, "Miss Rosa J. Young's Answer to the 'Open Letter,'" 10 February 1961, papers of the Synodical Conference Missionary Board, supplement 5, box 23, CHI, St. Louis MO.

expand Alabama Lutheran to a four-year college after decades of being a two-year junior college. Today, Concordia University Selma is an integrated school with about a 10 percent white student body.

Included in the Lutheran Human Relations Association's "Open Letter" was recently reported information about voter registration in Dallas and Wilcox counties, which despite their black majorities, had only six black citizens registered to vote. It was precisely these local conditions in Selma that eventually made it a focal point of national attention during the civil rights movement.[71] Lutheran institutions in both Greensboro and Selma were located in communities that played a significant role in the civil rights movement.

Many people who were concerned about improving the nation's race relations were inspired by the success of the Montgomery Bus Boycott. But there had been somewhat of a lull in civil rights activities in the late 1950s. It was a wave of spontaneous sit-ins at segregated lunch-counters that brought forth a burst of new civil rights protests in the early 1960s. The wave of sit-ins began on 1 February 1960 when a group of college students "sat-in" at the white-only lunch counter at a Woolworth's store in Greensboro, North Carolina. As Taylor Branch noted, "No one had time to wonder why the Greensboro sit-in was so different. In the previous three years, similar demonstrations had occurred in at least sixteen other cities. Few of them made the news, all faded quickly from public notice, and none had the slightest catalytic effect anywhere else. By contrast, Greensboro helped define the new decade."[72] The major organizations of the civil rights movement—the National Association for the Advancement of Colored People (NAACP), the Congress of Racial Equality (CORE), the Southern

---

[71] During the Kennedy administration, officials from the Justice Department began looking for cases of voter discrimination in the South. "They learned quickly that they needed predominately rural counties, with lots of farmers, because teachers and other middle-class urban Negroes felt too much economic pressure to testify. Large counties offered a higher pool of potential witnesses than small ones, and the degree of discrimination tended to vary directly with the proportion of Negroes in the county.... In Alabama the maps led them to stick a pin in Dallas County. By this selection method, the Justice Department went to work in Selma, the local county seat, long before SNCC or Martin Luther King" (Branch, *Parting the Waters*, 410).

[72] Ibid., 272.

Christian Leadership Council (SCLC), and the Student Non-violent Coordination Committee (SNCC)—all showed new levels of activism during the 1960s.

There was also a new level of activism among church organizations in the 1960s. A number of other denominations formed organizations to combat racial injustice. Two examples were the National Catholic Conference for Interracial Justice (NCCIJ), formed in 1958, and the Episcopal Society for Cultural and Racial Unity (ESCRU), formed in 1959.[73] Throughout the 1960s, these religious organizations came in increasing contact as they found common cause in their desire to achieve greater integration in church and society. The LHRAA's newsletter, *The Vanguard*, began to give regular mention to the activities of its "sister" organizations, the NCCIJ and the ESCRU. However, the policies and activities of these independent organizations were not always approved of by the official hierarchy and by the membership of their church bodies at large.

Some Lutherans viewed the Lutheran Human Relations Association as a radical or extremist organization. In general, the small percentage of Lutherans in the South was particularly suspect of the Lutheran Human Relations Association.[74] Schulze's role as executive secretary of the LHRAA involved traveling to different parts of the country to speak on the topic of race relations in the church. The Lutheran Human Relations Association was not particularly welcomed in the South, and Schulze's presence sometimes caused controversy.

---

[73] The National Catholic Conference for Interracial Justice grew out of local Catholic organizations with earlier roots. One of the great Catholic pioneers in race relations was Father John LaFarge, S. J., who was behind the development of the Catholic Interracial Council in New York in 1934. For more on NCCIJ and ESCRU, see John T. McGreevey, *Parish Boundaries: The Catholic Encounter with Race in the Twentieth-Century Urban North* (Chicago: The University of Chicago Press, 1996) and Gardiner H. Shattuck, Jr., *Episcopalians and Race: Civil War to Civil Rights* (Lexington: The University Press of Kentucky, 2000).

[74] See Richard O. Ziehr, *The Struggle for Unity: A Personal Look at the Integration of Lutheran Churches in the South* (Milton FL: CJH Enterprises, 1999) 81. "The fact that the Lutheran Church was an obvious minority in the South—some would say it was an 'alien' church—made it even easier to justify a willingness to maintain the status quo" (Ziehr, *The Struggle for Unity*, 19).

In January 1960 Schulze caused a great stir at St. John's Evangelical Lutheran Church in Winston-Salem, North Carolina, when members of St. Mark's, a nearby black Lutheran congregation, were invited to attend his evening presentation. Days later, the pastor of St. John's felt it necessary to write a letter to his congregation explaining the "slip-up." As he explained, "The meeting was intended only for our own members…[the invitation to St. Mark's] was done without the knowledge consent, or approval of myself, the Board of Elders, or any members of our congregation…. The Elders and myself wish to commend you for being hospitable."[75] The pastor also wrote to Schulze and to Valparaiso's president, O. P. Kretzmann, to complain about the "crash program" of integration.[76] While the pastor of St. John's attributed the presence of St. Mark's members to an invitation by Schulze, Schulze explained that his presentation at St. John's was already advertised in St. Mark's church bulletin. Schulze's letter expressed some regret for the negative feelings about the evening, but also expressed the need to show courage and convictions in these matters.[77] The incident illustrated what former Senator Paul Simon considered one of Schulze's strengths, his ability to offend people gently when needed.[78]

Schulze and the board of the LHRAA regularly received letters criticizing their positions. In 1960 the LHRAA endorsed the "Kneel-In" Movement as having special significance because "they are directed at our churches which have the greatest moral and ethical potential to remove discrimination and its source—sinful and unwarranted prejudice."[79] Just as civil rights protesters "sat-in" on businesses conforming to segregated practices, civil rights protesters began to "kneel-in" on congregations conforming to segregated practices. As Martin Luther King, Jr. often liked

---

[75] Letter to Members of St. John's from Pastor Steyer, with the approval of the Board of Elders, 18 January 1960, Andrew Schulze Papers, CHI, St. Louis MO.

[76] Martin W. Steyer to Rev. Andrew Schulze, 19 January 1960 (copy); Rev. M. Steyer to Dr. O. P. Kretzmann, 19 January 1960, Andrew Schulze Papers, CHI, St. Louis MO.

[77] Andrew Schulze to Brother Steyer, 21 January 1960 (copy), Andrew Schulze Papers, CHI, St. Louis MO.

[78] Paul Simon, interview by author 12 November 1999.

[79] "LHRAA Issues 'Kneel-In' Statement," Information Services, Valparaiso University, 7 October 1960, Valparaiso University Archives, Valparaiso IN.

to remind people, the most segregated hour in America was on Sunday morning as Americans predominately worshiped in all-white or all-black congregations. Churches served as important social centers in American life and so in some ways it is not surprising that churches did not rise above the social trends of mainstream America. Local churches were often "the most segregated major institution in American life."[80] The kneel-ins began in the border states and spread throughout the South, attracting a good deal of both positive and negative attention from various religious leaders and religious communities.[81] The LHRAA's endorsement of the "kneel-ins" especially upset a Lutheran pastor from Savannah, Georgia. The pastor criticized the board's decision to affirm the "kneel-ins" and accused the board of making pronouncements from their "theological ivory towers."[82]

But despite criticism, Schulze and others involved with the Lutheran Human Relations Association continued to take an active interest in events in the South. In March 1961 a white Lutheran vicar in Tuscaloosa, Alabama, James Fackler, was beaten by the Ku Klux Klan. The Klan was upset about Fackler's willingness to promote improved race relations. In February 1961 Vicar Fackler hosted a meeting on "The Church and Human Relations" that featured a white Lutheran pastor from Birmingham and member of the LHRAA, Joseph Ellwanger, and two of his young black parishioners. On 12 March Fackler included a brief reference about race relations in his Lenten sermon. Then on 16 March the Klan burned a cross on the lawn of the house where James Fackler and his wife were staying. Later that night, James Fackler was grabbed when about to enter his home and taken outside of town and beaten. In the midst of beatings and all sorts of invectives, Fackler was told to get out of Tuscaloosa. In response to the beating, local

---

[80] David Reimers, *White Protestantism and the Negro* (New York: Oxford University Press, 1965) 158. Reimers' study also pointed out that after the South, the Midwest was the region of the country that was slowest in terms of integrating its churches (Reimers, *White Protestantism and the Negro*, 174).

[81] See Michael B. Friedland, *Lift up Your Voice Like a Trumpet: White Clergy and the Civil Rights and Antiwar Movements, 1954–1973* (Chapel Hill: The University of North Carolina Press, 1998) 51–52.

[82] Pastor William B. Reinhardt to the Board of Directors of the Lutheran Human Relations Association of America, 8 December 1960, Andrew Schulze Papers, CHI, St. Louis MO.

Lutheran leaders confronted known Klan leaders who acted impervious to their concerns. Fackler was reassigned to complete his year of vicarage as an institutional chaplain in New Orleans.[83]

Andrew Schulze responded to the Fackler incident by publicizing the incident in *The Vanguard* and also bringing it to the attention of sister organizations, such as the ESCRU and NCCIJ.[84] Less than a year later, in January 1962, another white Lutheran pastor serving a black Lutheran congregation, Robert Faga, was also beaten by a group of local white men in Montgomery, Alabama. Schulze believed that God was working behind these events to stir up compassion not only for the Facklers and the Fagas, but also for black Americans who were constantly subjected to similar brutalities.[85] There was violent local resistance throughout the South as individuals and groups worked to change the racial status quo. During the early 1960s, civil rights activists met with violence on integrated "Freedom Rides" into the South and while working to register new black voters in states such as Mississippi.

The Cold War was constantly in the background of American life during the years of the civil rights movement. On the one hand, the larger context of the Cold War put greater stress on the need for improved race relations. America was in an ideological conflict representing concepts such as "liberty and justice for all," and therefore it was important that American

---

[83] Ziehr, *The Struggle for Unity*, 70–74. Also see James David Fackler, "The Peace That Passeth All Understanding," *The Cresset* 24 (June 1961): 16–17.

[84] Andrew Schulze to Father Morris, 13 May 1961 (copy), Andrew Schulze Papers, CHI, St. Louis MO. Andrew Schulze to Mr. Matthew Ahmann, 13 May 1961 (copy), papers of the National Catholic Council for Interracial Justice, ser. 20, box 16, Marquette University Archives, Milwaukee WI. Schulze suggested that the ESCRU, NCCIJ, and representatives of the National Council of Churches (NCC) work together on the basis of the Fackler incident and other such occurrences to lobby the federal government to ensure greater racial justice and security in American society. But Schulze added in a postscript to Ahmann that "Mr. Wofford, special consultant to the President in the area of civil rights, informed Mr. Paul Simon, a member of our Board of Directors, that no Federal law was violated in the Fackler case and hence the Federal government can take no action. What a mess we are in! How long, O Lord, how long!" (ibid). Due to schedule conflicts, the suggested meeting never took place.

[85] Andrew Schulze, "We're All Involved," *The Vanguard* 9 (February 1962): 1.

society should act upon these ideals.[86] But on the other hand, some used communist accusations to attempt to discount the individuals and the organizations that were working to bring about change during the civil rights movement. The ideology of communism included concerns about social and economic equality. So the very small number of communists in America, as well as communists overseas, embraced the cause of racial justice decades before most Americans. There were some individuals with communist sympathies who were involved with the civil rights movement. Martin Luther King, Jr. was repeatedly under federal pressure to distance himself from any individuals who had even remote communist connections so as not to jeopardize the Movement.[87] But these worries about communist connections were miscalculated. As a contemporary of the times pointed out, the civil rights movement was generally "a Christian movement, and Christians and Communists just don't mix."[88]

While Catholics were much more known for their anti-communist views, there was also a considerable strain of Lutheran anti-communism.[89] Over the years, Schulze occasionally received letters from fellow Lutherans who expressed concerns about the connections between race relations and communism. A couple of letters expressed suspicion that communists were behind recent federal decisions regarding race relations and the civil rights disturbances in the South. One letter accused the LHRAA of supporting supposedly communist-infiltrated organizations such as the NAACP.[90]

---

[86] See Mary L. Dudziak, *Cold War Civil Rights: Race and the Image of American Democracy* (Princeton: Princeton University Press, 2000).

[87] See Branch, "Hoover's Triangle and King's Machine," in *Parting the Waters*, 562–600.

[88] Franklin McCain quoted in *My Soul Is Rested: The Story of the Civil Rights Movement in the Deep South*, ed. Howell Raines (New York: Penguin Books, 1977 81.

[89] For more on Catholic anti-communism, see Charles R. Morris, "Stalin, the Pope, and Joe McCarthy," in *American Catholic: The Saints and Sinners Who Built America's Most Powerful Church* (New York: Times Books, 1997) and Patrick Carey, "Alienation and Activism: 1920–1945" and "Cold War Catholicism: 1945–1965," in *The Roman Catholics* (Westport CT: Greenwood Press, 1993). Prominent Lutherans who were vocal about their anti-communism included Walter A. Maier, Theodore Graebner, and Alfred M. Rehwinkel.

[90] Julian E. Williams to Andrew Schulze, 13 May 1960, Andrew Schulze Papers, CHI, St. Louis MO.

Schulze also saw communism as an immoral and atheistic force in the world and held strongly anti-communist views. However, Schulze believed that the way to counter communism was to work toward the elimination of unjust social conditions that made communism an attractive alternative to some.[91] For Schulze, the promotion of better race relations was the best way to work against the influence of communism, for he believed that race was one of the communist's strongest weapons of propaganda.[92]

In 1961 the LHRAA's Summer Institute was dedicated to the theme of "Communism, Christianity, and Race Relations." A portion of the institute involved a symposium on communism. Among the speakers were the Rev. Ralph Moellering; the renown Lutheran theologian, George W. Forell; the Pulitzer-prize winning journalist, Louis P. Lochner; professor of Concordia Seminary, Martin H. Scharlemann; and, a representative of the Federal Bureau of Investigation, Fern C. Stukenbroeker. In some correspondence, Schulze noted that Stukenbroeker was personally assigned to address the institute by the director of the FBI, J. Edgar Hoover.[93]

A major thrust of the institute was the need for social action and social justice to counter the appeal of communism. While Catholic social action often put an emphasis on communal organization and action, Lutheran social action stressed the need for individual involvement.[94] George Forell was well-known for his contributions to the development of Lutheran ethical thought.[95] Forell's address at the Summer Institute reflected the

---

[91] "American anticommunism was a complex, pluralistic movement, as pluralistic as the culture in which it was rooted. Memory's image of anticommunism was painted by its enemies, a monolithic projection of McCarthyism writ large. But the myth of monolithic anticommunism obscures the fundamental nature of American anticommunism: that it was a diverse movement of Americans of very different beliefs and goals who disagreed among themselves almost as much as they disagreed with communism" (Richard Gid Powers, *Not Without Honor: The History of American Anticommunism* [New York: Free Press, 1995] 426).

[92] Andrew Schulze to A. F. Twenhafel, 16 November 1963 (copy), Andrew Schulze Papers, CHI, St. Louis MO.

[93] Ibid.

[94] For more on Catholic social action, see McGreevey, *Parish Boundaries*, 38–47.

[95] See George Wolfgang Forell, *Faith Active in Love: An Investigation of the Principles Underlying Luther's Social Ethics* (Minneapolis: Augsburg Publishing House, 1959).

Lutheran emphasis on individual ethics, stressing the need for personal, parabolic action. Forell stressed that "we should not be discouraged but act in the small arena which is ours, showing our faith active in love, without letting the complexities of an ultimate solution paralyze us into inaction."[96] The Missouri Synod did show increasing support for social action at its national convention in 1962. While the synod had traditionally supported social welfare agencies, it now voted to create its first Commission on Social Action.[97]

Andrew Schulze continued to be confronted with concerns about the connections between civil rights and communism. The Lutheran Human Relations Association made arrangements for a new theater production, "Black Nativity," to be performed on the campus of Valparaiso University in January 1962. Schulze and others received some criticism concerning the production and especially of its playwright, Langston Hughes. Hughes was suspected for his earlier writings that criticized Christianity and reflected his communist leanings. Schulze wrote a response to these concerns and pointed out that Hughes had converted to Christianity since his earlier writings and had proved his loyalty before the Senate's McCarthy Committee.[98] Schulze held the belief that communism "not only endangers the security of our nation and the freedom of the world, but the future of

---

[96] George W. Forell, "The Ethics of Communism," *Proceedings* of the Lutheran Human Relations Association of America, Summer Institute, 28–30 July 1961, 57.

[97] J. Russell Hale, "Lutherans and Social Action" in *The Lutheran Church in North American Life*, ed. John E. Groh and Robert H. Smith (St. Louis: Clayton Publishing House, 1979) 119.

[98] "A member of The Lutheran Church—Missouri Synod, who is deeply committed to the Scriptural viewpoint that the Christ born of the Virgin Mary is the universal Savior of all mankind, asked a playwright and author whom he has known intimately for ten or twelve years, to write BLACK NATIVITY. The author's name is Langston Hughes. Many years ago, as an embittered young Negro, Mr. Hughes wrote a number of poems which, to say the least, were not complimentary to Christianity. But, for that reason to reject what he wrote in 1961 could be similar to a rejection of all the Pauline Letters of the New Testament; for St. Paul at one time in his life persecuted the church of Jesus Christ and, consenting to the stoning of the first New Testament martyr, stood by, perhaps in fiendish glee, holding the garments of those who did the stoning" (Andrew Schulze, February 1962, Andrew Schulze Papers, CHI, St. Louis MO).

the church as an institution."[99] Still, some individuals continued to accuse Schulze of being "soft" on communism.[100]

In 1962 the LHRAA's Summer Institute took the theme, "Our Image Abroad," and again focused on the international implications of American race relations.[101] Speakers included representatives from the embassies of India and Nigeria who provided a more global perspective on race relations. India and Nigeria were important countries, with large populations, that had played significant roles in the decolonization movement in Asia and Africa in the decades after World War II. But India and Nigeria were also areas of interest to Lutherans, who had long supported mission work in these countries. A representative of the Lutheran Church in Nigeria had attended the previous Summer Institute. After the institute, E. A. Ubom, a leader among Nigerian Lutherans, wrote to Andrew Schulze. Ubom wrote, "Segregation in churches has now become a stumbling block in the furtherance of God's Kingdom among colored peoples overseas. And for this reason it is meet that most of us who from the Headquarters of our Nigerian Mission go back with an assurance that our Lutheran Church practices what she preaches. I therefore thank you and all those who labor under this cause for what has been done."[102] The work of the Lutheran Human Relations Association had even global implications.

Every year at the Summer Institute, Schulze provided some sort of report as executive secretary of the LHRAA to recall the activities and the accomplishments of the past year. His report in 1962 emphasized that, from

---

[99] Andrew Schulze to A. F. Twenhafel, 16 November 1963 (copy), Andrew Schulze Papers, CHI, St. Louis MO.

[100] H. C. Miessler to the Rev. Dr. Oliver Harms, 7 February 1966 (copy), Andrew Schulze Papers, CHI, St. Louis. MO.

[101] Despite the very political and ideological nature of the Cold War, social and economic concerns continued to drive the global agenda. As Robert F. Kennedy reflected on his term as attorney general, "No amount of East-West debate on the claims of democracy against communism would dispel the global preoccupation with race and economics. 'There wasn't one area of the world that I visited,' he said later, '...that I wasn't asked about the question of civil rights'" (Branch, *Parting the Waters*, 566).

[102] E. A. Ubom to Andrew Schulze, 18 August 1961, Andrew Schulze Papers, CHI, St. Louis MO.

the beginning, a major goal of the Lutheran Human Relations Association was to educate Lutherans and others in the area of race relations. Schulze believed that the LHRAA worked for this goal through the publications that it promoted and distributed. Schulze stated that the circulation figures for various LHRAA-supported publications were in the thousands and even the tens of thousands. He mentioned materials such as the *Vanguard*, the annual proceedings of the Summer Institutes, and "Grace and Race in the Lutheran Church," the pamphlet published by the National Lutheran Council. Schulze made special mention of Clemonce Sabourin's *Let the Righteous Speak*, a poignant account of the Sabourin family's experiences with prejudice during their travels through the Southern United States.[103] Schulze believed that all of these publications were working to make people more informed and aware.

However, Schulze's report went on to stress the need, not only for education, but also for action. Schulze wrote, "Words alone are not strong enough.... There has been an ever-growing consciousness of the need for action that would change words and thoughts into a way of life."[104] Schulze's report was dated 28 July 1962. Exactly one month later, Andrew Schulze became involved in direct action himself, becoming one of several Northern white clergymen who were arrested in Albany, Georgia, for their participation in civil rights demonstrations.

In the summer of 1961, representatives of the Student Non-Violent Coordinating Committee (SNCC) initiated a campaign of civil rights activities in southwest Georgia. SNCC representatives based their local headquarters in the small city of Albany, Georgia. The city of Albany had a large minority of black citizens, about 40 percent of the population. Yet these black citizens, like other black Americans throughout the South, and all over America, were continually denied their basic rights as United States citizens. The civil rights campaign in Albany, which became known as the "Albany Movement," consisted primarily of black voter registration and

---

[103] See Clemonce Sabourin, *Let the Righteous Speak* (New York: Pageant Press, 1957).

[104] Andrew Schulze, "Perspective: A Year's End Report of the Lutheran Human Relations Association of America," in *Proceedings* of the Lutheran Human Relations Association of America, Summer Institute, 27–29 July, 57.

boycotts against segregated facilities. Eventually Martin Luther King, Jr. and representatives of the Southern Christian Leadership Council (SCLC) joined the campaign there.

At the heart of the civil rights movement was the idea of civil disobedience. Civil rights activists peacefully broke local laws to demonstrate their commitment to a "higher law." Through non-violent protests, activists hoped to bring latent hostilities to the surface. But the practice of civil disobedience was frustrated in Albany by the restrained response of the local chief of police, Laurie Pritchett. Pritchett understood the tactics of civil disobedience and kept order without resorting to violence against the protesters. After months of protests and over 1,000 arrests, including the arrest of Martin Luther King, Jr., the Albany Movement was stalling. In August 1962 King decided to make an appeal to religious leaders throughout the nation to come to Albany and participate in the protests.

Andrew Schulze, Karl Lutze, and Valparaiso University's president, O. P. Kretzmann had a conversation about Martin Luther King's appeal. Kretzmann encouraged someone from the Lutheran Human Relations Association to respond to the appeal. Lutze suggested that someone stay behind to watch the situation from the LHRAA office. After some discussion, Schulze concluded, "I have been writing about this all this time, and if I can only write and I can't put my body where my words are, then I'm not much of a writer."[105] Shortly afterwards, Schulze left for Chicago to meet other religious leaders who were going to Albany. Margaret Schulze and Karl Lutze went to Chicago to see Andrew off. In Chicago, the group was given a brief orientation by a man relatively new to the civil rights movement, someone who eventually became one of Martin Luther King's closest associates and friends, the Rev. Andrew Young.

As the group of religious leaders traveled by bus from Chicago, they were denied service in one Tennessee restaurant because there were a few black individuals in the group. There were no other incidents along the trip, but the group did have a sense of foreboding as they traveled deeper into the South.[106] At the same time, another group of religious leaders traveled from

---

[105] Lutze, Oral History Collection, 32.

[106] "After leaving Atlanta, Georgia, the atmosphere grew tense…. When they passed Americus, Georgia, site of the famed Koinonia farm where a racial integration

New York to Albany. Altogether over seventy individuals responded to King's appeal, including a significant number of Protestant, Catholic, and Jewish leaders. Andrew Schulze was one of five Lutheran pastors who went to Albany. Andrew Schulze and Lawrence Halvorson from the National Lutheran Council, headquartered in Chicago, stayed with the same black host family on their first night in Albany. Even though there were other Lutherans pastors involved, Schulze remained a somewhat unique figure in the group. At sixty-six, Andrew Schulze was much older than the rest of the religious leaders in Albany and had decades of experience with the struggle against racial injustice.

On 26 August 1962 the group of religious leaders met at Bethel AME Church in the morning for a briefing on the local situation from Martin Luther King, Ralph Abernathy, and a local leader, Dr. William Anderson. The group made plans for a gathering that afternoon at Albany's city hall. They hoped to have a meeting with city officials in order to urge further negotiation and reconciliation over matters of civil rights. At the very least, they intended to make a statement by their presence that they were concerned about the rights of Albany's black citizens. When the group arrived at city hall, Police Chief Pritchett and the national news media were waiting for them. There was a brief time of prayer and of reading from the scriptures, from the Psalms and from Galatians 5. Then Pritchett ordered the group to disperse and when they did not, he ordered that they be arrested for "disorderly conduct."

The religious leaders were arrested and sent to nearby jails. The majority of religious leaders spent only a couple days in prison before posting bond and returning home for their weekly religious duties. But Schulze and a few others were able to stay a couple of days longer. He spent six days in the Dougherty County Jail. These were hot summer days, spent in crowded and filthy facilities. It was an intense experience for him and the other religious leaders. A few of the religious leaders, including Schulze, drafted a letter to President John F. Kennedy. The letter expressed moral

program had been attempted several years previously, they had the eerie feeling that perhaps they were in for abusive treatment similar to that which the Koinonia members had received" (Alfred P. Klausler, "Six Days in Jail," *The Walther League Messenger* 71 [November 1962]: 6).

outrage against the system of segregation. The letter stated that "a way of life which distorts personality, destroys freedom, and perpetuates falsehood must not be permitted to endure."[107] Schulze was appalled by some of the conditions and some of the treatment to which he and others were exposed. In the Baker County Prison, there was an incident in which the guards ordered a couple of the black prisoners to urinate on the religious leaders who were jailed there.[108] While many Americans had a certain reverence for religious leaders, some Southerners merely saw these religious leaders as meddling outsiders.

But Schulze and the others also received words of encouragement in jail. The arrest of the religious leaders made national news. A few people sent telegrams and letters to Schulze as soon as they heard he was in jail. One couple sent a telegram that stated, "Congratulations You Are Privileged." Schulze was especially glad to receive a letter from a former youth of his congregation in St. Louis, Sam Hoard. Sam Hoard, now a pastor from Brooklyn, New York, noted, "If I don't end up in a jail cell soon myself, via a peaceful demonstration or prayer pilgrimage, I won't know how to attempt to explain it to my son years from now…it seems necessary to give this kind of witness so that the Gospel may be preached more effectively to ALL men."[109]

Shortly after his time in Albany, Schulze reflected on his experience in his column in *The Vanguard* and in an interview for *The Walther League Messenger*. He and others who were imprisoned during the movement found

---

[107] Andrew Schulze, typescript of notes written while in Dougherty County Jail, Albany, Georgia, 30 August 1962, Andrew Schulze Papers, CHI, St. Louis MO.

[108] The group intended to keep this incident confidential, but the story was picked by France Runge of the "Milwaukee Journal" (Lutze, Oral History Collection, 36). Schulze did not publicly reveal the worst details of their experience because their time in Albany was "but a token of the suffering inflicted on the 1,100 who had gone before them into the same jails, as well as the suffering that crushes the spirits of millions of Negroes in the south and in the north who by a cruel society overtly and otherwise are denied the right to be fully human" (Andrew Schulze, "I Was In Prison," *The Vanguard* 9 [September–October 1962]: 3).

[109] Bill and Janet Wenholz to Andrew Schulze, 29 August 1962 (Western Union Telegram); Sam, Alice, and "Larry" Hoard to Andrew Schulze, 29 August 1962, Andrew Schulze Papers, CHI, St. Louis MO.

spiritual meaning in their time in jail. Schulze noted that he could better understand St. Paul's letters written from a Roman prison. Some of the religious leaders, including Andrew Schulze, fasted during their time in jail for reasons of either protest or penitence. The religious leaders spent some of their time in jail discussing theology and singing "freedom songs" from the movement. The "freedom songs" often had spiritual overtones. Schulze was especially moved by the song phrase, "We are not alone." As Schulze recalled, "I applied that phrase to the comforting knowledge that God was with me during those trying days. In the filth, heat, and over the obscene and blasphemous language from the regular prisoners, I had the sustaining comfort that my Lord would never forsake me."[110]

Though Schulze's time in Albany was a trying experience, it was also a profoundly inspiring experience. After he and the others were released from prison, local leaders of the Albany Movement brought them to a black church rally. The crowd warmly welcomed the Northern religious leaders. It was a high point in Schulze's life. Karl Lutze recalled that Schulze said he had "never been so deeply, emotionally, and spiritually moved in my life as when these black brothers and sisters were expressing their gratitude for what we had done in identifying with them."[111]

Michael Friedland believed that white clergy involvement in Albany was an important development in the civil rights movement. This was the first time that a significant group of Northern white clergy became involved in civil rights protests in the South, and such involvement only increased over the next few years. As Friedland explained, "Despite the brevity of the white outsider's visit, as well as its lack of any palpable gains (including favorable publicity), SCLC's explicit invitation to northern clergy represented a significant shift in tactics… Footage of whites in clerical collars or yarmulkes made interesting copy, but it also conveyed the message that the movement was as much a moral and ethical issue as it was a political, social, and economic matter and, as such, affected all Americans."[112] While black pastors and black churches were at the heart of the civil rights movement, some white clergy and white lay leaders also played important roles.

---

[110] Klausler, "Six Days in Jail," 7–8.
[111] Lutze, Oral History Collection, 37.
[112] Freidland, *Lift up Your Voice Like a Trumpet*, 64–65.

But at the time, the Albany Movement, and the brief involvement by Northern white religious leaders, was considered a failure. Because of the restraint of the local law enforcement, Albany was seen as "the triumph of sophisticated segregation"; none of the expectations raised in 1961 and 1962 were realized.[113] Martin Luther King, Jr. came under criticism that he had not made any significant achievements since the Montgomery Bus Boycott. The civil rights movement seemed to be stalled. Because the demonstrations and arrests in Albany made no immediate gains, Schulze was asked if his time spent in prison was in vain. He emphasized that he had no regrets. He was glad to be a part of "the determined effort to overcome prejudice and awaken Christian consciences to the sin of segregation all over America." Despite frustrated goals in the short term, Schulze was confident that the "ultimate victory will be ours."[114]

O. P. Kretzmann actively supported Schulze's involvement in Albany. Upon Schulze's arrest, O. P. Kretzmann and Karl Lutze sent telegrams to President John F. Kennedy, Attorney General Robert F. Kennedy, and John A. Hannah of the federally-appointed Civil Rights Commission in support of Schulze and the other religious leaders who were arrested in Albany.[115] Kretzmann also contacted the president of the nearby University of Notre Dame, Theodore Hesburgh, C. S. C., and asked him to use his influence to support the Albany demonstrators. Hesburgh responded affirmatively and had important contacts in the federal government and, later, served on the national Civil Rights Commission.[116] Kretzmann provided the Lutheran Human Relations Association with the $200 needed for bond money for Schulze's release from jail. Kretzmann received a significant number of complaints that a member of Valparaiso's faculty was involved in this

---

[113] Quoted by David J. Garrow in *Bearing the Cross: Martin Luther King Jr. and the Southern Christian Leadership Conference* (New York: William Morrow and Company, Inc., 1986) 279.

[114] Klausler, "Six Days in Jail," 8.

[115] Information Services, Valparaiso University, 6 September 1962, Valparaiso University Archives, Valparaiso IN.

[116] O. P. Kretzmann and Theodore Hesburgh, (telegrams), Andrew Schulze Papers, CHI, St. Louis MO. For more on Father Hesburgh, see Michael O'Brien, *Hesburgh: A Biography* (Washington DC: Catholic University of America Press, 1998).

protest.[117] On this occasion and others over the years, Kretzmann needed to defend Schulze and his position at Valparaiso University.[118]

Other Lutherans did not support the religious demonstration in Albany. Schulze's involvement in Albany generated considerable interest among Lutherans at the time. The Rev. Dr. Edgar Homrighausen, president of the Southern District of the Lutheran Church—Missouri Synod, which included the states of Louisiana, Mississippi, Alabama, and parts of Florida, publicly criticized the participation of Northern religious leaders in Albany. Homrighausen was quoted in an article in the *Birmingham Post-Herald* saying that the demonstrators have "become engaged in a matter of which they have little or no understanding.... Surely there must be enough work to keep these men busy in their own areas."[119] This was a common criticism used by opponents of civil rights activists. Schulze responded to this general criticism in his article in *The Vanguard*. Schulze explained that the religious leaders from other parts of the country were also actively involved in trying to confront racial prejudice in their own communities. But they came to Albany because they were asked to come to Albany.[120]

As Schulze's story was told in Lutheran periodicals over the next few months, his involvement in Albany continued to be a matter of discussion among Lutherans. Schulze and other Lutheran officials received a significant amount of mail about the situation, which included both praise and criticism for his participation in Albany. The Missouri Synod had recently passed a resolution in favor of direct action at its national convention in the summer of 1962. It was a resolution that was promoted by the Lutheran

---

[117] Correspondence on Albany, Andrew Schulze Papers, CHI, St. Louis MO.

[118] Schulze concluded in his memoirs that "there was no other person in a position of high administrative authority in the Lutheran Church, at least in the Missouri Synod, who understood the seriousness of the race issue and was willing, if necessary, to put his career into jeopardy by an almost unprecedented commitment to a change for the better than O. P. Kretzmann" (Schulze, *Race against Time*, 132).

[119] "Lutheran Leader Flays Pilgrimages to Albany," clipping from the *Birmingham Post-Herald*, 31 August 1962, Andrew Schulze Papers, CHI, St. Louis MO. Homrighausen did help to bring about the administrative integration of the Southern District in 1961, but he generally stood against the activism of the civil rights movement. For more on Homrighausen, see Ziehr, *The Struggle for Unity*.

[120] Schulze, "I Was In Prison," 4.

Human Relations Association. The resolution stated that the synod should "commend and encourage those of its members who...have engaged in lawful and peaceful demonstrations for the furtherance of racial justice." It also suggested that church members should "exercise the greatest care in judging one another in their individual and different responses to complex social problems."[121] But church pronouncements sometimes had little influence on church practice.

After his participation in the Albany Movement, some people wanted to hold up Schulze as a great Lutheran example while others wanted to marginalize him as a rare exception to mainstream Lutheranism. Letters of praise noted Schulze's "outstanding and heroic success," his "forthrightness and positive leadership," and his "distinctive Christian witness." Letters of criticism implied that Schulze was "an extremist," "a strange character," "a troublemaker," and "a crack pot." A considerable number of letters implied that there was some communist connection to the events in Albany.[122] However, the letters of criticism did include some substantive arguments. Some individuals were concerned about the mix of religion and politics. Others were concerned about the inter-faith nature of the demonstration.

Lutherans have traditionally been very respectful of government authority. This perhaps had as much to do with the socio-economic and ethnic background of Lutherans as with Lutheran theology.[123] Nonetheless, Lutherans have generally held to the principle found in Romans 13:1, "Everyone must submit himself to the governing authorities, for there is no authority except that which God has established." Additionally, Lutherans in America seemed to especially embrace the concept of separation of church and state because it seemed to relate to Martin Luther's theological concept of the two kingdoms. Many Lutherans have greatly valued the apolitical nature of Lutheran theology and practice. So some of the criticism about Albany and the civil rights demonstrations related to general Lutheran

---

[121] *Human Relations: Resolutions of the Lutheran Church—Missouri Synod* (Lutheran Church—Missouri Synod and the Lutheran Human Relations Association, 1969) 13.

[122] Correspondence on Albany, Andrew Schulze Papers, CHI.

[123] See Frederick C. Luebke, "German Immigrants and American Politics: Problems of Leadership, Parties, and Issues," in *Germans in the New World: Essays in the History of Immigration* (Urbana: University of Illinois Press, 1990).

attitudes about religion and politics. Several letters suggested that religious leaders should not inject themselves so directly in political affairs. Other letters took issue with the concept of civil disobedience. As one letter expressed, "Imagine the Apostle Paul agitating in the Roman Empire for the freedom of the slaves! To use force in a situation by arms or non-resistance measures is one and the same, disobedience to civil authorities... Reform by the Gospel and not by the law is our business."[124]

But other Lutherans rejected this traditionally "quietistic" approach to politics. A few letters promoted the idea of increased Lutheran political and social activity. One letter suggested that if politicians failed to act effectively in such moral matters, it was essential that clergymen become involved.[125] When *The Lutheran Laymen* published two letters criticizing Schulze's participation in Albany, others wrote back in defense of the principle of civil disobedience. One letter pointed out that a careful reading of the entire chapter of Romans 13 did make allowances for the practice of civil disobedience. It also suggested that the concept of absolute submission to the authorities was the same concept that allowed so many Lutherans to unquestioning submit to Nazi authority in Germany.[126] Schulze rejected what he saw among some Lutherans as a rigid separation between theology

---

[124] Oswald Skor to Field Secretary Lutze, 17 September 1962, Andrew Schulze Papers, CHI, St. Louis MO.

[125] Chaplain Major George O. Taylor to Dr. Oliver Harms, president of the Lutheran Church—Missouri Synod, 17 September 1962 (copy), Andrew Schulze Papers, CHI, St. Louis MO.

[126] N. E. Kabelitz to The Lutheran Laymen, 10 May 1963 (copy), Andrew Schulze Papers, CHI, St. Louis MO. While many German Lutherans did support the Nazi regime, that was also true of many Germans of different religious persuasions. Lutheran support for the Nazi regime has sometimes been overstated. See Uwe Simon-Netto, *The Fabricated Luther: The Rise and Fall of the Shirer Myth*, foreword by Peter L. Berger (St. Louis: Concordia Publishing House, 1995). It was fitting that the works of the great Lutheran theologian Dietrich Bonhoeffer, the most famous Lutheran opponent of the Nazi regime, were popular reading among civil rights activists of various religious backgrounds. See James F. Findlay, Jr., *Church People in the Struggle: The National Council of Churches and the Black Freedom Movement, 1950–1970* (New York: Oxford University Press, 1993) 121.

and political and social matters. As Schulze expressed, "A theology is never true unless it relates itself to life."[127]

Schulze wrote a general letter of response that explained the reasons for his participation in Albany and his profound commitment to improved race relations. Schulze began with national and international implications of race relations. He described the emergence of newly independent, non-white nations around the world and believed that improved race relations were essential for "our own national security, even our future existence as a nation." But he went on to say that his primary motivation came not from being a citizen of the United States or as a citizen of the world, but from being a Christian. As far as addressing the legality of his actions, Schulze turned to the parable of the Good Samaritan. He pointed out that the priest and the Levite who passed by the wounded man could have found some justification for their actions in rabbinic law. Schulze stressed, "There is a higher law...than the Constitution of the State of Georgia and even the Constitution of the United States. I am not referring to the law of Moses which in itself is devastating in its condemnation of injustice, but rather to the 'law of love,' 'the new commandment' given to us by Christ, 'that ye love one another.'"[128]

Another concern about the events in Albany had to do with Schulze's involvement in a public event with leaders of other religious backgrounds. Schulze was originally surprised that there were not more letters criticizing him on this account.[129] The Missouri Synod had a relatively strict concept of religious fellowship. This position developed out of the early history of the Missouri Synod. Some of the first members of the Missouri Synod had left Europe because the Lutheran churches there were being forced by governing authorities to unite with Reformed churches. Missouri Synod Lutherans opposed "unionism," the joining of churches despite doctrinal differences. But exclusive religious fellowship was not only a matter of the history

---

[127] Andrew Schulze to Rev. Albert Jesse, 12 October 1962 (copy), Andrew Schulze Papers, CHI, St. Louis MO.

[128] Andrew Schulze to my dear Mr. —, 5 January 1963 (copy), Andrew Schulze Papers, CHI, St. Louis MO.

[129] Andrew Schulze to Rev. and Mrs. Samuel L. Hoard, 11 September 1962 (copy), Andrew Schulze Papers, CHI, St. Louis MO.

and the practice of Missouri Synod Lutheranism, it was also a matter of theology. By strictly limiting church fellowship, Missouri Synod Lutherans hoped to maintain the purity of their religious beliefs. They opposed church fellowship with other Christian denominations and even with some of their fellow Lutherans. However, there was some latitude to working with other Christians outside of the formal worship of Word and Sacrament.

In the demonstration in Albany, Schulze joined with religious leaders from various backgrounds, including Catholics, Baptists, Presbyterians, Methodists, Unitarians, and Jews. Lutheran theology, as well as traditional Christian theology, was based on a strong Christological foundation. So Lutherans were generally critical of a theology that was primarily centered on the promotion of good ethical behavior. Some Lutherans were critical of Martin Luther King, Jr. because of his theological background. While he had a deep religious faith, some Christians did not agree with his liberal theology and his modernist views of the Bible.[130] Schulze acknowledged that "Martin Luther King may be a bit weak in his theology." However, he also described King as "a great leader in the cause of justice and equity; he is a boon to our nation."[131]

The main concern that was expressed in letters to Schulze about Albany was not the involvement with other Christian denominations, but the inter-faith nature of the Albany protest. The involvement of Jewish religious leaders in the Albany demonstration made Schulze's participation a controversial issue for some Lutherans. A few individuals were especially concerned that he joined in a public prayer with Jewish believers.[132] Schulze responded to a few of the specific complaints, explaining that the demonstration involved a period of silent prayer.[133] Schulze had been conscious of inter-faith matters during his imprisonment. Schulze was impressed with what he saw as "true Jewish leadership, deeply committed to a 'community

---

[130] For more on King's religious background and experiences, see Garrow, *Bearing the Cross* and Stephen B. Oates, *Let the Trumpet Sound: A Life of Martin Luther King, Jr.* (New York: Harper Perennial, 1994).

[131] Andrew Schulze to John V. Egan, 26 September 1962 (copy), Andrew Schulze Papers, CHI.

[132] Correspondence on Albany, Andrew Schulze Papers, CHI.

[133] Andrew Schulze to Mark F. Bartling, 6 December 1962 (copy), Andrew Schulze Papers, CHI.

of righteousness.'" But his strict religious background also made him sensitive to the fact that the experience involved some "theological ambiguity."[134] He continued to deal with these issues over the next few years as he met with others of various religious backgrounds to promote improved race relations.

In settings with people of mixed religious backgrounds, Schulze gave witness to his religious beliefs. When he was honored for his involvement in Albany by a local chapter of the American Civil Liberties Union, Schulze explained his motivation for participating. In a setting with few traditional Christian believers, he explained that he went to Albany "not in spite of my conservative theology, but *because* of it; I went *because* I believed that Jesus Christ is God incarnate in the flesh of man; *because* I believed that He died and rose again; *because* I believed that through faith He had given me a new life which was my privilege to live out to the glory of God and in the interest of my fellowman, especially those against whom our white society had practiced inhumane injustice for centuries."[135] This was the faith that guided Andrew Schulze throughout his life.

In January 1963 Schulze participated in the National Conference on Religion and Race held at the Edgewater Beach Hotel in Chicago. It was a gathering of hundreds of religious leaders from various religious organizations and various religious traditions. While black churches and black religious organizations had been invited, few participated. The conference was largely a white gathering, dedicated to mobilize white religious groups to a greater promotion of racial equality. The conference was planned and organized by Matthew Ahmann, the young lay leader of the National Catholic Council for Interracial Justice (NCCIJ). Speakers at the conference included Rev. Will Campbell of the National Council of Churches; Rabbi Abraham Heschel, Professor of Ethics and Mysticism at the Jewish Seminary of America; Dr. Benjamin Mays, President of Morehouse College; Cardinal Albert Meyer, the Catholic Archbishop of

---

[134] Andrew Schulze, typescript of notes written while in Dougherty County Jail, Albany, Georgia, 30 August 1962, Andrew Schulze Papers, CHI, St. Louis MO.

[135] Schulze, *Race against Time*, 110–11.

Chicago; and the Rev. Dr. Martin Luther King, Jr.[136] The conference was held on the 100th anniversary of the Emancipation Proclamation, with the understanding that the task that Abraham Lincoln had begun had yet to be completed.[137]

This unprecedented religious gathering on race drew criticism from some of the press and some of the participants that the effort was "too little, too late." Organized religion had not done nearly enough to counter racism in America and in many ways had sanctioned racism in America. William Stringfellow, an Episcopal lay theologian and a white attorney working in Harlem, told the assembly, "The only practical and decent thing it could do at this late hour was weep."[138] But other participants countered attitudes of pessimism and fatalism. Rabbi Abraham Heschel, remembering the legacy of the Holocaust, stressed the need for hope, emphasizing "the greatest heresy is despair." Both Heschel and Martin Luther King appealed to the prophetic tradition of the Judeo-Christian heritage and quoted the words of the ancient prophet Amos in their speeches, "Let justice roll down like waters, and righteousness like a mighty stream."[139]

---

[136] See Matthew Ahmann, ed., *Race, Challenge to Religion: Original Essays and an Appeal to the Conscience from the National Conference on Religion and Race* (Chicago: Henry Regnery Company, 1963).

[137] Benjamin Mays, introduction to *Race, Challenge to Religion: Original Essays and an Appeal to the Conscience from the National Conference on Religion and Race*, ed. Matthew Ahmann (Chicago: Henry Regnery Company, 1963) 4.

[138] Friedland, *Lift up Your Voice Like a Trumpet*, 74. William Stringfellow was also a featured speaker at the LHRAA's Summer Institute in 1965. See *Proceedings* of the Lutheran Human Relations Association of America, Summer Institute, 23–29 July 1965.

[139] See Taylor Branch, "Prophets in Chicago," *Pillar of Fire: America in the King Years, 1963–65* (New York: Simon & Schuster, 1999) 31. King and Heschel came from vastly different backgrounds. "King the Baptist of Atlanta, descended from Negro preachers back into chattel slavery, Heschel the Orthodox Jew of Warsaw, descended from dynastic generations of Hasidic rabbis whose names remained luminous in East European Jewry…the two men were drawn to each other by a shared commitment to the language and experience of the Hebrew prophets. The lasting bond that grew between King and Heschel was among many historical legacies of the ecumenical conference" (Branch, "Prophets in Chicago," 21–22).

Several Lutherans participated, some associated with the Lutheran Human Relations Association and others with the National Lutheran Council.[140] Schulze led the delegation from the Lutheran Human Relations Association. During the conference, he was able to meet and visit various religious leaders from across the country. Schulze had contact with some of the prominent figures at the conference, such as Benjamin Mays and Abraham Heschel.[141] Schulze was also involved in some of the activities of the conference. He initiated a significant change to the conference's main statement, "An Appeal to the Conscience of the American People."

Schulze saw a paradox in these inter-faith opportunities. As he expressed in *The Vanguard*, regarding the National Conference on Religion and Race, "For Lutherans to participate in such an undertaking means to live dangerously...there may be an effort...to reduce everything to the least common denominator as far as faith and confession are concerned."[142] On the other hand, Schulze pointed out that not participating would be missing the opportunity for a greater Christian witness. Lutheranism, and traditional Christianity, is rooted in the idea of confessions of faith.[143] Schulze was concerned that "An Appeal to the Conscience of the American People," which called for a greater religious commitment to racial justice, was lacking any Christological content. He believed that "the elimination of all Christology must of necessity violate the conscience of those who take the New Testament seriously."[144] Due to the concern of Schulze and a few other individuals, a prefatory comment was added to "An Appeal to the

---

[140] See Andrew Schulze, "National Conference on Religion and Race," *The Vanguard* 10 (February–March 1963): 3–4, 6, 8.

[141] In a photograph published in *The Detroit News*, Schulze was pictured with Bishop Francis J. Schench of the Roman Catholic diocese in Duluth, Minnesota; Dr. Benjamin E. Mays; and Rabbi Abraham Heschel. Copy of a newspaper clipping, *The Detroit News*, 15 January 1963, Andrew Schulze Papers, CHI, St. Louis MO.

[142] Andrew Schulze, "Other Centennial Notes," *The Vanguard* 10 (January 1963): 4.

[143] L. DeAne Lagerquist noted that the concept of confession was important for understanding Lutheran theology and Lutheran piety. "These two—confession as a statement of religious belief and confession of sin as a component of religious behavior—are central to Lutheranism" (L. DeAne Lagerquist, *The Lutherans* [Westport CT: Praeger, 1999] 3).

[144] Schulze, *Race against Time*, 113.

Conscience of the American People."[145] The prefatory comment explained, "Coming as we do out of various religious backgrounds each of us has more to say than can be said here. But this statement is what we as religious people are moved to say together."[146]

Schulze's desire to clarify a Christian theological position did sometimes cause tension with Jewish leaders. One Jewish leader wrote both to praise and criticize Schulze for his description of the National Conference on Religion and Race in *The Vanguard* of February–March 1963. The Jewish leader was glad that Schulze acknowledged "that Jews have given moral and financial support toward the eradication of racism in our land far out of proportion to their numerical strength." However, there was objection to *The Vanguard's* depiction of Jewish theology and "the rather rigid insistence on the part of the Missouri Lutheran Synod that no man can come to the Father but by Jesus."[147] The civil rights movement brought about greater inter-faith activity and dialogue, but not necessarily greater inter-faith agreement. The National Conference on Religion and Race was meant to continue its work in local commissions, but these commissions were often inhibited by their religious and racial differences.[148] Some believed that the conference achieved little aside from its symbolic value. But looking back, Schulze believed that the it laid the groundwork for greater religious support of the civil rights legislation of the mid-1960s.[149]

On the front page of the issue of *The Vanguard*, which discussed the National Conference on Religion and Race, was a cover letter from Dr. Oliver R. Harms, the new president of the Lutheran Church—Missouri

---

[145] "Schulze Suggests Change in 'Appeal to Conscience:' Synod Men Attend Race Conference," *The Lutheran Layman* 34 (1 February 1963): 2.

[146] Ahmann, *Race, Challenge to Religion*, 171.

[147] Rabbi Arthur Gilbert to the Rev. Andrew Schulze, 29 March 1963 (copy), papers of the National Catholic Council for Interracial Justice, ser. 20, box 16, Marquette University Archives, Milwaukee WI.

[148] "Intramural differences kept popping up even among the subdivisions of the major white groups, especially Protestants and Jews, and hostile archbishops all but shackled Catholics in Los Angeles and Philadelphia. A Catholic leader of the organizing coalition reported that no city began with even a communicating familiarity between the white and Negro clergy" (Branch, *Pillar of Fire*, 32).

[149] Schulze, *Race against Time*, 114.

Synod. Harms wrote to congratulate the LHRAA on its tenth anniversary as an organization working on behalf of human relations.[150] At the Missouri Synod's national convention in 1962, Harms was elected to succeed John Behnken (1935–1962). Harms was also from Texas and served as a top advisor to Behnken, but he was more responsive than Behnken to the need for improving race relations. Harms was not in the forefront of the struggle for greater racial equality in church and society, but he was willing to listen and work with the LHRAA on racial matters.[151] It was helpful that the Missouri Synod had more racially sensitive leadership in the racially charged atmosphere of the 1960s.

The year 1963 was a watershed year in the history of American race relations. It was the year that public sympathy shifted in favor of the civil rights movement. Growing public support for civil rights activities came about largely because of the events that took place in one Southern city, Birmingham, Alabama. "But for Birmingham," American race relations may have never made the strides that they did in the twentieth century.[152] Martin Luther King's image as a civil rights leader had faltered in the early 1960s. After failure in Albany, King needed to achieve something of significance. Other movement leaders advised King to take a stand in Birmingham, a city infamous for its civil rights abuses and its reactionary chief of police, Bull Connor. In the spring of 1963, Martin Luther King and the others in the Southern Christian Leadership Conference committed themselves to the local struggle for racial justice in Birmingham, Alabama.

Civil rights activists in Birmingham followed a strategy that was similar to what had been tried in Albany. Through local protests they hoped to fill the jails to the point where local officials would realize that the system of segregation was unenforceable. But the protests in Birmingham got off to a

---

[150] Letter from Oliver R. Harms, *The Vanguard* 10 (February–March, 1963): 1.

[151] Lutze, Oral History Collection, 40–41.

[152] See Glenn T. Eskew, *But for Birmingham: The Local and National Movements in the Civil Rights Struggle* (Chapel Hill: University of North Carolina Press, 1997); Diane McWorter, *Carry Me Home: Birmingham, Alabama: The Climatic Battle of the Civil Rights Revolution* (New York: Simon & Schuster, 2001); Bobby M. Wilson, *America's Johannesburg: Industrialization and Racial Transformation in Birmingham* (Lanham MD: Rowman & Littlefield, 2000).

shaky start.[153] Then, during Holy Week of April 1963, Martin Luther King decided to break a local injunction against demonstrations and go to jail for the cause of racial justice in Birmingham. It was hoped that King's imprisonment would bring more national attention and more local volunteers to the civil rights protests. But King's actions in Birmingham brought him more immediate criticism than he had expected. Even some of the national news coverage suggested that King's activities in Birmingham were ill-timed. He was most disturbed by the criticism that came from local Birmingham clergymen.[154]

Local Birmingham clergy, who were of a liberal religious persuasion, were featured in an article in the Birmingham *News* criticizing the local acts of civil disobedience.[155] As a response, King wrote his famous "Letter from a Birmingham Jail," the most famous document of the civil rights movement. The "Letter from a Birmingham Jail" was a passionate defense of the tradition of civil disobedience from ancient times to the present. It was a bold condemnation of the white moderate, who believed that time alone would solve the problems of race relations.[156] The letter also expressed

---

[153] "Their grand Birmingham campaign showed signs of terminal weakness. In eight days, they had put fewer than 150 people in jail. By comparison, nearly twice than number had gone to jail in tiny Albany on the first day of mass protest alone" (Branch, *Parting the Waters*, 727–28).

[154] Ibid., 737–38.

[155] "The thirteen short paragraphs transfixed King. He was being rebuked on his own chosen ground...the history of the early Christian church made jail the appropriate setting for spiritual judgments—that buried within most religious Americans was an inchoate belief in persecuted spirituality as the natural price of their faith" (ibid., 738, 740).

[156] "There is nothing new about this kind of civil disobedience. It was evidenced sublimely in the refusal of Shadrach, Meshach, and Abednego to obey the laws of Nebuchadnezzar, on the grounds that a higher moral law was at stake. It was practiced superbly by the early Christians, who were willing to face hungry lions and the excruciating pain of chopping blocks rather than submit to certain unjust laws of the Roman Empire... I have reached to regrettable conclusion that the Negro's great stumbling block in his stride to freedom is not the White Citizen's Counciler or the Ku Klux Klanner, but the white moderate, who is more devoted to 'order' than to justice; who prefers a negative peace which is the absence of tension to a positive peace which is the presence of justice" (Martin Luther King, Jr., "Letter from a

King's profound disappoint with the white church.[157] But King's letter actually drew little immediate attention. The "Letter from a Birmingham Jail" was not widely published in newspapers and magazines until about a month later. As Taylor Branch pointed out, "In hindsight, it appeared that King had rescued the beleaguered Birmingham movement with his pen, but the reverse is true: unexpected miracles of the Birmingham movement later transformed King's letter from a silent cry of desperate hope to a famous pronouncement of moral triumph."[158]

The turning point in Birmingham came with what Branch called "The Children's Miracle." On 2 May 1963, Birmingham's schoolchildren began to be involved in Birmingham's civil rights protests. Movement leaders were desperate to find more volunteers who were willing to go to jail for the cause of civil rights, but there was considerable debate as to whether youth should be recruited for the protests. Finally, the Movement leaders came to an agreement. Any child old enough to be considered a full member of a church would be allowed to participate in the protests.[159] The result was

---

Birmingham Jail" in *Why We Can't Wait*, with a new afterword by the Reverend Jesse L. Jackson, Sr. [New York: Signet Classic, 2000] 72–73).

[157] "There can be no deep disappointment where there is not deep love. Yes, I love the church.... Yes, I see the church as the body of Christ. But, oh! How we have blemished and scarred that body through social neglect and through fear of being nonconformists.... But again I am thankful to God that some noble souls from the ranks of organized religion have broken loose from the paralyzing chains of conformity and joined us as active partners in the struggle for freedom. They have left their secure congregations and walked the streets of Albany, Georgia, with us...they have gone to jail with us. Some have been dismissed from their churches, have lost the support of their bishops and fellow ministers. But they have acted in the faith that right defeated is stronger than evil triumphant. Their witness has been the spiritual salt that has preserved the true meaning of the gospel in these troubled times" (ibid, 78, 81).

[158] Branch, *Parting the Waters*, 744.

[159] Civil rights leaders James Bevel came up with the formula. "Nearly all the young volunteers were Baptists.... Baptist doctrine required only a conscious acceptance of the Christian faith as a condition of both church membership and personal salvation. By common practice, churches allowed the youngest school-age children to become members.... How could [Bevel] and King tell six-year-old church members that they were old enough to decide their eternal destiny but too young to march against segregation?" (ibid., 755).

thousands of new volunteers willing to fill the jails of Birmingham. The real change in public opinion came when America saw all over its television news and newspapers the reaction of Bull Connor's policemen to the demonstrating children. Images of children being pressured with fire hoses and attacked by police dogs disturbed Americans across the country. Suddenly, many Americans saw the issue of civil rights with greater moral clarity and greater moral urgency.[160]

The federal government also took a stronger stand after witnessing the events in Birmingham. On 9 June 1963 President John F. Kennedy went on television to address the nation. While Kennedy had been somewhat sympathetic to the issue of civil rights, this speech was the first time he boldly committed himself and the nation to the cause of civil rights. Kennedy declared, "We are confronted with a moral issue…. It is as old as the as the Scriptures and is as clear as the Constitution. The heart of the question is whether we are going to treat our fellow Americans as we want to be treated." Kennedy then went on to announce plans for the development of national civil rights legislation to bring an end to the system of segregation in America.[161]

A few days later, to build support for the new civil rights legislation, President Kennedy invited about 250 of the nation's religious leaders to the White House to discuss civil rights. As Robert Mann observed, "Never before had a large group of American religious leaders gathered to plot strategy for a major legislative initiative."[162] Andrew Schulze was among the religious leaders who were invited and attended the White House reception on 17 June 1963. Other Lutherans who participated in the reception included the Rev. Dr. Walter F. Wolbrecht, the Rev. Norman Temme, and the Rev. Dr. O. P. Kretzmann.[163] Schulze's commitment to race relations had brought him into political and religious circles that he could have scarcely imagined at earlier stages in his life.

---

[160] See Branch, "The Children's Miracle," in *Parting the Waters*, 756–802.

[161] Branch, *Parting the Waters*, 823–24.

[162] Robert Mann, *The Walls of Jericho: Lyndon Johnson, Hubert Humphrey, Richard Russell, and the Struggle for Civil Rights* (New York: Harcourt Brace & Company, 1996) 370.

[163] "President Prompts Churches to Form Committee on Race: Missouri Synod Men At Meeting," *The Lutheran Layman* 34 (1 July 1963): 9.

Andrew and Margaret Schulze were honored in another way in the summer of 1963. At the LHRAA's Summer Institute in 1963, which celebrated the tenth anniversary of the LHRAA, the organization designated that their Mind of Christ Award should be bestowed on Andrew and Margaret Schulze. Many LHRAA supporters were glad that Margaret was also publicly recognized for all of her support and contributions behind the scenes. Valparaiso University professor Dr. John Strietelmeier noted at the presentation, "Our century, too, has had its prophets, for God does not leave himself without witness in any generation."[164] It was a happy occasion as Andrew and Margaret were recognized by their peers, other Lutherans who were also committed to the cause of racial harmony in both church and society.

From mid-July to mid-August 1963, Schulze was one of the leaders of an "Interracial Good Will Tour" to Europe. The main leader and organizer of the tour was the Rev. Ralph L. Moellering, who had long been associated with Schulze and the LHRAA. Andrew and Margaret joined several other couples for the tour; it was their first trip to Europe together. Besides visiting several European countries, the tour group also attended the Assembly of the Lutheran World Federation, held in Helsinki, Finland. The Missouri Synod was not an official part of the Lutheran World Federation as it did not agree with some of its theological positions. Still, the Missouri Synod could not ignore this organization that represented the vast majority of the world's Lutherans. The tour was a great opportunity for Schulze as he saw race relations as a global issue and something that was of importance to Lutheranism worldwide. The tour also included a few days in the Soviet Union, in the cities of Leningrad and Moscow, which Schulze found particularly fascinating.

While President Kennedy was trying to build support for civil rights legislation through meetings and negotiations, black civil rights leaders were planning to show their support for civil rights by organizing a march on Washington. The idea of a march on Washington to address racial concerns had a long history. The black activist and union organizer A. Philip Randolph first suggested a march on Washington when Franklin Delano

---

[164] "Mind of Christ Award—1963," *The Vanguard* 10 (July 1963): 3.

Roosevelt was president.[165] The idea now came to fruition in the summer of 1963. Many federal officials were worried that the March on Washington would become unruly. But the March on Washington proved to be success beyond most people's expectations and one of the most memorable events in twentieth-century American history.

As Schulze was in Europe in the weeks prior to the March on Washington, Karl Lutze and leaders of the local chapters of LHRAA worked to coordinate Lutheran participation. But Schulze was back in the United States in time to take part. He noted in some of his correspondence that the March on Washington was scheduled to take place on 28 August 1963, exactly one year after he and other religious leaders had been thrown in prison in Albany, Georgia.[166] On that day, hundreds of thousands of black and white Americans gathered on the Mall on Washington and listened to a series of speeches held at the Lincoln Memorial. The program of speeches ended with Martin Luther King, Jr.'s memorable "I Have a Dream" speech.

Clemonce Sabourin recalled that there was quite a bit of Lutheran participation in the March on Washington. The Rev. Richard John Neuhaus, then a Lutheran pastor in the New York area and now an influential Catholic priest, organized busloads of Lutherans to come down from New York City to Washington. But Sabourin also noted that he was disappointed that more black Lutheran pastors and more Lutheran church officials did not participate.[167] Still, the Lutheran presence at the March on Washington was noted. Lutherans from all over the country gathered at local Lutheran churches in the Washington, DC area prior to the march. Photographs from the day showed individuals holding dozens of placards with the words "Lutherans Marching!" and "Lutheran Human Relations Association."[168] Martin Luther King, Jr. took note of the presence of white

---

[165] Randolph agreed to cancel his plans for a march when President Roosevelt established the Committee on Fair Employment Practices.

[166] Andrew Schulze to Mr. Matthew Ahmann, 23 August 1963 (copy), Papers of the National Catholic Council for Interracial Justice, ser. 20, box 16, Marquette University Archives, Milwaukee WI.

[167] Oral History from Clemonce Sabourin, Oral History Collection, 173–74.

[168] Karl Lutze, "Washington: Love in Deed and in Truth," *The Vanguard* 10 (November 1963): 3.

churches in the March on Washington, including the presence of Lutherans in his book, *Why We Can't Wait*.[169]

While Schulze had been away on his tour in Europe, there had been a convention of the Missouri Synod's national youth organization, the International Walther League in Washington, DC. A major feature of the convention was a "Dialog on Race" between LHRAA Field Secretary Karl Lutze and black comedian Dick Gregory.[170] The International Walther League also designated the offerings from their convention's closing service to the work of the LHRAA. In his words of thanks to the Walther Leaguers, Schulze highlighted some of the work of the LHRAA. Andrew noted, "Exactly one month after the Walther League Convention began in Washington, D. C., a demonstration took place in that same city—the March on Washington—a demonstration unprecedented in the annals of U.S. history...our Association organized an all-Lutheran participation which involved over five hundred members of the three major Lutheran bodies."[171] Schulze, like many other civil rights supporters, had the sense that real progress was being made with regard to race relations in both church and society.

In the days that immediately followed the March on Washington, civil rights supporters had a brief sense of euphoria that real strides had been made toward putting race relations on the national agenda. But the deep and persistent nature of racial tensions soon brought a tragic turn in the civil rights movement. On Sunday morning, 15 September 1963, a bomb

---

[169] "One significant element of the March was the participation of the white churches. Never before had they been so fully, so enthusiastically, so directly involved.... It was officially endorsed by the National Council of Churches of Christ in the U.S.A., the American Baptist Convention, the Brethren Church, the United Presbyterian Church in the U.S.A., and by thousands of congregations and ministers of the Lutheran and Methodist Churches" (King, *Why We Can't Wait*, 113–14).

[170] "Dialog on Race at Youth Convention," *The Vanguard* 10 (August 1963): 2. Also see John Pahl, *Hopes and Dreams of All: The International Walther League and Lutheran Youth in American Culture, 1893–1993* (Chicago: Wheat Ridge Ministries, 1993) 263–64.

[171] Andrew Schulze to the executive secretary of the Lutheran Human Relations Association of America, 30 August 1963 (copy), box 37, Executive Office files, CHI, St. Louis MO.

exploded in the Sixteenth Street Baptist Church, killing four black girls.[172] The Sixteenth Street Baptist Church and Birmingham's children had played a significant role in the local demonstrations. Birmingham's churches and children therefore became targets of racial hatred. Birmingham had experienced so many previous racially motivated bombings, the city was sometimes referred to as "Bombingham." But the bombing which took the lives of four little girls was especially shocking.

The bombing of the Sixteenth Street Baptist Church also had a profound impact on the Lutheran community in Birmingham. Two of the girls who were killed in the bombing, Denise McNair and Cynthia Wesley, had significant ties to two of Birmingham's Lutheran churches. Denise McNair's father, Chris McNair, was a member of St. Paul's Lutheran Church and Cynthia Wesley was a regular visitor at a new Lutheran mission in the city.[173] The Rev. Joseph Ellwanger was the white pastor of the all-black St. Paul's Lutheran Church. Shortly after the bombing, he described the difficult morning during which he and his congregation were startled by the sound of a loud blast. Once Ellwanger found out that the Sixteenth Street Baptist Church had been bombed, he informed his parishioner and Sunday School superintendent, Chris McNair, and later comforted his congregation once they heard the news that Denise McNair and three other girls had been killed in the blast.[174]

Joseph Ellwanger had already been long familiar with Lutheran race relations. Joseph Ellwanger was the son of the Rev. Walter Ellwanger, who

---

[172] See Spike Lee, "Four Little Girls" (New York: HBO Home Video, 1998).

[173] "Lutheran Father of Bombing Victim Sees Gospel as 'Answer,'" *The Lutheran Witness* 82 (15 October 1963): 19. Chris McNair had a strong sense of loyalty to the Lutheran Church. As he once explained in Karl Lutze's presence, "When I was a little boy back in Arkansas there was no Lutheran church in our town. Now we had a little box on the shelf and we listened, and the voice would come, 'Bringing Christ to the Nations,' and then Dr. Walter A. Maier would preach the Lutheran Hour sermon.... I was a little boy, but I said, 'If I ever get to a city where there's a Lutheran church I'm going to join the Lutheran church'.... I've been very proud to be a Lutheran and I'll never forget what the Lutheran Hour meant in the life of my family" (Lutze, Oral History Collection, 49–50). Denise was the only child of Chris and Maxine McNair.

[174] Joseph Ellwanger, "The Birmingham Sunday School Bombing," audiotape recording at the Concordia Seminary Library, St. Louis MO.

was the long-time president of the historically black Alabama Lutheran Academy and College in Selma, Alabama. Ellwanger had been pastor at Birmingham's St. Paul's Lutheran since 1958 and was also a dedicated member of the Lutheran Human Relations Association.[175] Joseph Ellwanger had been involved with the recent civil rights demonstrations in Birmingham and was committed to working to improve race relations in Alabama as the leader of the Alabama Council on Human Relations.[176] In the aftermath of the bombing, he and other local pastors sought to comfort the families of the victims of the Sixteenth Street bombing.[177]

As funeral arrangements were made for the victims of the bombing, Martin Luther King, Jr. was asked to preach at the joint funeral for three of the four girls. Joseph Ellwanger was also asked by the McNairs to read a lesson at the service. When the president of the Southern District of the Missouri Synod, the Rev. Dr. Edgar Homrighausen, heard about the request, he advised Ellwanger not to participate in the funeral. Homrighausen stated that he was concerned that Ellwanger's participation might make him a target of local segregationists. Homrighausen was also

---

[175] Joseph Ellwanger and Emory Jackson were speakers at the LHRAA's Summer Institute in 1961. They were featured as "Voices from the South: A Report on how the Deep South is accepting, and resisting, integration." *Proceedings* of the Lutheran Human Relations Association of America, Summer Institute, 28–30 July 1961. Ellwanger also served for some time on the board of the Lutheran Human Relations Association.

[176] Joseph Ellwanger and other local pastors had also responded to the article in the Birmingham *News* that inspired King's "Letter from a Birmingham Jail." "Five white pastors from the Alabama Council on Human Relations risked social opprobrium by joining four black ministers in issuing a public statement sympathetic to the demonstrations. The leader of the council, thirty-three-year-old Joseph W. Ellwanger, was the white pastor of the all-black St. Paul's Lutheran Church and had been the only white minister who participated in the demonstrations, marching alongside members of his congregation...their suggestions were dismissed by Birmingham whites and ignored by most of the national media" (Friedland, *Lift up Your Voice Like a Trumpet*, 78).

[177] Ellwanger noted, "I could not help but marvel at the hopeful and forgiving spirit of these people whose entire lives have been under the white man's oppression in varying degrees and who had just experienced the ultimate of the system of prejudice" (Joseph Ellwanger, "Birmingham Pastor Recounts Bombing...," *The Vanguard* 10 [November 1963]: 4).

concerned that such participation was in opposition to the Missouri Synod's stance against inter-denominational unionism. But Ellwanger refused to heed Homrighausen's advice. As he explained, "I am serving as pastor of the father of one of these girls. He asked me—he and his wife asked me—to lead their family in prayer before the funeral and to participate in the funeral, and I am going there as a witness to the Gospel; and I will be there."[178] The funeral, held on 18 September 1963, attracted thousands of people and hundreds of the city's black and white clergymen.[179]

Race relations had become such a prominent concern that *The Lutheran Witness* included a two-part feature on the "Color Crisis" in its two issues in September 1963. The first part was titled "The Problems Are Opportunities." In the middle of the article in bold print was the statement, "Since integration is morally right, it is morally wrong for a Christian to oppose it or refuse to promote it on social or economic grounds."[180] It was the clearest expression to date in *The Lutheran Witness* against the practice of segregation in both church and society. The second part was titled "What Churches Are Doing" and highlighted the work of integrated Lutheran congregations in communities throughout the country.[181]

Future issues of *The Lutheran Witness* published several letters to the editor that reacted to the two articles on the "Color Crisis." Many of the letters were critical of the articles; there were many requests to cancel subscriptions to the magazine. One letter to the editor stated, "I just about have enough of the Negroes with the *Lutheran Witness* pushing the matter further; so I will ask you to send the *Lutheran Witness* to someone who loves

---

[178] Ziehr, *The Struggle for Unity*, 134–35.

[179] "King spoke over but three of the four coffins from the Birmingham church bombing. 'At times, life is hard,' he said, 'as hard as crucible steel.' Eight thousand people braved the vigilantes and jeep patrols to attend the giant funeral that overflowed Rev. John Porter's church. No elected officials attended. Among the mourners were eight hundred Birmingham pastors of both races, making them many times over the largest interracial gathering of clergy in the city's history" (Branch, *Parting the Waters*, 892).

[180] "Color Crisis, Part I: The Problems Are Opportunities," *The Lutheran Witness* 82 (3 September 1963): 4.

[181] "Color Crisis, Part II: What Churches Are Doing," *The Lutheran Witness* 82 (17 September 1963): 3–8.

the Negroes." Another letter stated, "*The Lutheran Witness* is not fit for us to read. It is very degrading to the white race."[182] But others wrote in support of the articles in *The Lutheran Witness* and were appalled by the reaction of some of their fellow Lutherans to the articles. One Lutheran summarized the situation by asking, "How can we promote mission work abroad and yet want segregation at our front door?"[183]

Another source that was critical of *The Lutheran Witness's* clear stance on the matter of segregation and integration was a new arch-conservative, tabloid-style newspaper titled *Lutheran News*. *Lutheran News* began to be published in 1962 by Herman Otten, an uncertified pastor of a small Missouri Synod congregation in Missouri. *Lutheran News* responded to articles on race relations in *The Lutheran Witness* by stating, "The integration issue is not a moral question at all. It is a practical matter."[184] Otten was alarmed by what he saw as a growing trend toward liberalism in the Missouri Synod. Otten's newspaper aimed to promote very conservative theological and social positions. Over the next several years, Andrew Schulze and the Lutheran Human Relations Association were occasionally criticized in the pages of *Lutheran News*, which was later renamed *Christian News*.

The year 1963 ended with more violence as an assassin's bullet took the life of President John F. Kennedy in late November. Many civil rights supporters were apprehensive about how the new president from Texas, Lyndon Baines Johnson, would handle the issue of civil rights. In the December 1963 issue of *The Vanguard*, O. P. Kretzmann, shared his thoughts on the central tragedy of the year in an article titled, "From Birmingham to Bethlehem." Kretzmann reflected, "It is a long and weary road—the way of the human heart and mind from all the Birminghams of the post-modern world to the cave at Bethlehem. In one place a Child is born in quietness and peace; in the other, children are killed in the unbelieving noise of a bomb...On the journey we may learn again that God

---

[182] "Letters," *The Lutheran Witness* 82 (1 October 1963): 21.

[183] "Letters," *The Lutheran Witness* 82 (12 November 1963): 22.

[184] Quoted in Ralph L. Moellering, *Christian Conscience and Negro Emancipation* (Philadelphia: Fortress Press, 1965) 95. The quote came from an article published in *Lutheran News* on 23 September 1963.

is, that Christ died, and that there can be no hope and no peace in Birmingham without Him."[185]

Beginning in 1964, the nature of Schulze's position within the LHRAA began to change. The LHRAA's board of directors granted him a one-year leave of absence. Schulze wanted to concentrate on a manuscript that he had on his mind for some time. When he later returned to his work at the LHRAA, he did so on a part-time basis. Karl Lutze took over as the executive secretary of the LHRAA in 1964, a position that he held until 1979. When Schulze returned from his leave of absence, he was given the new position of Director of Research for the LHRAA. With Schulze's leave, he also ended his position as editor of *The Vanguard*. Various individuals edited *The Vanguard* over the next few years.[186] *The Vanguard* continued to report on race relations among Lutherans and in American society. However, with Schulze no longer serving as editor, *The Vanguard* did seem to lose some of its strong theological substance.

The major focus of civil rights supporters in 1964 was the passage of national civil rights legislation that aimed to bring an end to the formal system of segregation in America. Because of a powerful bloc of Southern congressmen, passage of civil rights legislation required the backing of a significant number of congressmen from other regions of the country. The votes of Midwestern congressmen proved to be especially important for the passage of the Civil Rights Act of 1964. Because the Midwest had a comparably small minority population, the region sometimes seemed indifferent to racial issues. But even though this region of the country was lacking a natural constituency for civil rights, various religious organizations helped to create one.[187] Religious organizations such as the National Council of Churches put considerable effort into mobilizing grassroots support for civil rights legislation in the Midwest. As James Findlay described, "In a region with deep religious roots, moral arguments pressed

---

[185] O. P. Kretzmann, "From Birmingham to Bethlehem," *The Vanguard* 10 (December 1963): 2.

[186] "Schulze 1–Year Leave among LHRAA Shifts," *The Vanguard* 10 (November 1963): 1. "Appointments Announced," *The Vanguard* 11 (October-November 1964): 1.

[187] Mann, *The Walls of Jericho*, 412.

by church people might be especially effective.... For many midwestern churchpeople the civil rights issue was not a burning concern...there was a 'kind of irony' in the fact that the fate of the bill might rest with such people."[188]

Lutherans were highly concentrated in the Midwest and the Lutheran Human Relations Association worked to generate support among their fellow Lutherans for the proposed national civil rights legislation. In early 1964 Clemonce Sabourin, as president of the LHRAA, wrote a letter to all the pastors of the Lutheran Church—Missouri Synod. Sabourin encouraged pastors to have their parishioners express their support, in writing, to national politicians favoring the passage of civil rights legislation.[189] Lutheran publications also promoted passage of the civil rights bill. *The American Lutheran* reported on the LHRAA's efforts and noted that the National Catholic Conference of Interracial Justice was making similar efforts. *The American Lutheran* concluded its article on the need to support the civil rights bill with a quote from Andrew Schulze, "It is up to Christian citizens to stand up and be counted."[190]

There were other Lutheran efforts to promote the passage of civil rights legislation. The Lutheran Church of the Reformation in Washington DC, which was situated just a block away from the nation's capitol, held daily services for the passage of the legislation from April to June 1964, when the legislation was officially passed. A parish of the Lutheran Church of America, the Lutheran Church of the Reformation, did not have the same concerns about unionism as did Missouri Synod congregations. Protestant and Orthodox clergy were invited to conduct the services as well as

---

[188] Findlay, *Church People in the Struggle*, 51.

[189] Clemonce Sabourin to "Fellow Pastors," 20 February 1964 (copy), Andrew Schulze Papers, CHI, St. Louis MO.

[190] "The Civil Rights Bill," *The American Lutheran* 47 (April 1964): 88. While *The Lutheran Witness* made generally positive comments about the civil rights legislation, it emphasized, "there is a higher law that must receive passage in the heart's inner chamber of each individual. That law, says the Word of God, is wrapped up in a single commandment: "You shall love your neighbor as yourself" ("Civil Rights: Human Dignity," *The Lutheran Witness* 83 [14 April 1964]: 4).

Lutheran clergy.[191] Religious leaders from various backgrounds made their presence felt in the nation's capital during the ongoing debate over the legislation.[192]

The Civil Rights Bill made it through Congress by the end of June 1964. President Johnson signed the bill into law on 2 July 1964 in the presence of Martin Luther King, Rosa Parks, and other civil rights activists. The Civil Rights Act of 1964 was the first major piece of civil rights legislation passed since the era of Reconstruction. Many of America's religious leaders and religious organizations played a significant role in assisting passage of the bill. But despite the new prominence of white religious leaders in the national struggle for civil rights, many white denominations remained divided over the question of civil rights.[193]

Despite the number of Lutherans who actively supported civil rights, many remained indifferent or opposed to the spirit of the civil rights movement. In late 1964 many attitudes about the civil rights movement focused specifically on Martin Luther King, Jr. At a press conference in November 1964, J. Edgar Hoover, director of the FBI, publicly criticized King. Reflecting on King's complaints about some of the FBI workers in the South, J. Edgar Hoover remarked, "I consider King to be the most notorious liar in the country." The comments generated a significant

---

[191] Friedland, *Lift up Your Voice Like a Trumpet*, 100. The Lutheran Church of the Reformation also held special services for the passage of the Civil Rights Act of 1965 (Findlay, *Church People in the Struggle*, 64).

[192] "During the House debate the gallery sometimes seemed to overflow with ministers, priests, and rabbis—most of them voluntary watchdogs, or 'gallery watchers,' who tracked the votes and other activities of House members...'You couldn't turn around where there wasn't a clerical collar next to you.... It made all the difference in the world'" (Mann, *The Walls of Jericho*, 412–13).

[193] Taylor Branch noted that "a number of religious bodies nearly split apart at their national conventions" (*Pillar of Fire*, 299). Several recent histories look at how religion was used on both sides of the civil rights movement. See Charles Marsh, *God's Long Summer: Stories of Faith and Civil Rights* (Princeton NJ: Princeton University Press, 1997); Andrew Michael Manis, *Southern Civil Religions in Conflict: Black and White Baptists and Civil Rights, 1947–1957* (Athens: The University of Georgia Press, 1987); and Donald E. Collins, *When the Church Bell Rang Racist: The Methodist Church and the Civil Rights Movement in Alabama* (Macon GA: Mercer University Press, 1998).

amount of attention as Americans across the country tended to take sides either with Hoover or King.[194]

The Lutheran Witness had recently editorialized that America should thank God for Martin Luther King and his Christian leadership in the movement for racial equality.[195] In a later edition of *The Witness*, the magazine qualified and clarified its position on King in light of the comments made by J. Edgar Hoover. *The Witness* stated that King was not "without his faults," but also suggested that Hoover used "intemperate" language. *The Witness* defended itself, concluding that it could "scarcely serve the church during this social revolution by maintaining silence or by mumbling pious generalities calculated to make everybody happy and comfortable." Several of the letters to the editor made negative comments about *The Witness's* positive stance on King. Letters to the editor criticized King for his theology, his civil disobedience, and his supposed communist connections. One letter to the editor viewed King as "nothing more or less than a rabble-rouser."[196]

The Lutheran Human Relations Association thought it was important to defend the reputation of Martin Luther King. The board of directors of the LHRAA responded to J. Edgar Hoover's remarks about King by writing letters to Hoover and to the attorney general. These letters stressed King's commitment to nonviolence and his commitment to justice. The LHRAA asked that Hoover publicly apologize to King and asked the attorney general to guard against such "reckless outbursts." LHRAA president Clemonce Sabourin commented on why the board decided to speak out on behalf of Dr. King. Sabourin explained "As Christians we are called upon to defend

---

[194] Branch, *Pillar of Fire*, 526. "Mass polls favored Hoover three to one over King, while a smaller sample of letters to the White House favored King two to one. Johnson assumed a high posture...saying that both King and Hoover 'have exercised their freedom of speech on occasions,' and vowing to make sure that friction 'would not degenerate into a battle of personalities" (Branch, *Pillar of Fire*, 532).

[195] "Prizewinner: There is reason to thank God for the likes of Martin Luther King," *The Lutheran Witness* 83 (10 November 1964): 4.

[196] "Ask the Witness," *The Lutheran Witness* 83 (22 December 1964): 11. "Letters," *The Lutheran Witness* 83 (22 December 1964): 14.

out brother, to put the best construction on everything and to speak well of him."[197]

The Lutheran Human Relations Association had not previously generated much attention from the FBI. Many civil rights activists and organizations were targeted for surveillance by the FBI.[198] But Andrew Schulze and the Lutheran Human Relations Association only accumulated very small FBI files.[199] Perhaps this was because the LHRAA was a largely white organization and Lutherans were generally known to be basically socially conservative. When a representative from the FBI was asked to participate in the Summer Institute on "Christianity, Communism, and Race Relations," the FBI was most willing to participate. An FBI official noted that the LHRAA was "a highly respectable organization and the audience will undoubtedly include influential churchmen."[200] The majority of pages in the FBI's file on the LHRAA contained letters that criticized the LHRAA for the letter it wrote to J. Edgar Hoover on behalf of Dr. King.[201] A few Lutherans wrote to Hoover to explain that the LHRAA was not representative of the majority of Lutherans. One letter described the LHRAA as a group that "works in all sorts of ways to force social mixing and comes right out and says that there is no solution other than intermarriage."

---

[197] "LHRAA Writes Hoover On Behalf of Dr. King," *The Vanguard* 11 (December 1964): 1. "LHRAA Letters," *The Vanguard* 11 (December 1964): 1.

[198] See Kenneth O'Reilly, *"Racial Matters:" The FBI's Secret File on Black America, 1960–1972* (New York: Free Press, 1989).

[199] The extent of Schulze's file concerning his civil rights activities were four pages which documented his involvement in the demonstration in Albany, Georgia. "Andrew Schulze," FBI file 14–863, Federal Bureau of Investigation, Washington, DC.

[200] Mr. W. C. Sullivan to Mr. A. H. Belmont, 11 May 1961 (copy of memorandum); "Lutheran Human Relations Association of America," FBI file 94–55390, Federal Bureau of Investigation, Washington, DC.

[201] A number of letters were also sent directly to the LHRAA. As Karl Lutze noted to a colleague, the LHRAA was "getting a goodly share of letters for daring to suggest that this hero should be asked to apologize to a scoundrel like King. (Wouldn't you know it, one letter even took exception to calling King Martin Luther!)" (Karl Lutze to Mr. Matthew Ahmann, National Catholic Council for Interracial Justice, 21 December 1964, papers of the National Catholic Council for Interracial Justice, ser. 20, box 16, Marquette University Archives, Milwaukee, WI.

Another letter called the LHRAA a "leftist group" and reassured Mr. Hoover that the majority of Lutherans were not "falling for this group."[202]

The Lutheran Human Relations Association had grown in size and influence by the mid-1960s, but it was still an organization that included only a couple thousand members, a very small minority of Lutherans. Though largely Missouri Synod in its roots, the organization had expanded to include other branches of Lutheranism. Almost from the beginning, non-Missouri Synod Lutherans were invited to support the organization and participate in its annual Summer Institutes. Early in the organization's history, some of the local chapters of the LHRAA had a membership that was largely comprised of members of other Lutheran church bodies.[203] In the early 1960s *The Vanguard* included a column by the Rev. L. W. Halvorson of the National Lutheran Council titled "On Other Lutheran Fronts" that reported on race relations in other major Lutheran church bodies.

In 1964 there was an All-Lutheran Conference on Race held in Detroit, Michigan. Due to two recent Lutheran mergers, there were now three large Lutheran church bodies of comparatively equally size. Representatives of all three major Lutheran church bodies, The Lutheran Church in America (LCA), The American Lutheran Church (ALC), and The Lutheran Church—Missouri Synod (LCMS), were all in attendance. Even though the conference was planned by the National Lutheran Council, it supported a resolution that named the LHRAA as a possible "rallying center for a combined Lutheran blow at discrimination."[204] The president of the Lutheran Church—Missouri Synod, Dr. Oliver Harms, supported the idea of Lutherans working together on race relations. Karl Lutze recalled that Harms said, "It's absolutely silly that you should have three organizations doing this one thing.... If you can't get together on this issue...I think it would be a very sorry state." Since the Missouri Synod had the strictest concept of religious fellowship among the three major Lutheran

---

[202] Copy of letters, "Lutheran Human Relations Association of America," FBI file 94–55390, Federal Bureau of Investigation, Washington, DC.

[203] Lutze, Oral History Collection, 16–17.

[204] "All-Lutheran Conference on Race: Michigan Leaders Hail NLC-Sponsored Meet," *The Vanguard* 11 (January–February 1964): 1.

church bodies, Harm's openness on this matter helped the LHRAA to become a pan-Lutheran organization.[205] In 1965 the Lutheran Human Relations Association officially became a pan-Lutheran organization. During summer 1965, non-Missouri Synod Lutherans were first elected to the LHRAA's board of directors. Mr. William Ellis of the LCA and the Rev. Robert Graetz of the ALC were the first non-Missouri members to serve on the board.[206]

The focus of civil rights activities in 1964 and 1965 was the push for black voter registration, especially in the states of Alabama and Mississippi. The Student Non-Violent Coordinating Committee (SNCC) led the drive for voter registration in the South. SNCC, an organization of young leaders committed to racial justice, was the most dynamic of all the major civil rights organizations.[207] All across the South, youth took great risks to work for the cause of racial justice. On 18 February 1965, in Marion, Alabama, a young black man, Jimmy Lee Jackson, was killed as state troopers used force to break up a peaceful march from a local church to the nearby courthouse.

Partly in reaction to Jackson's death and partly to show support for the local voter registration drive, the Rev. Joseph Ellwanger, pastor of St. Paul's Lutheran Church in Birmingham, led a group of Concerned White Citizens of Alabama in a demonstration in Selma. On Saturday, 6 March 1965, Ellwanger led a group of about seventy white persons to the steps of the Selma courthouse to read a statement against the brutality of local law enforcement and in favor of black voter registration. While local civil rights activists supported the march, Ellwanger and the others were heckled by a crowd of local whites. His demonstration also lacked the support of some of his fellow Lutheran pastors. Earlier that day, the Rev. L. James Rongstad, of St. John's Lutheran Church in Selma, confronted Ellwanger and the group of demonstrators and criticized him and the others for interfering in the

---

[205] Lutze, Oral History Collection, 18.

[206] "LHRAA's Relations with Other Lutheran Bodies," Lutheran Human Relations Association Correspondence, box 37, Executive Office Files, CHI, St. Louis MO.

[207] See Clayborne Carson, *In Struggle: SNCC and the Black Awakening of the 1960s* (Cambridge MA: Harvard University Press, 1995).

affairs of the local community.[208] The story of Ellwanger's march and his confrontation with other Lutheran pastors made the front page of *The New York Times* on 7 March 1965.[209]

The incident at the Selma courthouse was soon overshadowed by another pivotal event in the civil rights movement. On Sunday, 7 March 1965, a day that became known as "Bloody Sunday," civil rights leaders John Lewis of SNCC and Hosea Williams of SCLC led hundreds of demonstrators in a march that was intended to start in Selma and culminate at the state capitol in Montgomery. The governor of Alabama, George Wallace, a committed segregationist, threatened that he would not allow the march to take place.[210] As the group of demonstrators crossed the Edmund Pettus Bridge that led out of Selma, they were attacked by state troopers.

---

[208] At the courthouse, a deputy read aloud a telegram that had been sent to the local sheriff by the Rev. Dr. Edgar Homrighausen, president of the Southern District of the Missouri Synod. The telegram stated, "The demonstration being led today in Selma by the Reverend Joseph Ellwanger does not have the official endorsement or sanction of The Lutheran Church—Missouri Synod.... He appears in his role and right as a citizen." Homrighausen had consulted with Missouri Synod president Oliver Harms before sending the telegram (Ziehr, *The Struggle for Unity*, 175). Ellwanger had consulted with LHRAA's Karl Lutze. Lutze recalled, "Joe was on the phone with me...beforehand. I was a sort of colleague at his side across the miles. That was one of the roles LHRAA served: when people were all alone and didn't have many allies about, we would talk with them and try to give them our perspective as best we could, and encourage them" (Lutze, Oral History Collection, 43).

[209] Roy Reed, "White Alabamians Stage Selma March to Support Negroes," *The New York Times*, 7 March 1965. The story was also covered in the next issue of *The Lutheran Witness*. *The Lutheran Witness* tried to show the perspective of all sides, suggesting that all the parties involved struggled with "lonely battles of conscience" ("Alabama Illustrates The Church's Dilemma and Dedication," *The Lutheran Witness* 84 [30 March 1965]: 13). "In This Instance," *The Lutheran Witness* 84 (30 March 1965): 4. Also see "Clergymen Back Civil Rights Cause By Joining Alabama Protest Marches," *The Vanguard* 12 (March–April, 1965): 1, 4.

[210] George Wallace attained national prominence and popularity for his public stands against integration. When he later ran for president, he gained significant support from the Midwest. See Dan T. Carter, *The Politics of Rage: George Wallace, The Origins of the New Conservativism, and The Transformation of American Politics* (New York: Simon & Schuster, 1995) and Stephen Lesher, *George Wallace: American Populist* (New York: Addison Wesley Longman, Inc., 1994).

The sight of state troopers clubbing, whipping, and using teargas against peaceful demonstrators was broadcasted to television viewers across America. As with the scenes of violence in Birmingham, Americans across the nation responded with a tremendous outpouring of public sympathy in favor of the civil rights demonstrators.[211]

Over the next few days, hundreds of religious leaders converged on Selma at the request of Martin Luther King, Jr. Other religious leaders, including Joseph Ellwanger, met with President Johnson to stress the need for federal involvement in securing voting rights for American minorities.[212] On 14 March 1965 President Johnson addressed the nation on television. Johnson poignantly explained, "At times history and fate meet at a single time in a single place to shape a turning point in man's unending search for freedom. So it was at Lexington and Concord. So it was a century ago at Appomattox. So it was last week in Selma, Alabama." Johnson then went on to propose federal legislation to secure voting rights for American minorities. Johnson ended his speech by invoking the words of the movement, "And we shall overcome."[213] The small city of Selma, the location of the Missouri Synod's historically black institution of higher education, had become an American landmark. But Alabama Lutheran Academy and College did not play a significant role in the civil rights activities that surrounded it. The Board of Control, chaired by the District

---

[211] There were many parallels between what happened in Birmingham and Selma. Just as the events in Birmingham in 1963 led to the Civil Rights Act of 1964, the events in Selma in 1965 led to the Civil Rights Act of 1965. There was a connection between what had happened in Birmingham and what happened in Selma. One young couple, with ties to both SNCC and SCLC, Diane Nash and James Bevel, were particularly influential in the drive for voter registration in Alabama. After the murder of the four girls in Birmingham, Nash and Bevel wanted to do something of equal magnitude to vindicate the deaths of the girls. Their plan was to rally a massive non-violent army to secure minority voting rights all across Alabama. The vision of Nash and Bevel was partly realized in the events around Selma and with the Voting Rights Act of 1965 (Branch, *Pillar of Fire*, 553).

[212] Friedland, *Lift up Your Voice Like a Trumpet*, 127.

[213] Quoted by John Lewis, with Michael D'Orso, *Walking with the Wind: A Memoir of the Movement* (San Diego: Harcourt Brace & Company, 1998) 353.

President, the Rev. Dr. Edgar Homrighausen, banned students from participating in the local demonstrations.[214]

Beginning on 21 March 1965, Martin Luther King and other civil rights leaders led a march from Selma to Montgomery. On this occasion, the marchers were under the protection of the Alabama National Guard. Thousands of people joined in the march, including many religious leaders.[215] Lutherans were again represented in the Selma-to-Montgomery March. Karl Lutze participated along with several students from Valparaiso University.[216] Other participants included Martin Marty and Will Herzfeld, a black Lutheran pastor who was also a local leader of the Southern Christian Leadership Conference.[217]

Andrew Schulze did not participate in the historic march from Selma to Montgomery, but was no doubt encouraged by the demonstration and the large numbers of participants, which included some of Valparaiso's students. This was a high point of the civil rights movement and it was somewhat unusual that Schulze was not a part of it. He had earlier responded to King's call for participation in the demonstration at Albany and stated his willingness to do so again. Karl Lutze believed that Schulze did not participate out of deference to him and his relatively new role as the main

---

[214] "Alabama Illustrates the Church's Dilemma and Dedication," *The Lutheran Witness* 84 (30 March 1965): 13. "Nevertheless the students on campus were keenly aware of what was going on in their community. The local newspaper carried an article about Rongstad's opposition to the demonstrations. He taught a class in Old Testament at the school, and after the students learned of his viewpoint, they walked out of his class. That, in turn, led to a four-day walk out for the entire student body. None of the students participated in the demonstrations, but during that walk-out they held a variety of discussion forums on the race issue as well as other problems" (Ziehr, *The Struggle for Unity*, 176–77).

[215] "The high-water mark of the white clergy's support for the civil rights movement arrived in the spring of 1965, with the highly visible presence of hundreds of priests, nuns, rabbis, and ministers in the SCLC-led Selma-to-Montgomery March" (Friedland, *Lift up Your Voice Like a Trumpet*, 113).

[216] Dave Sheriff and Tim Warfield, "31 VUers Participate: Students March in Alabama," *The Torch* (student newspaper of Valparaiso University), 26 March 1965.

[217] Oral History from Will Herzfeld, interview by Lee H. Wesley, 21 January 1982 and 13 May 1982, Archives of Cooperative Lutheranism, Lutheran Council in the USA, ELCA Archives, Chicago IL, 28.

leader of the LHRAA. Schulze did not participate as a way to step aside and let Lutze come into his own as the head of the LHRAA.[218]

Though Schulze's work with the LHRAA was now part-time, he still was very actively involved with the Summer Institutes. The Summer Institute in 1965 was dedicated to the issues of "Church, State, Race." It was an appropriate topic as the federal government was becoming more and more involved in consolidating some of the achievements of the civil rights movement. In the foreword to the *Proceedings* of the Summer Institute, Schulze criticized the record of the church in society. He wrote, "For too long the church has bypassed its total responsibility toward society by first establishing and then hiding behind a false concept of separation of church and state."[219] The institute emphasized the importance of the Christian's responsibility as a citizen to work for a more just society. Speakers included Senator Paul Simon and his brother, the Rev. Arthur Simon. Another guest speaker at the institute was a young black attorney from Texas, a woman who later became a famous American congresswoman, Barbara Jordan.[220]

On 6 August 1965 President Johnson signed the Voting Rights Act in to law. Just as the bombing of Birmingham's Sixteenth Street Baptist Church ended the mood of optimism that followed the March on Washington, just five days after signing of the Civil Rights Act of 1965, a riot erupted in Watts, a black neighborhood in Los Angeles. There had been a few riots during 1964, but they were not on the scale of the Watts Riot.[221] The Watts Riot, and other riots all across American cities, brought new attention to the problem of America's urban ghettos and helped to shift the focus of the civil rights movement away from the Deep South. The

---

[218] Karl Lutze, interview by author, 15 November 2001, telephone.

[219] Andrew Schulze, foreword to *Proceedings* of the Lutheran Human Relations Association of America, Summer Institute, 23–29 July 1965, 5.

[220] See Mary Beth Rogers, *Barbara Jordan: American Hero* (New York: Bantam Books, 2000).

[221] The Watts Riot was "the bloodiest riot since the Detroit outbreak of 1943…. The riot in the Watts district of that city lasted six days and left thirty-five people dead; in its duration and destructuctiveness it dwarfed the Harlem riot of 1964" (Adam Fairclough, *To Redeem the Soul of America: The Southern Christian Leadership Conference and Martin Luther King Jr.* [Athens: The University of Georgia Press, 1987] 274–75).

nature of the civil rights movement also changed as new, more aggressive black leaders emerged to make new demands of American society.

The next edition of *The Vanguard* included a feature article on "Why Los Angeles?" The author was the Rev. Dr. Jeff Johnson, a black Lutheran pastor and sociologist. Johnson was an active member of the LHRAA and had recently been hired as a professor at Valparaiso University. Johnson pointed out that "two of the oldest churches (one Lutheran), which presumably were capable of offering both moral and social leadership, actually pulled out of the Watts area." Johnson criticized the church because it too often reached out to some people, rather than all people, as God commanded. Johnson concluded by stressing that a commitment to racial justice involved more than just public sympathy for the civil rights movement. The Christian commitment to justice should influence decisions about "where to buy a house, how to train one's children, where to seek a job."[222]

The Missouri Synod gave new attention and new emphasis to racial issues in 1966. The president of the Missouri Synod, the Rev. Dr. Oliver Harms, set up a Race Relations Advisory Council to help the synod better respond to racial issues in both church and society. Appointed members of the council included Chris McNair, William Griffin, Jeff Johnson, and Karl Lutze.[223] After decades of racial insensitivity and institutionalized racism, the institutional church was making an attempt to come to grips with the racial situation in its midst.

Andrew Schulze's career also found a new measure of recognition within the Missouri Synod. Concordia Seminary in St. Louis awarded Andrew Schulze a Doctor of Divinity degree in 1966. This was an especially significant honor for Schulze as it came from one of the Missouri Synod's official seminaries. After decades of being on the "outskirts" of the church, advocating what was once an unpopular cause, recognition now came from the church's respected seminary. Schulze preached the sermon in the service in which he was awarded his doctorate. Schulze's sermon message warned that the church's "obsession with words...spoken without relating them to

---

[222] Jeff Johnson, "Why Los Angeles?" *The Vanguard* 12 (September 1965): 2.

[223] "Race Relations Advisory Council Named for Missouri Synod," *The Vanguard* 13 (March 1966): 1.

the total human situation [creates] a false dichotomy between body and soul; it is a heresy recognized by many and still very much alive in the Lutheran Church—Missouri Synod."[224] Even toward the end of his career, Schulze still acted as a prophet to his church. As he was awarded the doctorate, the president of Concordia Seminary, Alfred Fuerbringer, reflected that the doctorate was being bestowed on "a prophet's voice housed in a gentle spirit."[225]

The Summer Institute in 1967 was dedicated to the theme, "Who Will Listen?" Speakers included professors from the University of Chicago, the Rev. Dr. Martin Marty and Dr. John Hope Franklin, a pioneer in the field of African-American history. Another featured speaker was the Rev. Will Campbell, who had long been associated with the civil rights efforts of the National Council of Churches. The schedule of the institute was interrupted that summer as those gathered heard news about a riot in Detroit.[226] There were hundreds of riots across America in the hot summers of the late 1960s, but the riot in Detroit in the summer of 1967 was the worst of them all. Schulze wrote about the situation to his sons, "The events in Detroit added a most sobering note to the Workshop.... I was more or less speechless as I bid our Detroit friends farewell.... Tomorrow is Sunday. The Gospel Lesson—and it couldn't be more appropriate—is Christ weeping over Jerusalem."[227] Schulze and others continued to be concerned with how the problems of race relations were damaging both church and society.

The civil rights movement in the mid-to-late 1960s was marked by an intensified black consciousness. The change was reflected in the increasing popularity of groups such as the Nation of Islam and the growing radicalism of the Student Non-Violent Coordinating Committee. In 1966 Stokely Carmichael, who popularized the "Black Power!" slogan, replaced John Lewis as

---

[224] Andrew Schulze, "The New Life in Christ: Ministry and Race," audiotape of sermon for the Founder's Day Service, Concordia Seminary, St. Louis MO, 9 December 1966, Concordia Seminary Library, St. Louis MO.

[225] "Concordia Seminary Honors Andrew Schulze," *The Vanguard* 13 (December 1966): 1.

[226] *Proceedings* of the Lutheran Human Relations Association of America, Summer Institute, July 21–27, 1967, 26.

[227] Andrew Schulze to the boys, 29 July 1967, Schulze family papers, in the possession of Raymond Schulze.

the leader of SNCC. Carmichael and other more radical civil rights leaders were not necessarily committed to the idea of integration or to the method of nonviolence. While Schulze did not agree with the purpose or the philosophy of these more radical black leaders, he understood black radicalism as an outgrowth of the bitter legacy of racism.[228]

There was also growing black activism within the church.[229] At the end of the summer of 1967, black Lutheran pastors met in an All-Negro Lutheran Pastors Conference in Chicago to discuss the formation of an all-black Lutheran organization. The conference in Chicago was related to events that surrounded the Detroit Riot. The weekend of the riot, most of the white pastors of black Lutheran congregations in the city hesitated to come into the city to conduct worship services because of the violence. This situation motivated Detroit's black pastors, under the leadership of the Rev. Albert Pero, to call for a gathering of black Lutheran clergy to discuss the challenges of black Lutheran ministry. The conference of black Lutheran pastors was held at Schulze's former church in Chicago, Christ the King Lutheran Church.[230]

The Rev. Richard Dickinson was another leader behind the Chicago conference. In August 1967 Dickinson wrote to Andrew Schulze and others to inform them about the conference. He explained that an organization of black Lutherans could be "a powerful force for good within our Church, a valuable supplement to the efforts of the LHRAA."[231] Schulze tried to be supportive with his response, even sending a check to help defray the costs of the conference. However, he also voiced some concerns about the creation of an all-black Lutheran organization. He believed that such an organization might be helpful for a time, but he did not want it to become a permanent organization. Schulze stressed the need for unity in the church, and an all-black organization would only be helpful if it were a means to one

---

[228] See Andrew Schulze, *Fire from the Throne: Race Relations in the Church* (St. Louis: Concordia Publishing House, 1968) 57–60.

[229] Some activists applied the idea of Black Power to theology. See James H. Cone, *Black Theology and Black Power* (New York: Seabury, 1969).

[230] See Richard Dickinson, Sr., *This I Remember* (St. Louis MO: Richard Dickinson, Sr., 1995) 27–33.

[231] R. C. Dickinson to Dr. Andrew Schulze, 23 August 1967, Andrew Schulze Papers, CHI, St. Louis MO.

day achieving greater unity. Schulze referred to the 450th anniversary of the Reformation, noting that Luther did not wanted to start a sect, but wanted to keep the Church pure and whole. Schulze wanted Dickinson and the other black pastors who gathered at the conference to recognize that "the Conference itself is contrary to everything that is meant by the words '*one holy Catholic and apostolic church.*'"[232] Clemonce Sabourin was also discouraged by the efforts to create an all-black Lutheran organization. As one who had fought so hard to end segregation in the church, he also saw these efforts as a step backwards for the church.[233]

The conference held in 1967 led to another conference of black Lutheran clergy in 1968. The 1968 conference of black Lutheran included pastors from the Lutheran Church in America and the American Lutheran Church. This meeting of black Lutheran pastors led to the formation of the Association of Black Lutheran Clergy (ABLC), a pan-Lutheran organization that became more active over the next couple years. But the ABLC did not prove to be a long-standing organization. Because of the concern about unionism, some of the Missouri Synod's black pastors were hesitant about the pan-Lutheran nature of the organization. Instead of concentrating on the joint ABLC, many of the black pastors of the Missouri Synod turned their efforts into developing the Black Clergy Caucus of the Missouri Synod.[234]

In the spring of 1968, the book that Schulze had been working on for the past few years was finally completed. Concordia Publishing House, the official publishing agency of the Lutheran Church—Missouri Synod, published Schulze's *Fire from the Throne: Race Relations in the Church*. At the heart of *Fire from the Throne* was the idea that the church does have social obligations and that the words of the church must be accompanied by deeds. However, Schulze's book also stressed that "the church has a higher goal than social reform. In serving man, God is to be served."[235] *Fire from the*

---

[232] Andrew Schulze to Rev. R. C. Dickinson, 25 August 1967 (copy), Andrew Schulze Papers, CHI, St. Louis MO.

[233] Clemonce Sabourin to Andrew Schulze, 2 December 1970, Andrew Schulze Papers, CHI, St. Louis MO.

[234] Dickinson, *This I Remember*, 44–45. Also see Johnson, *Black Christians*, 203–204.

[235] Schulze, *Fire from the Throne*, 11

Throne had a strong Christological emphasis. As Schulze explained, "What makes the Christian religion distinctive...is not merely a distinctive teaching—although it is that—but a person. That person is Christ." Schulze believed that if the church only preached and did not act, it denied the incarnational nature of Christianity. [236]

Fire from the Throne also stressed the doctrine of the church. Schulze explained, "The church is always a togetherness, never a separation; and segregation therefore is the direct opposite of what the church is."[237] The title *Fire from the Throne* was a reference to God's judgment and God's mercy in the racial tensions and turmoil of the present. Schulze believed that God was acting through history and saw the present racial crisis as the judgment of God. But he also believed that there was "no reason for despair or hopelessness. The judgment is rather a sign that God has not abandoned His people."[238] Schulze also saw hope for the future. He believed that the young Christian churches of Africa and Asia might provide Christian leadership for the future if Western Christianity did not renew itself.[239]

In the mid-to-late 1960s, Martin Luther King, the overarching leader of the civil rights movement, turned his attention to the problems in America's urban ghettos, issues of poverty, and America's involvement in Vietnam. In early April 1968, King went to Memphis, Tennessee, to lend his moral support to the city's striking garbage workers. While in Memphis, King was shot to death on the balcony of the Lorraine Motel on 4 April 1968. While some groups and individuals continued to promote civil rights, King's death marked the end of the civil rights movement of the 1950s and 1960s.

---

[236] Ibid., 80.

[237] Ibid., 150.

[238] Ibid., 195.

[239] Schulze's vision of the future of Christianity is relevant today. The Christian Church "is growing fastest in the Third World. Indeed, the center of Christianity is no longer Europe and North America. There are now more Lutherans on the continent of Africa than there are in North America.... The Africanization of Lutheranism and Anglicanism, the Asiafication of Protestantism, and the Hispanicization of Roman Catholicism are significantly changing the complexion of these churches" (John Nunes, *Voices from the City: Issues and Images of Urban Preaching* [St. Louis: Concordia Publishing House, 1999] 33).

Schulze met with students, colleagues, and friends at Valparaiso in private gatherings and in memorial services to reflect on the death of Martin Luther King, Jr. Schulze recognized the profound implications of King's death. He wrote to one of his sons, "No one knows how many blacks are going to heed Stokely Carmichael's words that they will 'have to get guns'...and how many are going to follow King's philosophy of nonviolence. It seems that the hour of God's judgment has come. Lord, have mercy."[240] The next edition of *The Vanguard* featured articles by Andrew Schulze, Clemonce Sabourin, and Joseph Ellwanger, reflecting on the legacy of Martin Luther King, Jr. Schulze saw King's greatest contribution as helping "the church, its clergy and its people...to see once again the social implications of the gospel and the church's role as the conscience of society."[241] Andrew Schulze had found inspiration in the life and the legacy of Martin Luther King, Jr.

The president of the Lutheran Church—Missouri Synod, the Rev. Dr. Oliver Harms, sent a telegram of sympathy on behalf of the synod to King's widow, Coretta Scott King. The next edition of *The Lutheran Witness* reported on King's death and on President Harms's response.[242] Once again, the following *Lutheran Witness* included letters to the editor complaining about the comments made about Martin Luther King.[243] Harms also received personal letters that complained about the telegram he sent to Coretta King and the fact that he participated in a memorial service for Dr. King. Individuals criticized King for his theology, his lawlessness, and his supposed communist connections.[244]

---

[240] Andrew Schulze to Herb Schulze, 5 April 1968, Schulze family papers, in the possession of Raymond Schulze.

[241] Andrew Schulze, "Heritage, Sorrow, Strength," *The Vanguard* 15 (April 1968): 2.

[242] "In Perspective," *The Lutheran Witness* 87 (May 1968): 3.

[243] "Letters," *The Lutheran Witness* 87 (June 1968): 22. The previous *Lutheran Witness* included an article on the racial situation in Milwaukee. One Milwaukee activist was a controversial Catholic priest, James Groppi. One letter to the editor asked, "Was Dr. Martin Luther King, Jr., a man of God? Is Father Groppi a Christian?" Ibid., 22.

[244] Letters concerning Martin Luther King, Jr., Martin Luther King Jr., box 29, Executive Office Files, CHI, St. Louis MO.

In 1968 the racial divide seemed as great as ever. Riots raged all across America in the wake of the assassination of Martin Luther King. Various black leaders spoke about black separatism and black power. With more and more discussion about "Black Power," the Summer Institute of 1968 explored the topic of "The Church and Power." The Rev. William Griffin's presentation asked the question, "Is There Room in the Church for Black Power?" The Rev. Will Herzfeld spoke on "The Gift of Power." The Lutheran Human Relations Association continued its tradition of addressing contemporary issues in the context of Christianity.

At the end of the summer in 1968, Schulze officially completed all his duties with Valparaiso University and with the Lutheran Human Relations Association of America. At seventy-two, Andrew Schulze finally retired. Schulze had worked with the LHRAA during the height of the civil rights movement. Now that era was over. At the end of August, Andrew and Margaret set sail for Germany, where they spent about a year before returning to their home in Valparaiso. Schulze's active work with the LHRAA and the university was over, but he continued to be engaged with race relations and the church until the end of his life.

Chapter 6

Later Years, 1968–1982

At the end of the summer of 1968, Andrew and Margaret Schulze set sail to spend a year in West Germany. The Schulzes stayed in Bad Driburg, located about fifty miles to the southwest of Hanover. The Schulzes always lived on a very modest income; they were able to arrange their year overseas through connections they made through Valparaiso University.[1] The Schulzes hoped to learn more about their family history during their time in Germany. They were not as successful as they hoped because they had little information on which to base their research.[2] During their stay in Germany, Andrew Schulze also began writing his memoirs, which became one of his major projects during the early years of his retirement.

The year in Germany allowed Andrew and Margaret to travel to various places in Europe to visit friends. A highlight of the year was when they visited friends in the Holy Land. Hans and Doris Liebenow were living in Jerusalem where Hans was completing Hebrew studies. The Schulzes and the Liebenows had been friends since their days in St. Louis, when Schulze was pastor of St. Philips and Liebenow was a student at Concordia Seminary. Besides seeing the sites of the Holy Land, Liebenow also made arrangements for Schulze to preach in Our Redeemer Lutheran Church, located near the Church of the Holy Sepulcher in the heart of Old

---

[1] George Hans Liebenow, interview by author, 19 October 1999.

[2] Mrs. Andrew Schulze to Mrs. George Reinhart, 10 October 1973 (copy), Schulze family papers, in the possession of Raymond Schulze. The Schulzes lacked information about their family origins, in part, due to a fire that destroyed many of the immigration records in the Cincinnati Courthouse.

Jerusalem.[3] With their visit to the Holy Land, the Schulzes were able to fulfill the dream of many Christians and visit the places where Christians believe that Jesus Christ lived, died, and rose again.

Andrew and Margaret returned to the United States in the summer of 1969. Before returning to their home in Valparaiso, they spent time with their family. In retirement, they were able to spend more time visiting their children and their grandchildren. The Schulze sons and their families were spread out across the country, from the East Coast to the West Coast, from New York to California. Paul, Herb, and Ray Schulze were influential pastors in the communities in which they served. At one time or another, like their father before them, all of the Schulze sons were involved in inter-racial ministries.

Though retired, Schulze continued to follow events and trends in his church body. The Missouri Synod's national convention held in Denver, Colorado, in the summer of 1969, proved to be a turning point in the synod's history. In the convention's first order of business, delegates to the convention elected a new president, the Rev. Dr. J. A. O. Preus, to replace the Rev. Dr. Oliver Harms. Preus was a favorite of Missouri Synod conservatives. He presided over the synod as it returned to its conservative moorings after a decade or so of increased openness. Preus was the dynamic and controversial president when the theological and political conflicts of the Missouri Synod resulted in a schism in the church body in the 1970s.

Even though Preus was considered a champion of conservative theology, he did not always embrace a conservative social agenda. Preus was fairly progressive when it came to race relations. It could be argued that he was the most racially sensitive of all Missouri Synod presidents to date. While the climate for race relations was different in the 1970s, and minorities could have been seen as a valuable asset during the in-fighting in the church, Preus's commitment to race relations was not a recent development.[4] Karl Lutze remembered Preus had far more enthusiasm for

---

[3] George Hans Liebenow, interview by author, 19 October 1999.

[4] Preus's sensitivity to race relations may have been related to his Norwegian-American heritage. Scandinavians and Scandinavian-Americans tended to hold more progressive attitudes concerning race relations. J. A. O. Preus was originally a

LHRAA's campus visits than most LCMS school administrators when he was president of Concordia Theological Seminary in Springfield.[5]

Prior to his election as president, Preus had made plans to participate in LHRAA's Mutual Enrichment Program. Through the Mutual Enrichment Program, theologians spent a couple of weeks living and working with inner-city pastors and their congregations. After being elected, Preus noted that "the experience should be even more valuable to me now."[6] As part of the program, Preus spent a week in Chicago, observing and participating in the work of Immanuel Lutheran Church on the West Side of Chicago. Through his tenure as president, Preus continued to be open and interested in supporting Lutheran race relations. Lutze observed, "We obviously were never a political threat to him, and he was very conscious of what a strong asset social ministry was to his administration.... I can't recall anything at all that he ever did, anything that was obstructive or at all a deterrence to the work of LHRAA's ministry."[7]

---

member of the small Norwegian synod, the Evangelical Lutheran Synod (ELS) before becoming a member of the Missouri Synod.

[5] "While we were in our early years, each spring we would always go to all the Missouri Synod schools.... And River Forest said, 'Sure, you all come.' They put a note on the board, and one or two would show up for interviews. At Seward I found a more helpful reception and would go to talk with more people.... St. Louis had me speak in chapel.... But at Springfield—Dr. Preus met me at the airport, put me up in a hotel, called off classes, had all the students listen to my presentation for two hours, had me speak in chapel, and arranged for all the students and their wives to gather while I interviewed them one-on-one and had a group session with them; and before I left town Dr. Preus and I went out to lunch and he wanted to know what, just between him and me, what the scene was in race relations. This happened several times at Springfield" (Oral History from Karl Lutze, interview by James Albers, 20 July 1981 and 26 October 1981, Archives of Cooperative Lutheranism, Lutheran Council in the USA, Oral History Collection, ELCA Archive, Chicago IL, 52.

[6] "New President to Experience Innercity 'Live-In,'" *The Vanguard* 16 (July–August 1969): 1.

[7] Lutze, Oral History Collection, 56. Still, Preus's time in office was mainly filled with other concerns. As St. Louis reporter James E. Adams noted, Preus seemed to offer "lavish support for evangelism, world missions, and social concerns...Preus never hedged on civil rights for blacks. He was attuned to the concerns of black churchmen.... Yet the Preus enthusiasm and leadership in these areas of churchmanship often had an unrealistic air. He sounded like a wartime president

The 1969 convention was the first Missouri Synod convention that included representatives of the new Association of Black Lutheran Clergy (ABLC). Representatives such as the Rev. Albert Pero—president of the ABLC—and the Rev. Will Herzfeld made a strong showing at the national convention.[8] Representatives of the ABLC were given time to address the delegates. After his message, Rev. Herzfeld invited the assembly to follow him outside the convention hall in a symbolic gesture to acknowledge "the world where God has sent us." Hundreds of delegates followed Herzfeld outside where they joined together in saying the Lord's Prayer and in singing "We Shall Overcome."[9] Nothing like this had ever happened at a convention of the Missouri Synod. Karl Lutze described it as "a very, very strong experience...people dramatically stood up to identify with this minority voice that was saying, we've got to see other people in the kingdom of God."[10]

Schulze, however, was no longer so involved with church politics on the national level. A couple years after Andrew and Margaret arrived in Valparaiso, they decided to join a developing Lutheran congregation to the north of Valparaiso, Faith Memorial. As Schulze then explained to his sons, "Mother and I have joined the little mission north of town. We hope that in some way we shall be able to render a bit more service to the Kingdom through this small congregation than through the large one in town."[11]

---

promising the nation both guns and butter.... The reality at hand was a theological civil war" (*Preus of Missouri: And The Great Lutheran Civil War* [New York: Harper & Row Publishers, 1977] 162–63).

[8] Both Pero and Herzfeld continued to be influential in Lutheran circles. Pero became a professor of theology at the Lutheran School of Theology in Chicago. For more on his contributions, see Albert Pero and Ambrose Moyo, eds., *Theology and the Black Experience: The Lutheran Heritage Interpreted by African and African-American Theologians* (Minneapolis: Augsburg Publishing House, 1998). Herzfeld served as the vice-president and the president of the Association of Evangelical Lutheran Churches (AELC), the body which broke away from the Missouri Synod in the 1970s.

[9] Karl Lutze, "Church Receives Gift from Black Members," *The Vanguard* 16 (July–August 1969): 1.

[10] Lutze, Oral History Collection, 65.

[11] Andrew Schulze to the boys, 18 October 1956, Schulze family papers, in the possession of Raymond Schulze.

During Schulze's years of retirement, he and Margaret had the time to become more active in their home congregation. As he wrote to one of his sons during the early years of his retirement, "We find ourselves more and more involved in the life of our local congregation; we participated in an every-member visitation and evangelism program." The small congregation was in many ways typical of other Missouri Synod congregations. In the same letter, Schulze also noted that their pastor was still hesitant about supporting social activism.[12]

Andrew and Margaret became interested in the charismatic movement in the later years of their lives. Charismatic Christians emphasized the gifts and power of the Holy Spirit. Charismatic belief and practice was central to congregations of a Pentecostal background. But in the 1960s and 1970s, the charismatic movement began to find followers among the major mainstream Christian denominations in America. Andrew and Margaret met occasionally with a group of charismatic Lutherans in the Valparaiso area. In 1971 the couple attended a charismatic renewal conference held at Concordia Seminary in St. Louis.[13] But ultimately, the Schulzes became disenchanted with the charismatic theology and practice.[14] While the charismatic movement did gain new attention in the 1970s, only a small strain of Lutherans today consider themselves charismatic believers.

Schulze's memoirs, *Race against Time: A History of Race Relations in the Lutheran Church—Missouri Synod from the Perspective of the Author's Involvement, 1920–1970*, were published in the fall of 1972. Because his memoirs included the sins and errors of the church, Schulze thought it was important that his memoirs be published by the church's official publishing agency, Concordia Publishing House.[15] But Concordia Publishing House as well as Augsburg Publishing House both declined publishing the memoirs, on the basis that the book would have only limited marketability. Instead, old friends and colleagues of Andrew Schulze led a fundraising drive that

---

[12] Andrew and Margaret Schulze to Ray and Margaret Schulze, 28 January 1970, Schulze family papers, in the possession of Raymond Schulze.

[13] Andrew and Margaret Schulze to Paul Schulze, 2 June 1971, Schulze family papers, in the possession of Raymond Schulze.

[14] Karl Lutze, interview by author, 29 January 2000.

[15] Andrew Schulze to Karl Lutze, 4 October 1968 (copy), Andrew Schulze Papers, Concordia Historical Institute, St. Louis MO.

enabled the Lutheran Human Relations Association to publish the memoirs. O. P. Kretzmann, Martin Marty, and Clemonce Sabourin led the effort to publish Schulze's memoirs.[16]

In the foreword to *Race against Time*, Schulze tried to prepare the reader for the sometimes shameful record of the church and various churchmen with regard to race relations. Schulze quoted St. Paul, who after listing the sins of the Israelites noted that these sins "were written down for our instruction." He also pointed out that "the story of the Missouri Synod in the main reflects the story of the other major denominations in the area of race relations."[17] Still, the memories from Andrew Schulze's ministry focused on the particular examples of Lutheran racism and indifference. Each chapter in *Race against Time* explored a different topic in Schulze's career from the "Ecclesiastical Power Structure" to "Church Periodicals" to "Friends and Mentors." In reflecting on the slowness of the church to deal with issues of race relations, Schulze suggested that it sometimes failed to recognize that its eternal concerns begin in the here and now. He concluded by stressing the "inseparable" nature of the gospel of salvation through Jesus Christ and the social implications of the gospel.[18]

Schulze's memoirs received positive reviews in various Lutheran and Christian periodicals. Professor Albert E. Jabs of Voorhees College in Denmark, South Carolina, noted that "the work issues from the

---

[16] "Kretzmann, Marty, Sabourin Join to Honor Dr. Schulze," *The Vanguard* 19 (August 1972): 4.

[17] Andrew Schulze, *Race against Time: A History of Race Relations in the Lutheran Church—Missouri Synod from the Perspective of the Author's Involvement* (Valparaiso IN: Lutheran Human Relations Association, 1972) 2, 1.

[18] Andrew Schulze, *Race against Time*, 151. Michael Friedland also noted the church's struggle to balance present and eternal concerns: "Martin Luther King Jr. had been fond of saying that if the churches were concerned only with the hereafter and not with the gospel imperatives dealing with the here and now, institutional religious bodies would become nothing more than 'country clubs with stained-glass windows.' Yet if the churches spent most of their time and budgets on secular and social problems, letting the world set the agenda, and not on issues concerning souls and personal morality, what would keep them from becoming social service agencies with altars?" (*Lift up Your Voice Like a Trumpet: White Clergy and the Civil Rights and Antiwar Movements, 1954–1973* [Chapel Hill: The University of North Carolina Press, 1998] 239).

geographical area of the mid-western United States, but its far-reaching theological and social implications extend far beyond these boundaries."[19] A review of *Race against Time* in the Christian magazine *Worldview* also put Andrew Schulze's life and work into a larger context. As the review stated, "Almost every predominantly white church body in the country has been blessed, infuriated, prodded, inspired, and changed by the Andrew Schulzes of America."[20]

In retirement, Schulze continued occasionally to write and contribute articles to *The Vanguard*. In the December 1972 issue of *The Vanguard*, during the Advent and Christmas seasons of the church year, he wrote about the significance of the Incarnation. The Incarnation, the Christian belief that God became man in Jesus Christ, is a central doctrine of the Christian faith. The Incarnation was also an essential aspect of Schulze's personal theology. As Schulze saw it, the life and the work of Jesus Christ "gives us a distinct reason for being involved in the social issues of our time."[21] Schulze found much of his inspiration and motivation in the miracle of Christ's incarnation.

During the 1970s, the Lutheran Human Relations Association began to get involved with other issues. The LHRAA began to show new interest in women's rights and new opposition to the war in Vietnam. Schulze opposed the Vietnam War and prepared a study of the war for the LHRAA prior to his retirement.[22] Schulze did not hesitate to voice his opinion on the war, but he did not become actively involved with protests against the war. One of Schulze's sons, Herb Schulze, and a close friend of the Schulze family, Sam Hoard, both served as military chaplains in Vietnam.[23] During the

---

[19] Prof. Albert E. Jabs, "Local Involvement Reflects Nation-Wide Racial Problems," *The Vanguard* 20 (June 1973): 2.

[20] "Briefly Noted," *Worldview* (February 1973): 56.

[21] Andrew Schulze, "The Grand Miracle," *The Vanguard* 19 (December 1972): 4.

[22] Andrew Schulze to Miss Jane Allison, 12 January 1968 (copy), Schulze family papers, in the possession of Raymond Schulze.

[23] Schulze wrote to his son Herb in 1968, "An understanding of the moral issue is more important than a plan for disengagement. If it is once established and accepted that our involvement in Vietnam is immoral—and I think it is—then a plan for withdrawal will soon be found…let me add once again the assurance that we continue in daily prayer in your behalf and for a God-pleasing early resolution of that

1970s, the LHRAA did occasionally publish statements against the war in *The Vanguard*.[24] While criticism of the war was never a primary focus of the LHRAA, its occasional criticism did cause controversy among some LHRAA supporters.[25]

The Missouri Synod experienced increased tensions and controversies in the early 1970s. At the 1973 convention of the Missouri Synod, held in New Orleans, delegates to the convention voted to censure the faculty of Concordia Seminary, St. Louis. The convention also directed specific criticism at the president of Concordia Seminary, the Rev. Dr. John Tietjen. There had been concerns for some time over the method and content of the theology being taught at the seminary. At the heart of the controversy was the historical-critical method of biblical interpretation. Many in the Missouri Synod saw the use of modern interpretive methods as undermining the divine authority and the content of Scripture. Missouri Synod "moderates" were open to using historical criticism while Missouri Synod "conservatives" held objections to using historical criticism. Missouri Synod "moderates" and "conservatives" solidified their positions in convention sometimes referred to as "the Second Battle of New Orleans."[26] The New

---

which all of us abhor" (Andrew Schulze to Herb Schulze, 15 March 1968, Schulze family papers, in the possession of Raymond Schulze).

[24] The April 1971 issue of *The Vanguard* included articles such as "Church Editors in Protest: Stop The War Now!" and "Assent to Dissent."

[25] Martin Scharlemann, who had been an important supporter of LHRAA in its early days, turned against the organization due to its criticism of Vietnam. In his later years, Scharlemann described the LHRAA as "a Marxist organization...the change took place...during the Viet Nam madness. They suddenly were using their materials for purposes other than trying to solve race relations. They were using their paper and their literature to help undermine the foreign policy of the United States"(Oral History of Martin Scharlemann, interview by Edith Rehbein [daughter], 9–10 August 1980, Archives of Cooperative Lutheranism, Lutheran Council in the USA, Oral History Collection, ELCA Archives, Chicago IL).

[26] E. Clifford Nelson, "The New Shape of Lutheranism," in *The Lutherans in North America*, ed. E. Clifford Nelson, rev. ed. (Philadelphia: Fortress Press, 1980). Martin Marty, who left the Missouri Synod during the 1970s controversy, observed, "Never in the twentieth century has a church been so torn" (Nelson, "The New Shape of Lutheranism," 529). For the most balanced account of the controversy, see

Orleans convention demonstrated that Concordia Seminary, the elite institution of the synod, had lost the trust of many of those whom it served.

Under increased scrutiny and with accusations of heresy, there was a charged atmosphere at Concordia Seminary. In protest, the vast majority of the faculty and students of Concordia Seminary staged a walk-out from the seminary in February 1974. With the help of Eden Seminary (United Church of Christ) and the Divinity School at St. Louis University (Roman Catholic), faculty and students from Concordia Seminary began a seminary-in-exile, which became known as Christ Seminary-Seminex. Concordia Seminary, St. Louis, struggled over the next few years to rebuild its faculty and its student body.

The controversies in the Missouri Synod continued as some Seminex graduates were ordained and placed in Missouri Synod congregations. The 1975 convention of the Missouri Synod resolved that Seminex graduates needed to go through colloquy training, like graduates of other seminary programs, to be ordained and placed in Missouri Synod congregations. Some district presidents did not comply with the synod's resolution. Eventually, President Preus dismissed four of the synod's district presidents who had ordained and placed Seminex graduates.

Already in 1973 moderates in the Missouri Synod began Evangelical Lutherans in Mission (ELIM), an organization that eventually formed the basis for a break-away church body, the Association of Evangelical Lutheran Churches (AELC). The AELC began to take shape after the Missouri Synod's convention in 1975. About 150 congregations left the Missouri Synod to form the AELC.[27] As James Adams observed, "The pattern of American Protestant history in the twentieth century had been inverted. Instead of battered and beaten Protestant conservatives leaving denominations controlled by liberals, battered and beaten 'liberals' were leaving Missouri."[28]

Byran V. Hillis, *Can Two Walk Together Unless They Be Agreed? American Religious Schisms in the 1970s* (Brooklyn NY: Carlson, 1991).

[27] Edgar R. Trexler, *Anatomy of a Merger: People, Dynamics, and Decisions that Shaped the ELCA* (Minneapolis: Augsburg Fortress, 1995) 4.

[28] Adams, *Preus of Missouri*, 222.

The Missouri Synod's struggle in the 1970s influenced the future shape of American Lutheranism. Another issue that surrounded the conflict was the question of Lutheran unity.[29] The moderates from Missouri were in favor of greater Lutheran unity and pushed for a merger of the major Lutheran church bodies in America. In 1987 the Association of Evangelical Lutheran Churches (AELC), the Lutheran Church in America (LCA), and the American Lutheran Church (ALC) joined to form a new church body. Today, the church body that they formed, the Evangelical Lutheran Church in America (ELCA), is the largest Lutheran church body in America with about five million members.[30] The Missouri Synod is the second largest Lutheran church body, with about half as many members.

Various individuals and organizations within Lutheran circles made their opinions known during the theological and political battles of the 1970s. Valparaiso University's board of directors made it clear that the University did not take an official stand on the conflict, but also made it clear that the University defended the principle of freedom of expression for members of its community. Over forty faculty and staff from Valparaiso University issued a statement of support for President John Tietjen and Concordia Seminary in the midst of the controversy.[31] Andrew Schulze did not sign this statement of support, but he did sign another statement which was issued by the Theology Department of Valparaiso University. Though

---

[29] The same Missouri Synod convention that elected President Preus in 1969 also approved church fellowship with the American Lutheran Church (ALC). The conservatives had gotten their way on the president, but the moderates had gotten their way on the issue of fellowship. The president of Concordia Seminary, John Tietjen, was also seen as a spokesperson for Lutheran unity. Tietjen authored the book, *Which Way to Lutheran Unity? A History of the Efforts to Unite the Lutherans of America* (St. Louis: Concordia Publishing House, 1966). The fellowship arrangement between the Missouri Synod and the ALC began to deteriorate in the late 1970s and ended the 1980s.

[30] See Trexler, *Anatomy of a Merger*.

[31] "Valparaiso University and The Crisis in the Church," February 1974; "Board Reaffirms University's Position Regarding Lutheran Church—Missouri Synod Tensions," News Release, 11 February 1974; "42 from Faculty-Staff at Valpo University Show Tietjen Support," University News files, Valparaiso University Archives, Valparaiso IN.

retired, Schulze was an emeritus faculty member and still had many friends and colleagues who were still active at the University.

During the 1970s controversy, Andrew Schulze showed sympathy for the moderate side. The statement from Valparaiso's Theology Department which Schulze signed, expressed that members of Valparaiso's Theology Department did not find conflict between their religious commitment and the process of critical inquiry. Valparaiso's theology professors were concerned that because of the criticism which surrounded Concordia Seminary in St. Louis, "the church will not be able to supply ministers who can ably relate the Gospel to modern life."[32]

As Schulze's son, Paul Schulze, recalled, his father had a basic conservative approach to theology prior to his years at Valparaiso University. But during his years there, he was influenced by other theology professors and became more of a moderate in his understanding of theology. Paul Schulze explained that in the process, his father "discovered that folks whose theology was a bit more 'free' and 'flexible' were also the more enthusiastic about challenging the church on the racial issue than were the more 'conservative' folks...as if a more hardened spirit permeated people's theology as well as their sociology."[33] Andrew Schulze's experiences and contacts during the civil rights movement also shaped his theology in the later years of his life.

In his later years, Schulze was one of the few individuals who held joint clergy status in both the Lutheran Church—Missouri Synod (LCMS) and the Association of Evangelical Lutheran Churches (AELC).[34] While Schulze became more of a moderate in the later years of his career, he never left the church body in which he had spent his life. All three of Schulze's sons eventually left the Missouri Synod; they left at different times and for different reasons.[35] But Andrew Schulze remained. He was already retired at

---

[32] "An Open Appeal to the District President of the Lutheran Church—Missouri Synod," 13 February 1974, Valparaiso University Archives, Valparaiso IN.

[33] Paul Schulze to the author, 7 June 2000, in author's possession.

[34] "LHRAA Founder, Andrew Schulze, Dies in California," *Lutheran Perspective* (3 May 1982).

[35] Paul Schulze left the Missouri Synod before the 1970s controversy and joined the Lutheran Church in America (LCA). Andrew Schulze advised his son to reconsider this decision, largely for practical reasons. But Schulze also noted that

the time of the controversy. This was the church body in which he was originally brought up in the Christian faith and had spent his entire ministry. It was the church body in which he spent decades battling for the cause of racial justice. He had known very well that it was an imperfect institution, but it was an institution that he cherished, despite its flaws.

One can generalize that theological liberals and theological moderates did tend to have a better record than theological conservatives concerning race relations. But this generalization can only be taken so far. As Charles Marsh pointed out, "An accurate picture of how religion shaped the civil rights movement cannot be drawn from a crude juxtaposition of good social gospelers on the one hand and bible thumping racists on the other. Over the course of the movement, some bible-thumpers appeared as social progressives, and some who were weaned on liberal theology championed segregation."[36] With regard to theological and social matters, Lutherans did not always act in seemingly consistent ways.[37]

The theological and political struggles of the 1970s caused tensions within black Lutheran ministry in the Missouri Synod. While many of the white Lutheran pastors in black ministry sided with the moderates during the 1970s struggles, the majority of black Lutheran pastors sided with the conservatives during the 1970s struggles. Many of the black Lutheran pastors had been trained in the conservative tradition at the Lutheran seminary in Greensboro, North Carolina, which had since been closed. The Missouri Synod's Black Clergy Caucus tried officially to stay out of the infighting of the synod. The Missouri Synod eventually lost fifteen of about 200 black congregations. However, fourteen of the fifteen black Lutheran

---

"this is where God has placed you in His Kingdom" (Andrew Schulze to Paul Schulze, 18 May 1968, Schulze family papers, in the possession of Raymond Schulze.

[36] Charles Marsh, *God's Long Summer: Stories of Faith and Civil Rights* (Princeton: Princeton University Press, 1997) 4.

[37] For example, *The Vanguard's* analysis of the Missouri Synod's convention in 1977 noted that the Missouri Synod passed resolutions that reached out to minorities while at the same time backed away from relationships with other Lutherans ("Missouri Synod Convention Opens Doors to Minorities, Backs away from Other Lutherans," *The Vanguard* 24 [August–September 1977]: 2).

congregations that joined the AELC were under the pastoral leadership of white Lutheran pastors.[38]

In the midst of this tumultuous decade in Missouri Synod history, the synod tried to give new attention to black Lutheran ministry. In 1977 the Missouri Synod celebrated the centennial anniversary of its black Lutheran history. While there was a history of black Lutheranism prior to 1877, this was the year in which the Missouri Synod became involved in black mission efforts through the Synodical Conference. The centennial was observed at the some of the local conferences and conventions of the Missouri Synod and through various publications. Richard Dickinson wrote a centennial history for the synod, *Roses and Thorns: The Centennial Edition of Black Lutheran Mission and Ministry in the Lutheran Church—Missouri Synod.*[39]

The Lutheran Human Relations Association did not comment on the controversies of the 1970s. Though many involved with the LHRAA were in sympathy with the moderate side during the Missouri Synod conflict, the LHRAA wanted to remain a pan-Lutheran organization and did not want to lose any of its support over the matter. But the Lutheran Human Relations Association did eventually get involved with some of the controversies within Lutheranism. As the LHRAA became more committed to women's issues in the 1970s, it also came to support women's ordination. While the Lutheran Church in America (LCA) and the American Lutheran Church (ALC) accepted women's ordination, the Missouri Synod opposed it.[40] This ultimately led to tensions within the Lutheran Human Relations Association.

---

[38] See Richard C. Dickinson, Sr., "Black Ministry and the Split in the Missouri Synod: Come What May We're Here To Stay," in *This I Remember* (St. Louis MO: Richard C. Dickinson, Sr., 1995).

[39] As the foreword to *Roses and Thorns* explained, this history examined "an aspect of black religion too often overlooked.... A substantial group of blacks have chosen to make their fight from inside of the American mainstream churches" (Armstead Robinson, foreword to *Roses and Thorns: The Centennial Edition of Black Lutheran Ministry and Mission in the Lutheran Church—Missouri Synod,* by Richard C. Dickinson [St. Louis: Concordia Publishing House, 1977] 8).

[40] For a history of women's issues in the Missouri Synod, see Mary Todd, *Authority Vested: A Story of Identity and Change in the Lutheran Church—Missouri Synod* (Grand Rapids: William B. Eerdmans Publishing Company, 2000).

For a time, Karl Lutze mediated over the tensions within the LHRAA. But eventually the tensions led to his resignation from the position of executive secretary of the LHRAA in 1979.[41] Some members of the board of the LHRAA were upset that Valparaiso University, as a university affiliated with the Missouri Synod, withdrew its sponsorship for the LHRAA's annual Summer Institute worship service because a female pastor led the worship service. In 1980 the board of the LHRAA decided to leave the campus of Valparaiso University and relocate its offices in Milwaukee. The move was also related to the criticism that the LHRAA's small town, more rural setting, made the LHRAA out-of-touch with inner-city, urban issues.[42] While some believe that it was a mistake for the LHRAA to lose its connection with Valparaiso University, the organization continues to maintain its offices in Milwaukee.

The Lutheran Human Relations Association eventually became more connected with the Evangelical Lutheran Church of America (ELCA) than with the Lutheran Church—Missouri Synod (LCMS). Though it is still an independent Lutheran organization, the membership of the organization, and the stance that the organization takes on various issues, ties the Lutheran Human Relations Association more closely to the ELCA. As the Lutheran Human Relations Association expanded its focus from race relations to women's issues and to issues of sexual orientation, it lost some of its traditional supporters. Despite its historic roots in the Missouri Synod, the organization lost many of its ties to the synod.

Some suggest that Andrew Schulze would be disappointed that the efforts of the Lutheran Human Relations Association are no longer primarily concentrated on race relations. Others suggest that the organization is acting in the spirit of Andrew Schulze by attacking the injustices of the day. As is true for the great reformer, Martin Luther, Lutherans interpret Andrew Schulze's legacy in different ways. While more liberal Lutherans emphasize the "destructive" legacy of Luther, his attack on

---

[41] Oral History from Karl Lutze, 88–89.

[42] "Lutheran Human Relations Board Takes Action on Location, New Director," news release, 3 November 1980. "Lutheran Action Group Severs University Tie," Religion News Service, 13 November 1980, University News files, Valparaiso University Archives, Valparaiso IN.

the abuses of the institutional church, more conservative Lutherans emphasize the "constructive" legacy of Luther, his development of a new theology and practice for the church. The same extremes can hold true for the supporters of Andrew Schulze.

In 1979, due to age and deteriorating health, Andrew and Margaret moved to California to live with their oldest son, Paul, and his wife, Elizabeth. Andrew and Margaret spent the last years of their lives in El Cerrito, California, just to the north of Berkeley, in the San Francisco Bay Area. Schulze grew increasingly frail in the last years of his life, yet he still retained his warmth and his sense of humor.[43] Andrew Schulze died on 30 March 1982 and Margaret Schulze died a few months later on 5 August 1982.[44]

The funeral service for Andrew Schulze was held at Prince of Peace Lutheran Church, his home congregation in Cincinnati, Ohio. He was buried with his relatives at Baltimore Pike Cemetery in Cincinnati. Additional memorial services were held at St. James Lutheran Church in Richmond, California, and at Valparaiso University's Gloria Christi Chapel. The service at Valparaiso was a special commemoration of the life and the work of Andrew Schulze. The Rev. Dr. Norman Nagel, Dean of the Chapel at Valparaiso, led the memorial service at the university. Schulze's longtime friend and colleague, Karl Lutze, delivered the homily on the text from John 10:9–16 ("I came that they may have life, and have it abundantly.") The memorial service included the hymns "We Know That Christ Is Raised," "For All the Saints," and "Lord of All Nations, Grant Me Grace," a hymn that had been specifically written for the Lutheran Human Relations Association.[45]

---

[43] Paul Schulze to the author, 7 June 2000, in the author's possession.

[44] Walter Heyne noted in a tribute to Andrew Schulze, "To speak of Andrew without immediately thinking of Margaret is to leave out an important ingredient in the development of his career as a leader of the Church and a champion of equal opportunities in that church." "Tributes to Andrew Schulze," *The Vanguard* 29 (May 1982): B.

[45] "The Memorial Service: Andrew Schulze, March 8, 1896—March 30, 1982," 15 April 1982, Gloria Christi Chapel, Valparaiso University. Valparaiso University Archives, Valparaiso IN.

The May 1982 issue of *The Vanguard* included several tributes to Andrew Schulze. Some of his closest friends and colleagues—Karl Lutze, Walter Heyne, George Hans Liebenow, Clemonce Sabourin, and Joseph Ellwanger—wrote about their memories of Andrew Schulze. Joseph Ellwanger remembered first hearing about Schulze when Ellwanger was at the seminary. Schulze was described as a "firebrand extremist on the race issue." So Ellwanger was shocked to discover "a very thin gaunt man who looked as though he might be swept to heaven by the next gentle breeze" and a man who spoke with "charitable phrasings and in such evangelical tones."[46] Another tribute came from Jody Kretzmann, who knew Andrew and Margaret Schulze as he was growing up. Kretzmann explained that he knew of no one, at least among Lutherans, to whom the label "saint" has been more universally attached.[47] Kretzmann praised Schulze for his "moral consistency," for his "absolute insistence that belief and reflection lead to action." He noted that "if power can breed arrogance, so too can righteousness," yet Andrew Schulze was even known for his humility. His ministry reflected an understanding of "both individual and institutional frailty."[48]

Other Lutheran publications made special note of Schulze's passing, but his death was only routinely mentioned in the synod's official publication, *The Lutheran Witness*.[49] To this day, many Lutherans are unaware of the life and legacy of Andrew Schulze. Though Lutherans remain a predominantly white denomination, the history of American Lutheranism would no doubt be different if it were not for him. Some suggest that black Lutherans would have formed their own church bodies had it not been for individuals such as Andrew Schulze.

---

[46] "Tributes to Andrew Schulze," *The Vanguard* 29 (May 1982): C.

[47] As Karl Lutze noted in his remarks at Schulze's memorial service, "People often referred to Andrew as 'Saint.' He would chafe under this tribute, because as he often confided—'impatience, pride, resentment can so easily replace our Lord's intent that we be patient, humble, and have love for all people. His saintliness he would insist—'if there is any at all—comes from the Lamb of God who takes away my sin too" (Karl E. Lutze, "Andrew Showed Us," 15 April 1982, Gloria Christi Chapel, Valparaiso University, Valparaiso University Archives, Valparaiso IN.)

[48] "Tributes to Andrew Schulze," *The Vanguard* 29 (May 1982): B.

[49] "Notices," *The Lutheran Witness* 99 (August 1982): 30.

Over the course of Andrew Schulze's life, Lutherans became more sensitive to racial issues and more involved with social issues. However, these changes did not come about primarily because of Schulze's influence. While he was an early promoter of Lutheran integration, the Lutherans who did integrate their churches did so as American society became integrated. Lutherans were shaped by the broader trends of twentieth-century American life. As the twentieth century began, Lutherans were still in their ethnic enclaves, but by the end of the century, Lutherans were a part of mainstream American life. Still, as Lutherans adjusted to the issues of modern American life, they needed leaders such as Andrew Schulze.

Andrew Schulze influenced many, many people over the course of his life. Through his speaking, his writings, his teaching, and his actions, Andrew Schulze had an impact on Lutherans throughout the country. But even more significant than his influence, was his example. As Michael Friedland concluded in his study of twentieth-century religious activists, "In the end, it was not the degree of success, or lack of it, that made the clerical activists noteworthy; nor was it their numbers, which were small; nor their influence, which was limited. What made these individuals important in both religious and historical terms was their very act of witness, their willingness and determination to back up their religious conviction with action."[50] Through his life and ministry, Andrew Schulze was an example of a twentieth-century Good Samaritan.

---

[50] Michael B. Friedland, *Lift up Your Voice Like a Trumpet: White Clergy and the Civil Rights and Antiwar Movements, 1954–1973* (Chapel Hill: The University of North Carolina Press, 1998) 252.

Bibliography

ARCHIVAL COLLECTIONS

Andrew Schulze Papers. Concordia Historical Institute (CHI), St. Louis, Missouri.

Clemonce Sabourin Papers. In the possession of William Carr, St. Louis MO.

Congregation and District Files. Archives of the Northern Illinois District of the Lutheran Church Missouri Synod, Chicago, Illinois.

Executive Office Files, Concordia Historical Institute (CHI), St. Louis, Missouri.

Fannie Cook Papers. Missouri Historical Society, St. Louis, Missouri.

Lutheran Human Relations Association of America (LHRAA) Papers. Evangelical Lutheran Church in America (ELCA) Archives, Chicago, Illinois.

Lutheran Human Relations Association of America (LHRAA) Papers. Valparaiso University Archives, Valparaiso, Indiana.

National Catholic Council for Interracial Justice (NCCIJ) Papers. Marquette University Archives, Milwaukee, Wisconsin.

National Lutheran Council Papers. Evangelical Lutheran Church in America (ELCA) Archives, Chicago, Illinois.

Sangamon Valley Collection. The Lincoln Library, Springfield, Illinois.

Schulze Family Papers. In the possession of Raymond Schulze, Spring Hill FL.

University papers. Valparaiso University Archives, Valparaiso, Indiana.

FBI FILES

"Andrew Schulze" No. 14–863. Federal Bureau of Investigation, Washington, DC.

"Lutheran Human Relations Association of America" No. 94–55390. Federal Bureau of Investigation, Washington, DC.

AUDIO AND VIDEO RESOURCES

Carson, Clayborne and Peter C. Holloran, ed. *A Knock at Midnight: Inspiration from the Great Sermons of Rev. Martin Luther King, Jr.* New York: Intellectual Properties Management in association with Warner Books, Inc., 1998.

Ellwanger, Joseph. *The Birmingham Sunday School Bombing.* Audiotape Recording at the Concordia Seminary Library, St. Louis, Missouri.

Hampton, Henry, creator and executive producer. *Eyes on the Prize: America's Civil Rights Years, 1954–1965.* Boston: Blackside, Inc., 1986.

———., creator and executive producer. *Eyes on the Prize: America at the Racial Crossroads, 1965–1985.* Boston: Blackside, Inc., 1990.

Lee, Spike. *Four Little Girls.* New York: HBO Home Video, 1998.

Schulze, Andrew. *The New Life in Christ: Ministry and Race.* Sermon Recording for the Founder's Day Service, Concordia Seminary, St. Louis, 9 December 9, 1966. Audiotape Recording at the Concordia Seminary Library, St. Louis, Missouri.

Sent Forth By God's Blessing: A History of the Lutheran Church—Missouri Synod. St. Louis: LCMS Video, 1997.

TRANSCRIPTS OF INTERVIEWS

Herzfeld, Will L. Interviewed by Lee H. Wesley. 21 January 1982 and 13 May 1982.

Lutze, Karl E. Interviewed by James W. Albers. 20 July 1981 and 26 October 1981.

Oral History Collection, Archives of Cooperative Lutheranism, Lutheran Council in the USA, ELCA Archives.Sabourin, Clemonce. Interviewed by Karl E. Lutze. 21–22 April 1983.

Scharlemann, Martin H. Interviewed by Edith Rehbein [daughter]. 9–10 August 1980.

Trout, Nelson W. Interviewed by Norman E. Minich. 19–20 August 1982.

INTERVIEWS

Dickinson, Richard C. Personal Interview. 5 October 1999, St. Louis MO.

Ellwanger, Joseph W. Personal Interview. 17 February 2000, Milwaukee WI.

Griffin, William H. Personal Interview. 27 January 2000, Chicago IL.

Herzfeld, Will L. Personal Interview. 26 January 2000, Chicago IL.

Hoard, Sam. Telephone Interview. 20 July 2000.

Liebenow, George Hans. Personal Interview. 19 October 1999, St. Louis MO.

Lutze, Karl E. Personal Interview. 29 January 2000, Valparaiso IN.

Marty, Martin. Personal Interview. 24 January 2000, Chicago IL.

Schulze, Herbert. Telephone Interview. 10 June 2000.

Schulze, Paul. Telephone Interview. 14 June 2000.

Schulze, Raymond. Personal Interview. 10 July 1999, Collegeville MN.

Simon, Paul. Personal Interview, 11 November 1999, Carbondale IL.

Strielemeier, John H. Personal Interview. 8 February 2000, Valparaiso IN.

REPEATEDLY CITED NEWSPAPERS AND PERIODICALS
American Lutheran
The Cresset
The Christian Century
Focus: Race Relations Bulletin The Lutheran Witness
The Lutheran Pioneer
Proceedings of the LHRAA Summer Institutes
The St. Louis Lutheran
The Vanguard
The Walther League Messenger

ARTICLES
Ahlstrom, Sydney. "The Lutheran Church and American Culture: A Tercentenary Retrospect." *Lutheran Quarterly* 9 (November 1957): 321–42.

Adams, Patricia L. "Fighting for Democracy in St. Louis: Civil Rights During World War II." *Missouri Historical Review* 80 (October 1985): 58–75.

Baepler, Richard. "Otto Paul Kretzmann (1901–1975)." *Concordia Historical Institute Quarterly* 73 (Fall 2000): 132–46.

———. "Otto Paul Kretzmann's Valparaiso University Presidency." *Concordia Historical Institute Quarterly* 74 (Winter 2000): 194–211.

Barnhart, John D. "Sources of Southern Migration into the Old Northwest." *Mississippi Valley Historical Review* 22 (June 1935): 49–62.

Corbert, Katharine T., and Mary E. Seematter. "No Crystal Stair: Black St. Louis, 1920–1940." *Gateway Heritage* 8 (Fall 1987): 8–15.

Dobbert, G. A. "The Cincinnati Germans, 1870–1920: Disintegration of an Immigrant Community." *Bulletin of the Historical and Philosophical Society of Ohio* 23 (October 1965): 230–42.

Ellwanger, Walter H. "Lutheranism in Alabama and Other Parts of the South." *Concordia Historical Institute Quarterly* 48 (Summer 1975): 35–43.

Fortenbaugh, Robert. "American Lutheran Synods and Slavery, 1830–1860." *Journal of Religion* 13 (January 1933): 72–92.

Galchutt, Kathryn M. "'A Beam of Light:' The Controversy Surrounding Andrew Schulze's *My Neighbor of Another Color*." *Essays and Reports of the Lutheran Historical Conference*, forthcoming.

Granquist, Mark. "Five American Lutheran Histories." *The Lutheran Quarterly* 12/2 (Summer 1998): 197–209.

Gude, George J. "Training of African-American Church Workers in the LCMS/Synodical Conference." *Concordia Historical Institute Quarterly* 68 (Fall 1995): 103–18.

Kelleher, Daniel T. "St. Louis' 1916 Residential Segregation Ordinance." *Missouri Historical Society Bulletin* 26 (April 1970): 239–48.

Kemper, Donald K. "Catholic Integration in St. Louis: Civil Rights During World War II." *Missouri Historical Review* 73 (October 1978): 1–22.

Kinnison, William A. "German Lutherans in the Ohio Valley." *Queen City Heritage* 42 (Fall 1984): 3–11.

Lawson, Steven F. "Freedom Then, Freedom Now: The Historiography of the Civil Rights Movement." *American Historical Review* 96 (Spring 1991): 456–71.

McArver, Susan. "Recent Trends in Denominational Historiography and Implications for American Lutheran Scholars." *Essays and Reports of the Lutheran Historical Conference* 17 (1999): 127–46.

Moellering, R. L. "Rauschenbusch in Retrospect." *Concordia Theological Monthly* 27 (August 1956): 613–33.

Mueller, J. T. "The Spiritual, Not the Social Gospel in the Church (With Special Reference to the Race Relations Problem)." *Concordia Theological Monthly* 14 (October 1943): 682–93.

Nohl, Frederick. "The Lutheran Church—Missouri Synod Reacts to United States Anti-Germanism During World War I." *Concordia Historical Institute Quarterly* 35 (July 1962): 49–66.

Noll, Mark. "The Lutheran Difference." *First Things* 20 (February 1992): 31–40.

Noon, Thomas R. "The Alpha Synod of Lutheran Freedmen (1889–1891)." *Concordia Historical Institute Quarterly* 50 (Summer 1977): 64–70.

Olson, Audrey. "The Nature of an Immigrant Community: St. Louis Germans, 1850–1920." *Missouri Historical Review* 66 (April 1972): 342–59.

Owen, Ralph Dornfield. "The Old Lutherans Come." *Concordia Historical Institute Quarterly* 20 (1947): 3–56.

Rose, Matthew. "Unremarkably Lutheran." *First Things* 29 (February 2001): 13–14.

Scheidt, David L. "The 'High Church Movement' in American Lutheranism." *Lutheran Quarterly* 9 (November 1957): 343–49.

Sernett, Milton. "Lutheran Abolitionism in New York State: A Problem in Historical Explication." *Essays and Reports of the Lutheran Historical Conference* 10 (1984): 16–37.

———. "A Question of Earnestness: American Lutheran Missions and Theological Education in Alabama's 'Black Belt.'" *Essays and Reports of the Lutheran Historical Conference* 9 (1982): 80–117.

Stevens, Leland. "Trends in the Missouri Synod As Reflected in *The Lutheran Witness*, 1882–1914." *Concordia Historical Institute Quarterly* 69 (Summer): 88–101.

———. "Trends in the Missouri Synod as Reflected in *The Lutheran Witness*, 1914–1960." Concordia Historical Institute Quarterly 69 (Fall): 116–32.

———. "Trends in the Missouri Synod as Reflected in *The Lutheran Witness*, 1960–Early 1990s." *Concordia Historical Institute Quarterly* 69 (Winter): 165–82.

Taylor, Henry Louis, Jr. "On Slavery's Fringe: City-Building and Black Community Development in Cincinnati, 1800–1850." *Ohio History* 95 (Winter/Spring 1986): 5–33.

Todd, Mary. "Historiography and the Uses of History in the Lutheran Church—Missouri Synod." *Essays and Reports of the Lutheran Historical Conference* 17 (1999): 147–66.

Webster, Ronald. "American Lutheran Opinion Makers and the Crisis of German Protestantism under Hitler." *Essays and Reports of the Lutheran Historical Conference* 17 (1999): 203–18.

Wittke, Carl. "Ohio Germans, 1840–1875." *Ohio Historical Quarterly* 66 (October 1957): 339–54.

BOOKS

Abell, Aaron I. *The Urban Impact on American Protestantism, 1865–1900*. Cambridge: Harvard University Press, 1943.

Adams, James E. *Preus of Missouri: And The Great Lutheran Civil War*. New York: Harper & Row Publishers, 1977.

Ahlstrom, Sydney. *A Religious History of the American People*. New Haven: Yale University Press, 1972.

Ahmann, Matthew, editor. *Race, Challenge to Religion: Original Essays and an Appeal to the Conscience from the National Conference on Religion and Race*. Chicago: Henry Regnery Company, 1963.

Albers, James W. *From Centennial to Golden Anniversary: The History of Valparaiso University from 1959–1975*. Valparaiso IN: Valparaiso University, 1976.

Allbeck, Willard Dow. *A Century of Lutherans in Ohio*. Yellow Springs OH: Antioch, 1966.

Arand, Charles P. *Testing the Boundaries: Windows to Lutheran Identity*. St. Louis: Concordia Publishing House, 1995.

Avella, Steven M. *This Confident Church: Catholic Leadership and Life in Chicago, 1940–1965*. Notre Dame: University of Notre Dame Press, 1992.

Ayers, Edward. *The Promise of the New South: Life After Reconstruction*. New York: Oxford University Press, 1992.

———, Patricia Nelson Limerick, Stephen Nissenbaum, and Peter S. Onuf. *All over the Map: Rethinking American Regions*. Baltimore: The Johns Hopkins University Press, 1996.

Baepler, Walter A. *A Century of Grace: A History of the Missouri Synod, 1847–1947*. St. Louis: Concordia Publishing House, 1947.

Behnken, John W. *This I Recall*. St. Louis: Concordia Publishing House, 1964.

Bodnar, John. *The Transplanted: A History of Immigrants in Urban America*. Bloomington: Indiana University Press, 1985.

Branch, Taylor. *Parting the Waters: America in the King Years, 1954–1963*. New York: Simon & Schuster Inc., 1988.

———. *Pillar of Fire: America in the King Years, 1963–1965*. New York: Simon & Schuster, 1999.

Carson, Clayborne. *In Struggle: SNCC and the Black Awakening of the 1960s.*
    Cambridge: Harvard University Press, 1981.
Carey, Patrick. *The Roman Catholics.* Westport CT: Greenwood Press, 1993.
Carmichael, Stokely, and Charles V. Hamilton. *Black Power: The Politics of*
    Liberation in America. New York: Vintage Books, 1967.
Carter, Dan T. *The Politics of Rage: George Wallace, the Origins of the New*
    Conservatism, and the Transformation of American Politics. New York:
    Simon & Schuster, 1995.
Cayton, Andrew R. L., and Peter S. Onuf. *The Midwest and the Nation:*
    Rethinking the History of an American Region. Bloomington: Indiana
    University Press, 1990.
Cincinnati Historical Society. *Cincinnati: The Queen City.* 3rd ed. Cincinnati:
    Cincinnati Historical Society, 1996.
Coates, Thomas, and Erwin L. Lueker, editors. "Four Decades of
    Expansion." In *Moving Frontiers: Readings in the History of the Lutheran*
    Church—Missouri Synod, edited by Carl S. Meyer. St. Louis: Concordia
    Publishing House, 1964.
Coburn, Carol. *Life at Four Corners: Religion, Gender, and Education in a*
    German-Lutheran Community, 1868–1945. Lawrence: University of
    Kansas Press, 1992.
Collins, Donald E. *When the Church Bell Rang Racist: The Methodist Church*
    and the Civil Rights Movement in Alabama. Athens: University of
    Georgia Press, 1987.
Cone, James H. *Black Theology and Black Power.* New York: Seabury, 1969.
Conzen, Kathleen Neils. "The Germans." In *Harvard Encyclopedia of*
    American Ethnic Groups, edited by Stephen Thernstrom et al.
    Cambridge: Harvard University Press, 1980.
Dickinson, Richard C. *Roses and Thorns: The Centennial Edition of Black*
    Lutheran Mission and Ministry in The Lutheran Church—Missouri Synod.
    St. Louis: Concordia Publishing House, 1977.
———. *This I Remember.* St. Louis MO: Richard C. Dickinson, Sr., 1995.
Drake, St. Clair, and Horace R. Cayton. *Black Metropolis: A Study of Negro*
    Life in a Northern City. Rev. ed. New York: Harper & Row, 1962.
Drews, Christopher F. *Half a Century of Lutheranism among Our Colored*
    People, 1877–1927. St. Louis: Concordia Publishing House, 1927.
DuBois, W. E. B. *The Souls of Black Folk*, with a foreword by Henry L.
    Gates. New York: Bantam Doubleday, 1989.

Duziak, Mary L. *Cold War Civil Rights: Race and the Image of American Democracy*. Princeton: Princeton University Press, 2000.

Eskew, Glenn T. *But for Birmingham: The Local and National Movements in the Civil Rights Struggle*. Chapel Hill: University of North Carolina Press, 1997.

Fairclough, Adam. *Better Day Coming: Blacks and Equality, 1890–2000*. New York: Viking, 2001.

———. *To Redeem the Soul of America: The Southern Christian Leadership Conference and Martin Luther King, Jr*. Athens: University of Georgia Press, 1987.

Fevold, Eugene L. "Coming of Age, 1875–1900." In *The Lutherans in North America*, revised edition, edited by E. Clifford Nelson. Philadelphia: Fortress Press, 1980.

Findlay, James F., Jr. *Church People in the Struggle: The National Council of Churches and the Black Freedom Movement, 1950–1970*. New York: Oxford University Press, 1993.

Forell, George Wolfgang. *Faith Active in Love: An Investigation of the Principles Underlying Luther's Social Ethics*. Minneapolis: Augsburg Publishing House, 1959.

Forster, Walter O. *Zion on the Mississippi: The Settlement of the Saxon Lutherans in Missouri, 1839–1841*. St. Louis: Concordia Publishing House, 1953.

Fox, Tim, editor. "The Ville." In *Where We Live: A Guide to St. Louis Communities*. St. Louis: Missouri Historical Society, 1995.

Franklin, John Hope, and Alfred Moss Jr. *From Slavery to Freedom: A History of African Americans*. New York: A. A. Knopf, 2000.

Friedland, Michael B. *Lift up Your Voice Like a Trumpet: White Clergy and the Civil Rights and Antiwar Movements, 1954–1973*. Chapel Hill: University of North Carolina Press, 1988.

Garrow, David J. *Bearing the Cross: Martin Luther King Jr. and the Southern Christian Leadership Conference*. New York: William Morrow and Company, Inc., 1986.

Gerber, David A. *Black Ohio and the Color Line, 1860–1915*. Urbana: University of Illinois Press, 1976.

Gleason, Philip. *The Conservative Reformers: German-American Catholics and the Social Order*. Notre Dame: University of Notre Dame Press, 1968.

———. *Speaking of Diversity: Language and Ethnicity in Twentieth-Century America*. Baltimore: Johns Hopkins Press, 1992.

Gordon, Milton M. *Assimilation in American Life: The Role of Race, Religion, and National Origins*. New York: Oxford University Press, 1964.

Graebner, Alan Niehaus. *Uncertain Saints: The Laity in the Lutheran Church—Missouri Synod, 1900–1970*. Westport CT: Greenwood Press, 1975.

Graebner, Norman A. "Lutherans and Politics." In *The Lutheran Church and North American Life*, edited by John E. Groh and Robert H. Smith. St. Louis: Clayton Publishing House, 1979.

Graetz, Robert S. *Montgomery: A White Preacher's Memoirs*. Minneapolis: Fortress Press, 1991.

Granquist, Mark. "Lutherans in the United States, 1930–1960: Searching for the 'Center.'" In *Reforming the Center: American Protestantism, 1900 to the Present*, edited by Douglas Jacobsen and William Vance Trollinger, Jr. Grand Rapids MI: Wm. B. Eerdmans Publishing Co., 1988.

Greene, Lorenzo J., Gary R. Kremer, and Antonio F. Holland. *Missouri's Black Heritage*. Rev. ed. Columbia: University of Missouri Press, 1993.

Groh, John E., and Robert H. Smith, editors. *The Lutheran Church in North American Life*. St. Louis: Clayton Publishing House, 1979.

Grossman, James R. *Land of Hope: Chicago, Black Southerners, and the Great Migration*. Chicago: University of Chicago Press, 1989.

Gustafson, David A. *Lutherans in Crisis: The Question of Identity in the American Republic*. Minneapolis: Fortress Press, 1993.

Hale, J. Russell. "Lutherans and Social Action." In *The Lutheran Church in North American Life*, edited by John E. Groh and Robert H. Smith. St. Louis: Clayton Publishing House, 1979.

Handy, Robert T., editor. *The Social Gospel in America*. New York: Oxford University Press, 1966.

Harlan, Louis R. *Booker T. Washington: The Making of a Black Leader, 1856–1901*. New York: Oxford University Press, 1972.

———. *Booker T. Washington: The Wizard of Tuskegee, 1901–1915*. New York: Oxford University Press, 1986.

Harrison, Shelby M., director. *The Springfield Survey: A Study of Social Conditions in an American City*. New York: Russell Sage Foundation, 1920.

Haselden, Kyle. *The Racial Problem in Christian Perspective*. New York: Harper & Bros., 1959.

Heintzen, Erich H. *Prairie School of the Prophets: The Anatomy of a Seminary, 1846–1976*. St. Louis: Concordia Publishing House, 1989.

Higham, John. *Strangers in the Land: Patterns of American Nativism, 1860–1925*. 2nd ed. New Brunswick NJ: Rutgers University Press, 1992.

Hill, Samuel S. "Religion and Region in America." In *Protestantism and Regionalism*, edited by Martin Marty. New York: K. G. Saur, 1992.

Hillis, Byran V. *Can Two Walk Together Unless They Be Agreed? American Religious Schisms in the 1970s*. Brooklyn NY: Carlson, 1991.

Hirsh, Arnold R. *Making the Second Ghetto: Race and Housing in Chicago, 1940–1960*. Chicago: University of Chicago Press, 1998.

Hoard, Samuel. *Almost A Layman*. Orlando FL: Drake's Publishing, 1981.

Hoffmann, Oswald C. J. *What More Is There To Say But Amen: The Autobiography of Dr. Oswald C. J. Hoffmann as told to Ronald J. Schlegel*. St. Louis: Concordia Publishing House, 1996.

Holt, Thomas C. "Afro-Americans." In *Harvard Encyclopedia of American Ethnic Groups*, edited by Stephen Thernstorm et al. Cambridge: Harvard University Press, 1980.

Hood, Robert E. *Begrimed and Black: Christian Traditions on Black and Blackness*. Philadelphia: Fortress Press, 1994.

Hough, Joseph C., Jr. *Black Power and White Protestants: A Christian Response to the New Negro Pluralism*. New York: Oxford University Press, 1968.

Human Relations: Resolutions of the Lutheran Church—Missouri Synod. St. Louis: The Lutheran Church—Missouri Synod and The Lutheran Human Relations Association of America, 1969.

Hurt, R. Douglass. "Ohio: Gateway to the Midwest." In *Heartland: Comparative Histories of the Midwestern States*, edited by James H. Madison. Bloomington: Indiana University Press, 1988.

Jackson, Kenneth T. *Crabgrass Frontier: The Suburbanization of the United States*. New York: Oxford University Press, 1985.

———. *The Ku Klux Klan in the City, 1915–1930*. New York: Oxford University Press, 1967.

Jacoby, Tamar. *Someone Else's House: America's Unfinished Struggle for Integration*. New York: Basic Books, 1998.

Johnson, Jeff G. *Black Christians: The Untold Lutheran Story*. St. Louis: Concordia Publishing House, 1991.

Johnson, Niel M. "Lutherans in American Economic Life." In *The Lutheran Church in North American Life*, edited by John E. Groh and Robert H. Smith. St. Louis: Clayton Publishing House, 1979.

Jonas, Gilbert. *Freedom's Sword: The NAACP and the Struggle Against Racism in America, 1909–1969*. London: Routledge, 2004.

Kraabel, Alf M. *Grace and Race in the Lutheran Church*. Chicago: National Lutheran Council, 1957.

Kellogg, Charles Flint. *NAACP: A History of the National Association for the Advancement of Colored People*. Baltimore: Johns Hopkins Press, 1967.

King, Martin Luther, Jr. *Why We Can't Wait*. New York: Signet Classic, 2000.

King, Robert H., ed. *African Americans and the Local Church*. St. Louis: Concordia Publishing House, 1996.

———. *Pastor Jenkin's Said "Hang on to Matthew 6:33": Autobiography of Robert H. King*. St. Louis: Concordia Publishing House, 1999.

Klein, Christa R. "Denominational History as Public History: The Lutheran Case." In *Reimagining Denominationalism: Interpretative Essays*, edited by Robert Bruce Mullin and Russell E. Richey. New York: Oxford University Press, 1994.

———. "Lutheranism." In *The Encyclopedia of American Religious Experience: Studies of Traditions and Movements*, edited by Charles H. Lippy and Peter W. Williams. New York: Scribner, 1988.

———. *Politics and Policy: The Genesis and Theology of Social Statements in the Lutheran Church of America*. Minneapolis: Fortress Press, 1989.

Krebs, Ervin E. *The Lutheran Church and the Negro in America*. Columbus OH: Board of American Mission of the American Lutheran Church, 1950.

Krohe, James, Jr. *Summer of Rage: The Springfield Race Riot of 1908*. Springfield IL: Sangamon County Historical Society, 1974.

Kuenning, Paul P. *The Rise and Fall of American Lutheran Pietism: The Rejection of An Activist Heritage*. Macon GA: Mercer University Press, 1988.

Lagerquist, L. Deane. *The Lutherans*. Westport CT: Praeger, 1999.

Lemann, Nicholas. *The Promised Land: The Great Black Migration and How It Changed America*. New York: Alfred A. Knopf, 1991.

Lesher, Stephan. *George Wallace: American Populist*. New York: Addison Wesley Longman, Inc., 1994.

Levine, Lawrence W. *Black Culture and Black Consciousness*. New York: Oxford University Press, 1977.

Lewis, David Levering. *W. E. B. DuBois: Biography of a Race, 1868–1919*. New York: Henry Holt and Company, 1993.

Lewis, John, with Michael D'Orso. *Walking with the Wind: A Memoir of the Movement*. San Diego: Harcourt Brace & Company, 1998.

Luker, Ralph E. *The Social Gospel in Black and White: American Racial Reform, 1985–1912*. Chapel Hill: University of North Carolina Press, 1991.

Luebke, Frederick C. *Bonds of Loyalty: German-Americans and World War I*. DeKalb: Northern Illinois University Press, 1974.

———. "German Immigrants and American Politics: Problems of Leadership, Parties, and Issues." In *Germans in the New World: Essays in the History of Immigration*. Urbana: University of Illinois Press, 1990.

———. *Germans in the New World: Essays in the History of Immigration*. Urbana: University of Illinois Press, 1990.

Luecke, Richard. "Themes of Lutheran Urban Ministry." In *Churches, Cities, and Human Community: Urban Ministry in the United States, 1945–1985*, edited by Clifford J. Green. Grand Rapids MI: Wm. B. Eerdmans Publishing Company, 1996.

Lueking, F. Dean. *A Century of Caring, 1868–1968: The Welfare Ministry among Missouri Synod Lutherans*. St. Louis: The Board of Social Ministry of The Lutheran Church—Missouri Synod, 1968.

———. *Mission in the Making: The Missionary Enterprise among Missouri Synod Lutherans, 1846–1963*. St. Louis: Concordia Publishing House, 1964.

Luther, Martin. *Selected Political Writings*, edited by J. M. Porter. Philadelphia: Fortress Press, 1974.

Lutze, Karl E. *To Mend the Broken: The Christian Response to the Challenge of Human Relations Problems*. St. Louis: Concordia Publishing House, 1966.

McGreevy, John T. *Parish Boundaries: The Catholic Encounter with Race in the Twentieth-Century Urban North*. Chicago: University of Chicago Press, 1996.

McWorter, Diane. *Carry Me Home: Birmingham, Alabama: The Climatic Battle of the Civil Rights Revolution*. New York: Simon & Schuster, 2001.

Madison, James H., editor. *Heartland: Comparative Histories of the Midwestern States*. Bloomington: Indiana University Press, 1988.

Maier, Paul L. *A Man Spoke, A World Listened: The Story of Walter A. Maier*.
St. Louis: Concordia Publishing House, 1963.

Malcolm X, with Alex Haley. *The Autobiography of Malcolm X*. New York:
Ballantine, 1965.

Manis, Andrew Michael. *Southern Civil Religions in Conflict: Black and White Baptists and Civil Rights, 1947–1957*. Athens: University of Georgia Press, 1987.

Mann, Robert. *The Walls of Jericho: Lyndon Johnson, Hubert Humphrey, Richard Russell, and the Struggle for Civil Rights*. New York: Harcourt Brace & Company, 1996.

Marable, Manning. *Black Leadership*. New York: Columbia University Press, 1998.

Marsh, Charles. *God's Long Summer: Stories of Faith and Civil Rights*. Princeton: Princeton University Press, 1997.

Marty, Martin. *Modern American Religion, Volume 1: The Irony of It All, 1893–1919*. Chicago: University of Chicago Press, 1986.

———. *Modern American Religion, Volume 2: The Noise of Conflict, 1919–1941*. Chicago: University of Chicago Press, 1991.

———. *Modern American Religion, Volume 3: Under God, Indivisible, 1941–1960*. Chicago: University of Chicago Press, 1996.

Marty, Myron A. *Lutherans and Roman Catholicism: The Changing Conflict, 1917–1963*. Notre Dame: Notre Dame University Press, 1968.

May, Henry F. *Protestant Churches and Industrial America*. New York: Harper & Bros., 1949.

Mays, Benjamin E. Introduction to *Race, Challenge to Religion: Original Essays and an Appeal to Conscience from the National Conference on Religion and Race*, edited by Matthew Ahmann. Chicago: Henry Regnery Company, 1963.

Meier, August and Elliott Rudwick. *CORE: A Study in the Civil Rights Movement, 1942–1968*. New York: Oxford University Press, 1973.

Meier, Everette and Herbert Mayer, editor. "The Process of Americanization." In *Moving Frontiers: Readings in the History of the Lutheran Church—Missouri Synod*, edited by Carl S. Meyer. St. Louis: Concordia Publishing House, 1964.

Meuser, Fred W. "Facing the Twentieth Century, 1900–1930." In *The Lutherans in North America*. Rev. ed., edited by E. Clifford Nelson. Philadelphia: Fortress Press, 1980.

Meyer, Carl S. *Log Cabin to Luther Tower: Concordia Seminary During 125 Years Toward a More Excellent Ministry, 1839–1964*. St. Louis: Concordia Publishing House, 1965.

———. "The Missouri Synod and Other Lutherans Before 1918." In *Moving Frontiers: Readings in the History of the Lutheran Church—Missouri Synod*, edited by Carl S. Meyer. St. Louis: Concordia Publishing House, 1964.

———, editor. *Moving Frontiers: Readings in the History of the Lutheran Church—Missouri Synod*. St. Louis: Concordia Publishing House, 1964.

———. "Ohio's Accord With Missouri, 1868." In *The Maturing of American Lutheranism*, edited by Herbert T. Neve and Benjamin A. Johnson. Minneapolis: Augsburg Publishing House, 1968.

Meyer, Ruth Fritz. *Women on A Mission: The Role of Women in the Church from Bible Times up to and including a History of the Lutheran Women's Missionary League during its First Twenty-Five Years*. St. Louis: Concordia Publishing House, 1967.

Miller, Randall M. Introduction to *States of Progress: Germans and Blacks in America Over 300 Years*. Philadelphia: The German Society of Pennsylvania, 1989.

———, editor. *States of Progress: Germans and Black in America over 300 Years*. Philadelphia: The German Society of Pennsylvania, 1989.

Miller, Zane L. *Boss Cox's Cincinnati: Urban Politics in the Progressive Era*. Chicago: University of Chicago Press, 1968.

———, and Bruce Tucker. *Changing Plans for America's Inner Cities: Cincinnati's Over-the-Rhine and Twentieth Century Urbanism*. Columbus: Ohio State University Press, 1998.

Moellering, Ralph Luther. *Christian Conscience and Negro Emancipation*. Philadelphia: Fortress Press, 1965.

Moore, Leonard. *Citizen Klansmen: The Ku Klux Klan in Indiana, 1921–1928*. Chapel Hill: University of North Carolina Press, 1991.

Morris, Charles R. *American Catholic: The Saints and Sinners Who Built America's Most Powerful Church*. New York: Times Books, 1997.

Mueller, John Theodore. *A Brief History of the Origin, Development, and Work of the Evangelical Lutheran Synodical Conference of North America, Prepared for Its Diamond Jubilee, 1872–1947*. St. Louis: Concordia Publishing House, 1948.

Mundinger, Carl S. *Government in the Missouri Synod: The Genesis of Decentralized Government in the Missouri Synod*. St. Louis: Concordia Publishing House, 1947.

Mydral, Gunnar, with Richard Sterner and Arnold Rose. *An American Dilemma: The Negro Problem and Modern Democracy*. New York: Harper & Bros., 1944.

Nelson, E. Clifford, editor. *The Lutherans in North America*. Rev. ed. Philadelphia: Fortress Press, 1980.

———. "The New Shape of Lutheranism, 1930–Present." In *The Lutherans in North America*. Rev. ed., edited by E. Clifford Nelson, Philadelphia: Fortress Press, 1980.

Nunes, John. *Voices form the City: Issues and Images of Urban Preaching*. St. Louis: Concordia Publishing House, 1999.

Oates, Stephen B. *Let the Trumpet Sound: A Life of Martin Luther King, Jr.* New York: Harper Perennial, 1994.

O' Brien, Michael. *Hesbergh: A Biography*. Washington DC: Catholic University of America Press, 1998.

O'Reilly, Kenneth. *"Racial Matters:" The FBI's Secret File on Black America, 1960–1972*. New York: Free Press, 1989.

Pahl, John. *Hopes and Dreams of All: The International Walther League and Lutheran Youth in American Culture*. Chicago: Wheat Ridge Ministries, 1993.

Pelikan, Jaroslav. "Lutheran Heritage." In *The Encyclopedia of American Religious Experience: Studies of Traditions and Movements*, edited by Charles H. Lippy and Peter W. Williams. New York: Scribner, 1988.

Pero, Albert, and Ambrose Moyo, editors. *Theology and the Black Experience: The Lutheran Heritage Interpreted by African and African-American Theologians*. Minneapolis: Augsburg Publishing House, 1998.

Peterson, Merrill D. *Lincoln in American Memory*. New York: Oxford University Press, 1994.

Poole, Stafford, and Douglas J. Slawson. *Church and Slave in Perry County, Missouri*. Lewiston NY: Edwin Mellen Press, 1986.

Powers, Richard Gid. *Not without Honor: The History of American Anticommunism*. New York: Free Press, 1995.

Primm, James Neal. *Lion of the Valley: St. Louis, Missouri, 1764–1980*. 3rd ed. St. Louis: Missouri Historical Press, 1998.

Raines, Howell, editor. *My Soul Is Rested: The Story of the Civil Rights Movement in the Deep South*. New York: Penguin Books, 1977.

Ralph, James R., Jr. *Northern Protest: Martin Luther King Jr., Chicago, and the Civil Rights Movement.* Cambridge: Harvard University Press, 1993.

Raboteau, Albert J. *Canaan Land: A Religious History of African Americans.* New York: Oxford University Press, 2001.

Reimers, David. *White Protestantism and the Negro.* New York: Oxford University Press, 1965.

Rippley, La Vern J. *The German-Americans.* Boston: Twayne Publishers, 1976.

Rogers, Mary Beth. *Barbara Jordan: American Hero.* New York: Bantam Books, 2000.

Rudnick, Milton. *Fundamentalism and the Missouri Synod: A Historical Study of Their Interaction and Mutual Influence.* St. Louis: Concordia Publishing House, 1966.

Rudwick, Elliott. *Race Riot at East St. Louis, July 2, 1917.* Carbondale: Southern Illinois University Press, 1964.

Russo, Edward J. *Prairie of Promise: Springfield and Sangamon County.* Woodlands CA: Windsor Publications, 1983.

Sabourin, Clemonce. *Let the Righteous Speak.* New York: Pageant Press, 1957.

Salley, Columbus, and Ronald Behm. *Your God Is Too White.* Downer's Grove IL: Inter-Varsity Press, 1970.

Schulze, Andrew. *Fire from the Throne.* St. Louis: Concordia Publishing House, 1968.

———. *My Neighbor of Another Color.* St. Louis MO: Andrew Schulze, 1941.

———. *Race against Time: A History of Race Relations in the Lutheran Church—Missouri Synod from the Perspective of the Author's Involvement, 1920–1970.* Valparaiso IN: Lutheran Human Relations Association of America, 1972.

Schwartzkopf, Louis J. *The Lutheran Trail: History of the Synodical Conference Lutheran Churches in Northern Illinois.* St. Louis: Concordia Publishing House, 1950.

Senechal, Roberta. *The Sociogenesis of a Race Riot: Springfield, Illinois in 1908.* Urbana: University of Illinois Press, 1990.

Sernett, Milton C., editor. *African American Religious History: A Documentary Witness.* 2nd ed. Durham NC: Duke University Press, 1999.

———. *Bound for the Promised Land: African American Religion and The Great Migration.* Durham NC: Duke University Press, 1997.

Shapiro, Henry D., and Jonathan D. Sarna, editors. *Ethnic Diversity and Civic Identity: Patterns of Conflict and Cohesion in Cincinnati Since 1820.* Urbana: University of Illinois Press, 1992.

Shattuck, Gardiner H., Jr. *Episcopalians and Race: Civil War to Civil Rights.* Lexington: University Press of Kentucky, 2000.

Simon-Netto, Uwe. *The Fabricated Luther: The Rise and Fall of the Shirer Myth.* Foreword by Peter L. Berger. St. Louis: Concordia Publishing House, 1995.

Smith, Timothy L. *Revivalism and Social Reform in Mid-Nineteenth Century America.* New York: Abingdon Press, 1957.

Solberg, Richard W. *Lutheran Higher Education in North America.* Minneapolis: Augsburg Publishing House, 1985.

Spear, Allan H. *Black Chicago: The Making of a Negro Ghetto, 1890–1920.* Chicago: University of Chicago Press, 1967.

Stange, Douglas C. *Radicalism for Humanity: A Study of Lutheran Abolitionism.* St. Louis: Oliver Slave, Ltd., 1970.

Stelzer, Ronald. *Salt, Light, and Signs of the Times: An Intimate Look at the Life and Times of Alfred (Rip) Rehwinkel.* New Haven MO: Lutheran News, Inc., 1993.

Strietelmeier, John. *Valparaiso's First Century: A Centennial History of Valparaiso University.* Valparaiso IN: Valparaiso University, 1959.

Suelflow, August R. "The Beginnings of 'Missouri, Ohio, and Other States' in America." In *Moving Frontiers: Readings in the History of the Lutheran Church—Missouri Synod*, edited by Carl S. Meyer. St. Louis: Concordia Publishing House, 1964.

———. *The Heart of Missouri: A History of the Western District of the LCMS, 1854–1954.* St. Louis: Concordia Publishing House, 1954.

———. *Heritage in Motion: Readings in the History of the Lutheran Church—Missouri Synod, 1962–1995.* St. Louis: Concordia Publishing House, 1998.

Taylor, Henry Louis, Jr. "City Building, Public Policy, the Rise of the Industrial City, and the Black Ghetto-Slum Formation in Cincinnati, 1850–1940." In *Race and the City: Work, Community, and Protest in Cincinnati, 1820–1970*, edited by Henry Louis Taylor, Jr. Urbana: University of Illinois Press, 1993.

———, ed. *Race and the City: Work, Community, and Protest in Cincinnati, 1820–1970.* Urbana: University of Illinois Press, 1993.

Teaford, Jon. *Cities of the Heartland: The Rise and Fall of the Industrial Midwest*. Bloomington: Indiana University Press, 1993.

Tietjen, John H. *Which Way To Lutheran Unity? A History of Efforts to Unite the Lutherans of America*. St. Louis: Concordia Publishing House, 1966.

Trexler, Edgar R. *Anatomy of a Merger: People, Dynamics, and Decisions that Shaped the ELCA*. Minneapolis: Augsburg Fortress, 1995.

Todd, Mary. *Authority Vested: A Story of Identity and Change in the Lutheran Church—Missouri Synod*. Grand Rapids MI: Wm. B. Eerdmans Publishing Company, 2000.

Tolzmann, Don Heinrich. *Cincinnati's German Heritage*. Bowie MD: Heritage Books, 1994.

Trotter, Joe William, Jr. *River Jordan: African American Urban Life in the Ohio Valley*. Lexington: University Press of Kentucky, 1998.

Tucker, Richard. *The Dragon and The Cross: The Rise and Fall of the Ku Klux Klan in Middle America*. Hamden CT: Archon Books, 1991.

Tuttle, William M., Jr. *Race Riot: Chicago in the Red Summer of 1919*. New York: Atheneum, 1970.

Walker, Mack. *Germany and the Emigration, 1816–1885*. Cambridge: Harvard University Press, 1964.

Washington, Booker T. *Up from Slavery*, with an introduction by Ishmael Reed. New York: Signet Classic, 2000.

Weisbrot, Robert. *Freedom Bound: A History of America's Civil Rights Movement*. New York: Norton, 1990.

Wentz, Abdel Ross. *A Basic History of Lutheranism in America*. Philadelphia: Muhlenberg Press, 1955.

Wentz, Frederick K. *Lutherans in Concert: The Story of the National Lutheran Council*. Minneapolis: Augsburg Publishing House, 1968.

White, Ronald C., Jr. *Liberty and Justice for All: Racial Reform and the Social Gospel*. San Francisco: Harper & Row, 1990.

Whitfield, Stephen J. *A Death in the Delta: The Story of Emmet Till*. New York: Free Press, 1988.

Wiederaenders, Robert. "History of Lutheranism in the Chicago Area." In *Chicago Lutheran Planning Study*. Chicago: National Lutheran Planning Study, 1965.

Williamson, Joel. *The Crucible of Race: Black-White Relations in the American South Since Emancipation*. New York: Oxford University Press, 1984.

Wilson, Bobby M. *America's Johannesburg: Industrialization and Racial Transformation in Birmingham.* Lanham MD: Rowman & Littlefield, 2000.

Wood, Forrest G. *The Arrogance of Faith: Christianity and Race from the Colonial Era to the Twentieth Century.* New York: Knopf, 1990.

Woodward, C. Vann. *The Strange Career of Jim Crow.* 3rd rev. ed. New York: Oxford University Press, 1974.

Wunthrow, Robert. *The Restructuring of American Religion: Society and Faith Since World War II.* Princeton: Princeton University Press, 1988.

Young, Rosa J. *Light in the Dark Belt: The Story of Rosa Young as Told by Herself.* Rev. ed. St. Louis: Concordia Publishing House, 1950.

Ziehr, Richard O. *The Struggle for Unity: A Personal Look at The Integration of the Lutheran Church in the South.* Milton FL: CJH Enterprises, 1999.

DISSERTATIONS

Bailey, Charles. "The Ville: A Study of a Symbolic Community in St. Louis." Ph.D. dissertation, Washington University, 1978.

Braun, Mark. "Changes within the Evangelical Lutheran Synodical Conference of North America which led to the Exit of the Wisconsin Evangelical Lutheran Synod." Ph.D. dissertation, Concordia Seminary, St. Louis, 2000.

Christensen, Lawrence Oland. "Black St. Louis: A Study in Race Relations, 1865–1916." Ph.D. dissertation, University of Missouri—Columbia, 1972.

Graebner, Alan Niehaus. "The Acculturation of an Immigrant Lutheran Church: The Lutheran Church—Missouri Synod, 1917–1929." Ph.D. dissertation, Columbia University, 1965.

Kohlhoff, Dean Wayne. "Missouri Synod Lutherans and the Image of Germany, 1914–1945." Ph.D. dissertation, University of Chicago, 1973.

Liebenow, George Hans. "Attitudes and Policies of the Lutheran Church Toward the Negro." Bachelor's Thesis, Concordia Seminary, St. Louis, 1957.

Moellering, Ralph Luther. "The Missouri Synod and Social Problems, A Theological and Social Analysis of the Relation to Industrial Tensions, War, and Race Relations from 1917 to 1941." Ph.D. dissertation, Harvard University, 1964.

Svendsbye, Lloyd. "The History of a Developing Social Responsibility among Lutherans in America from 1930 to 1960, With Reference to the American Lutheran Church, the Augustana Lutheran Church, the Evangelical Lutheran Church, and the United Lutheran Church in America." Th.D. dissertation, Union Theological Seminary, 1966.

White, Joseph Michael. "Religion and Community: Cincinnati Germans, 1814–1870." Ph.D. dissertation, University of Notre Dame, 1980.

Index

Abernathy, Ralph, 180
Adams, James, 230
Ahmann, Matthew, 189
Alabama Lutheran Academy and
    College (Alabama Lutheran
    College and Seminary), 52, 70,
    165, 167–69, 212–13
Albany Movement, 178–89
All-Lutheran Conference on Race,
    209
All-Negro Lutheran Pastors
    Conference, 217
Almost a Layman (Hoard), 108
Alpha Synod, 41n28
*An American Dilemma: The Negro
    Problem and Modern Democracy*
    (Mydral), 98
American Indian Movement (AIM),
    158n37
The American Lutheran, 95–97, 205
American Lutheran Church (ALC),
    136–37, 138, 156, 209, 231, 234
American Lutheran Publicity
    Bureau, 95–96
American Luther League, 147
Amt, Paul, 91, 108
Anderson, Marian, 82
Anderson, William, 180
anti-communism, 174–76
Antioch Baptist Church (St. Louis),
    67–68
Association of Black Lutheran
    Clergy (ABLC), 218, 224
Association of Evangelical Lutheran
    Churches (AELC), 230, 231
Augsburg Publishing House, 226

The Autobiography of a Colored Man
    (Johnson), 85

Bailey, Charles, 68
Bailey, Mrs. M., 64
Ballard, John C., 141
Barth, G. Christian, 106
Bates, George (Mr. and Mrs.), 52
Baur, John C., 147
Becker, Donald, 132n56, 163
Becker, William Dee, 100
Behnken, John W., 61, 74–75, 87,
    107, 109–10, 118, 141, 151, 166
Bevel, James, 212n211
Birmingham (AL) ; church bombing
    (1963), 199–200; protests (1963),
    193–96
*Black Christians: The Untold
    Lutheran Story* (Johnson), 3
black churches, negative view of, 40
Black Clergy Caucus of the
    Missouri Synod, 218
black culture, bias against, 42
black Lutheranism; centennial
    celebrated in 1977, 234; creating
    different structure for
    congregations, 109–13;
    geographic shift in, 42–43;
    meeting with resistance, 42;
    mission status, 43–44; organized
    on segregated basis, 43; pastors',
    role in forcing church to deal with
    racial issues, 108–109; predating
    Synodical Conference, 39
black Lutherans, organizing in
    1920s, 54–55

"Black Nativity," 176
Black Power, 217, 221
black voter registration, 210
Bloody Sunday (march across
    Edmund Pettis Bridge, Selma
    [AL]), 211–12
Boe, Paul, 158n37
Bonhoeffer, Dietrich, 186n126
Bowen, Trevor, 84
Branch, Taylor, 169, 195
Bronzeville (Chicago), 120
Brown v. Board of Education, 82, 142,
    149

Caemmerer, Richard R., 99, 106
Campbell, William, 189, 216
"Cards on the Table" (Sabourin),
    110–12
Carino, Alvaro, 160
Carmichael, Stokely, 216–17, 220
Carter, Marmaduke Nathanael, 65,
    72, 77, 80, 103, 122
Cartwright, Marguerite, 160
Carver, George Washington, 95
Catholics; as example in race
    relations, 110–11, 122; stand on
    discrimination, 114–16
Chicago; Catholic parishes in, 123;
    center of movement to form
    Association of Black Lutheran
    Clergymen, 132; presence of
    Lutherans in and around, 117–18;
    South Side, surpassing Harlem as
    "capital of Black America,"
    118–20; thriving religious center,
    123–24
Chicago Society for Better Race
    Relations, 133
The Christian Century, 87, 161
Christian day schools, 42, 50
Christian Dogmatics (Mueller), 88
Christian-Jewish relations, 160,
    188–92
Christ the King Lutheran Church
    (Chicago), 120

Christian News (*Lutheran News*), 203
Christ Seminary-Seminex, 230
Cincinnati; black Americans in,
    during Schulze's childhood,
    24–25; development of, 13;
    diverse religious environment of,
    17–18; favored place for German
    immigrants, 11–12; history of
    racial unrest in, 22–23;
    significance in African-American
    history, 22
Cincinnati Forty-eighters, 19
Cincinnati: The Queen City, 12
civil disobedience, 179, 194
civil rights, concern over link to
    communism, 174–77
Civil Rights Act of 1964, 204–206
civil rights movement, 6–7, 154–57,
    169–70, 173–74, 192–201. *See also*
    Albany Movement, Birmingham
    church bombing, Bloody Sunday,
    Civil Rights Act of 1964, Freedom
    Rides, Montgomery Bus Boycott,
    Voting Rights Act of 1965
Coates, Thomas, 83n84
Cold War, 173
communicant integration, 133–34
Concerned White Citizens of
    Alabama, 210–11
Concordia College, Fort Wayne,
    107–108
Concordia College, Milwaukee, 83
Concordia Publishing House,
    76–77, 86, 89–90, 218, 226
Concordia Seminary (St. Louis), 32,
    60, 215–16; desire to avoid
    controversy, 105; faculty
    censured, 229–30; growing
    sensitivity to racial issues, 106
Concordia Theological Monthly, 87
Concordia Theological Seminary
    (Springfield IL), 32–34, 36, 163;
    acceptance of black students, 106;
    training at, 47

Concordia University, Selma (AL), 52. *See also* Alabama Lutheran Academy and College

Congress of Racial Equality (CORE), 102, 169–70

Connor, Bull, 193, 196

Conzen, Kathleen, 14

Cox, George, B., 13

Craemer, F. August, 33

The Cresset, 86

Dau, W. H. T., 51, 85, 90

Daughters of the American Revolution, 82

Dickinson, Moses S., 131–32, 141

Dickinson, Richard, 113, 217, 234

Divine White Right (Bowen), 84

Doescher, John F., 38–39

Dominick, Albert, 139

Double Victory, 97

Drewes, Christopher F., 51, 128

DuBois, W. E. B., 9

Duden, Gottfried, 58n1

Eden Seminary, 230

Elleardsville (St. Louis), 67

Ellis, William, 210

Ellwanger, Joseph, 172, 200–202, 210–11, 212, 220, 237

Ellwanger, Walter H., 168, 200–201

Engelder, Theodore, 47, 49, 87–88

Episcopal Society for Cultural and Racial Unity (ESCRU), 170

Evangelical Lutheran Church in America (ELCA), 37n18, 117, 231

Evangelical Lutherans in Mission (ELIM), 230

Evangelical Lutheran Synod of Missouri, Ohio, and Other States, 59. *See also* German Evangelical Lutheran Synod of Missouri, Ohio, and Other States; Lutheran Church—Missouri Synod

Evangelical Lutheran Synodical Conference of North America. *See* Synodical Conference

Fackler, James, 172–73

Faga, Robert, 173

Feddersen, Esther, 103

Federal Bureau of Investigation, 208–209

Federal Council of Churches, 114

Federation of Lutheran Churches of the Missouri Synod in Cincinnati, 26

Fellowship of Reconciliation, 102

Fiehler, Gertrude, 141

Findlay, James, 204–205

Finley, Otis, 72–73

Fire from the Throne: Race Relations in the Church (Schulze), 218–19

First English Lutheran Church (Cincinnati), 17

Focus, 103, 141

Forell, George W., 175–76

Franckean Synod, 24, 53n68

Franklin, John Hope, 216

Freedom Rides, 173

Friedland, Michael, 182, 238

Fritz, John H. C., 129

Fuerbringer, Alfred, 216

Garvey, Marcus, 54

General Conference, 54–55

German Americans, 9–12, 14–15, 62; assimilation of, World War I's effect on, 28–29; attitudes on race and slavery, 23; feelings toward, 26–27

German Evangelical Lutheran Synod of Missouri, Ohio, and Other States, 15, 24, 37, 114. *See also* Evangelical Lutheran Synod of Missouri, Ohio, and Other States; Lutheran Church—Missouri Synod

German Forty-eighters, 18–19

Gilligan, Francis J., 84
Glennon, John J., 115
Goering, Emma, 48
Goering, Herman, 48
Goering, Margaret, 48. *See also* Schulze, Margaret
Gose, Paul E., 65
Grace Colored Lutheran Church (St. Louis), 64
Graebner, Alan, 28, 60, 96
Graebner, Theodore, 62, 87
Graetz, Robert, 154n27, 156–57, 210
Granquist, Mark, 3–4
Great Migration, 43, 63, 119
Gregory, Dick, 199
Griffin, William, 144–45, 215, 221

Halvorson, Lawrence (L. W.), 180, 209
Hansen, Marcus Lee, 21
Hansen's Law, 21n46
Harlem Renaissance, 54
Harms, Oliver R., 192–93, 209–10, 211n208, 215, 220
Heintzen, Erich, 36
Heithaus, Claude H., 115
Herberg, Will, 21
Herzberger, F. W., 64
Herzfeld, Will, 213, 221, 224
Hesburgh, Theodore, 183
Heschel, Abraham 189, 190
Heyne, Walter (Wallie), 105, 141, 144, 236n44, 237
Hoard, Samuel, 106–108, 181, 228
Hoffman, Oswald, 142
Holy Sacraments (St. Louis), 66
Holy Trinity Lutheran Church (Springfield IL), 32, 42–43; foundation of, 36–37; parochial school, 50; Schulze's growing involvement with, 48
Homrighausen, Edgar, 184, 201–202, 211n208, 212–13
Hoover, J. Edgar, 175, 206

Hughes, Langston, 176

Illinois State University, 33n5
Immanuel Lutheran Church (Chicago), 132
Immanuel Lutheran Church (Cincinnati), 26, 52
Immanuel Lutheran College, 89, 111–12, 113, 165, 166–67
immigrants, leaving Lutheran churches, 18
individual ethics, 175–76
Institute on Non-Violence and Social Change, 157
International Walther League, 199
interracial marriage, 90

Jabs, Albert E., 227–28
Jackson, Emory, 201n175
Jackson, Jimmy Lee, 210
Jackson, John H., 124n25
Jim Crow churches, 129–30
Johnson, James Weldon, 85
Johnson, Jeff, 39, 44, 106, 164, 215
Johnson, Lyndon Baines, 203, 206, 212, 214
Jones, Phyllis, 51
Jordan, Barbara, 214

Kaufmann, Aloys P., 100
Kennedy, John F., 196, 197, 203
Kennedy, Robert F., 177n101
Kettner, Elmer A., 162
KFUO (St. Louis), 66, 97
King, Martin Luther, Jr., 7, 155–57, 171–72, 174, 179–80, 183, 188, 190, 193–95, 198–99, 201, 206–207, 212, 219–20
Kinnison, William, 17
kneel-in movement, 171–72
Koehneke, Martin L., 143
Kraabel, Alf M., 160
Kramer, G. M., 91
Krebs, Ervin E., 103
Kretzmann, A. T., 149–50

Kretzmann, Jody, 237
Kretzmann, Otto Paul, 47, 83, 133, 147–48, 179, 183–84, 196, 203–204, 227
Ku Klux Klan, 45–46, 51n63, 146, 172–73
Kurth, Karl, 128, 132, 139

Laetsch, Theodore, 80
Lagerquist, L. Deane, 4
Lavalis, Joseph, 128
Lawson, Steven, 6
Lehman, P. D., 112n109
Lemann, Nicholas, 118–19
"Letter from a Birmingham Jail," 194–95
Lewis, David Levering, 35
Lewis, John, 211, 216
Liebenow, Doris, 222
Liebenow, George Hans, 105, 141, 222, 237
Lillegard, Geo., 139
Lincoln, Abraham, 33n5, 34–35
Lindemann, Paul, 96
Little Rock (AR) school desegregation, 160
liturgical renewal, 96
Lochner, John Frederick Carl, 159
Lochner, Louis P., 159–60, 164, 175
Loehe, Wilhelm, 32, 159
Luebke, Frederick, 26–27
Luecke, Richard, 3
lunch counter sit-ins, 169
Luther, Martin, 44–45, 52–53, 74, 136n62
Lutheran Church in America (LCA), 209, 234. See also United Lutheran Church in America
Lutheran Church of Christ the King (Chicago), 131
Lutheran Church and Indian People (LUCHIP), 158n37
Lutheran Church—Missouri Synod, 16, 37n18, 209, 231. See also

Evangelical Lutheran Synod of Missouri, Ohio, and Other States; German Evangelical Lutheran Synod of Missouri, Ohio, and Other States; acceptance of black congregations, 114; cautious in relations with other synods, 135–36; creating Commission on Social Action (1962), 176; criticism of, for anti-Americanism, 27–28; importance of Chicago to, 118; institutional spirit of deference and tradition, 166; leading role in developing American black Lutheranism, 137–38; making transition from German to English, 28; Mission Board of the Northern Illinois District, 120–30; nucleus of, 11n8; opposing women's ordination, 234; origins of, 18n33; parochial schools in, 50n61; passing resolution supporting direct action in Civil Rights Movement, 184–85; racial justice as issue at seminaries, 105; response to Brown decision, 142–43; seminaries of, 32–34; strict concept on religious fellowship, 187; supporting segregated education, 78–79; tensions within (1970s), 229–34; as truest exposition of Christian faith, 46; unique in American religious environment in 1920s, 60–61
Lutheran Church of the Reformation (Washington, DC), 205
"The Lutheran Hour," 66
Lutheran Human Relations Association of America (LHRAA), 1, 85, 135, 141; attention to Native Americans and other groups, 157–58; becoming a pan-Lutheran organization, 209–10;

belief in church's role in society,
150; defending King's reputation,
207–208; executive secretary
position, 148; generating support
for national civil rights legislation,
205; global implications of work,
177; growing association with
ELCA, 235; involvement in
women's rights and antiwar issues,
228; Mutual Enrichment
Program, 224; no comment on
1970s synod controversies, 234;
opposition to, 149; publishing
Schulze's memoirs, 226–27; on
reinvesting in Alabama Lutheran
College and Seminary, 167–68;
relocating to Milwaukee, 235;
resolutions regarding race
relations placed before national
conventions, 151–53; Schulze's
changing role in, 204; size and
scope of, 158–59, 209; summer
institutes, 156–57, 159–60,
175–76, 177–78, 201n175, 208,
214, 216, 221; tensions within,
regarding women's ordination,
234–35; viewed as extremist
organization, 170–72; working
with National Lutheran Council
on surveying Lutheran colleges
and seminaries, 165
Lutheran Ladies' Aid for Colored
Missions, 64–65
Lutheran News (*Christian News*), 203
The Lutheran Pioneer, 40–41, 42,
53–54
Lutheran publications, general
handling of racial matters,
128–29. *See also individual
publications*
Lutheran Race Relations Bulletin, 103,
128–29, 141
Lutheran Race Relations Institute,
103–104, 127

Lutherans; addressing ethical issues,
53; American, history of positions
on racial issues, 23–24; attitude
about religion and politics, 186;
attitudes toward political and
social action, 52–53; awakening
social consciousness, 93–94;
critical of theology centered
around promoting good ethical
behavior, 188; General Council,
37n18; General Synod, 37n18;
German immigrants, 10;
immigrants' adaptation to
America, 17; increased
urbanization and suburbanization,
123; Ohio history of, as
microcosm, 16–17; organization
in synods, 37–38; respectful of
government authority, 185–86;
segregated higher education for,
51–52; wariness of political and
social action, 92–93
The Lutherans (Lagerquist), 4
The Lutherans in North America
(Meuser), 92–93
Lutheran Society for Better Race
Relations in Chicago, 127
Lutheran theology, 2, 44–45
Lutheran University Association,
147
Lutheran Witness, 61n8, 87, 91, 97,
161–62, 164, 202–203, 207,
211n209, 220, 237
Lutheran Women's Missionary
League (LWML), 150–51
Lutheran World Federation, 197
Luther College, 52n64
Lutze, Karl, 127, 131–32, 143, 158,
165–66, 179, 182–83, 198, 199,
204, 209, 213–15, 223–24, 235–37

Maier, Walter A., 61, 66, 83, 97–98
Mandery, Andrew, 12
Mandery, Mary, 12
Mann, Robert, 196

Marbach, Franz Adolph, 59
March on Washington (1963), 197–99
Marsh, Charles, 233
Marty, Martin, 105, 144–45, 213, 216, 227
Mays, Benjamin, 189
McGreevy, John, 123
McNair, Chris, 200, 215
McNair, Denise, 200
Meissner, Edwin, 101
Meuser, Fred W., 92–93
Meyer, Albert, 189–90
Michel, Virgil, 96
middle-class, Lutherans' desire to reach, in black community, 70–71
Miller, Arthur, 142–43
mission work, with African Americans in US South, 24
Missouri Synod. *See* Lutheran Church—Missouri Synod
modernist-fundamentalist debates (1920s), 61–62
Moeller, Albert J. C., 78
Moellering, Ralph Luther, 66n24, 73n48, 82, 132, 175, 197
Moellering, Theodore, 20, 48
Montgomery (AL) Bus Boycott, 73n46, 145, 154–57, 169
The Morality of the Color Line (Gilligan), 84
Mount Zion Lutheran Church (New York City), 109
Mueller, John Theodore, 88–92, 139
Mueller, Martin W., 164
Muhammad, Elijah, 124
Muhlenberg, Henry Melchior, 17, 59
Mydral, Gunnar, 98
My Neighbor of Another Color (Schulze), 1, 74, 80–81, 84–92, 94–95, 104

Nagel, Norman, 236

Nash, Diane, 212n211
National Association for the Advancement of Colored Peoples (NAACP), 35–36, 54, 82, 102, 169–70
National Catholic Conference for Interracial Justice (NCCIJ), 170, 205
National Conference on Religion and Race (1963), 189–93
National Council of Churches, 204
National Lutheran Council (NLC), 136n62, 137, 138, 142, 165, 191
National Urban League, 54
Nation of Islam, 124, 217
Nau, Henry, 89, 103
Nazi regime, Lutheran support for, 97, 186
Nees, Martin E., 141
Neuhaus, Richard John, 198
Niebuhr, H. R., 87
Noll, Mark, 2n3
Northern Conference, 70–71
Norwegian Synod, 37n19, 38, 223–24n4

Ohio Synod, 37n19
Old Lutherans, 10n5, 16
Olivet Baptist Church (Chicago), 124
One Nation Under God? (Noll), 2n3
Otten, Herman, 203
Our Redeemer Lutheran Church (Jerusalem), 222–23
Over-the-Rhine, 11–12

Parks, Rosa, 154, 206
parochial schools, 42, 50
parsonages, 49–50
Pelikan, Jaroslav, 44–45, 105
periodicals, covering mission work in the South, 40n25
Pero, Albert, 217, 224
Pfotenhauer, (Johann) Friedrich, 53, 118

Phillips (Homer G.) Hospital, 68
Piepkorn, Arthur Carl, 134–35
Plessy v. Ferguson, 9
Predestination Controversy of the
    1880s, 37n19
Preisinger, Mrs. Arthur, 151
Preus, Herman Amberg, 38
Preus, J. A. O., 223–24, 230
Prince of Peace Lutheran
    (Cincinnati) Church, 26
Pritchett, Laurie, 179, 180
*The Promised Land: The Great Black
    Migration and How It Changed
    America* (Lemann), 118–19

Quillan, Frank U., 22–23

Race Relations Advisory Council,
    215
race relations, American;
    international implications of, 177;
    local nature of, 5
race riots, 214–15; Chicago (1919),
    120; Detroit (1943), 99, 100–101;
    Detroit (1967), 216; early
    twentieth century, 35; East St.
    Louis, 100; Watts, 214–15
*Race against Time: A History of Race
    Relations in the Lutheran
    Church—Missouri Synod from the
    Perspective of the Author's
    Involvement, 1920–1970* (Schulze),
    3, 226–28
Randolph, A. Frank, 197–98
Rauschenbusch, Walter, 93n118
Rehwinkel, Alfred M., 80, 89, 103,
    104–105, 106, 134
Resurrection Evangelical Lutheran
    Church (Chicago), 131
revolutions of 1848, émigrés from,
    18–19
Rincker, Leroy, 83
Ritter, Joseph E., 115–16
River Jordan (Trotter), 22
Rongstad, L. James, 210–11

Roosevelt, Eleanor, 82
Roosevelt, Franklin Delano, 197–98
*Roses and Thorns: The Centennial
    Edition of Black Lutheran Mission
    and Ministry in the Lutheran
    Church—Missouri Synod*
    (Dickinson), 234

Sabourin, Clemonce, 77–78, 87, 89,
    103, 108–13, 133, 139, 166, 198,
    205, 207–208, 218, 220, 227, 237
Saxon emigrants, settling in
    Missouri, 58–59
Saxon Lutheran Church, 58
Scharlemann, Martin H., 134, 143,
    152, 153–54, 175, 229n25
Schiebel, William, 105
Schultz, Verna, 125
Schulze, Andrew; accepting call at
    Christ the King (Chicago), 131;
    accused of un-American activities
    during World War II, *98*;
    advocate for black Lutherans, 51;
    arrested in Albany (GA) for
    participation in civil rights
    demonstration, 178, 179–85;
    association with Kretzmann,
    147–48; attractive church
    buildings, perceived need for, 67;
    awarded Doctor of Divinity
    degree from Concordia Seminary
    (St. Louis), 215–16; beginning
    involvement with black Lutheran
    congregations, 31–32; birth of, 9;
    changing role in LHRAA, 204;
    childhood, 9–10, 14–15, 24–25;
    childhood home, 13; chosen
    executive secretary for LHRAA,
    141–42, 144; concern over lack of
    civil rights leadership among
    religious conservatives, 155;
    concern over lack of leadership in
    church on race relations, 132–33;
    concern over segregation in
    Missouri Synod schools, 81–82;

Concordia Class of 1924, 44;
confirmation, 20; conflicts with
Northern Illinois District,
121–22, 124, 126–27, 130;
connecting domestic racism and
foreign missions, 86; connecting
World War II with domestic
events, 97; connection to Trinity
Lutheran (Springfield IL), 48;
contact with others in black
Lutheran ministry, 69–70; death
of, 236; on death of M. L. King,
220; decisions regarding
children's education, 83; desire to
become pastor, 20–21, 29;
differences in ministry from other
white pastors serving black
congregations, 48–50;
discouraged by attempt to create
black Lutheran conference,
217–18; drawing on Lutheran
tradition in commitment to racial
justice, 45; early conversion to
cause of race relations, 7; early
involvement with African-
American community, 21–22;
early jobs, 21; early work in
Chicago, 125–26; on Education
Committee of Mayor's
Commission on Race Relations
(St. Louis), 101–102; elected
member of Synodical
Conference's missionary board,
128; embracing awakening
Lutheran social consciousness,
93–94; emphasizing need for
action in addition to education,
177–78; ending career in small-
town setting, 148–49; ending of
St. Louis ministry, 116; explaining
ministry at St. Philip's, 71; family
lineage, 10–11; family's
immersion in black community,
69; frustration with church's
official response to race relations

(1952), 140–41; grandparents of,
12; growing network of
supporters, 7; growing realization
of need for integration and racial
justice, 72–73; growth in St.
Philip's Lutheran Church during
pastorate of, 65–66; guiding force
behind Lutheran Race Relations
Institutes, 103–104; home
congregation. *See* Trinity
Lutheran Church; honorary
doctorate from Valparaiso, 141;
hoping for end to black Lutheran
missions, 130; housing in
Chicago, 130; increased role after
Detroit riot of 1943, 100;
increasing activity to promote
better race relations among
Lutherans, 75–87; influence on
Lutherans, 237–38; installed at
Holy Trinity, 48; on integration,
50; interest in charismatic
movement, 226; interest in racial
situation in church's schools of
higher education, 164–65; internal
struggles over racial issues, 73–74;
interpretations of legacy, 235–36;
invitee to White House reception
on civil rights, 196; involvement
with Faith Memorial (Valparaiso),
225–26; involving next generation
of pastors in racial issues, 105; on
isolation of black Lutheran
congregations, 55–56; joint clergy
status in LCMS and AELC,
232–33; language training, 47;
lasting mark on American
Lutheranism, 7–8; leader of
Interracial Good Will Tour to
Europe, 197; living in Chicago,
125; locations of early ministry, 1;
Lutheran reaction to participation
in Albany, 184–89; measuring self
against other racial pioneers, 82;
meetings with mixed-religious-

background attendees, 188–89; military experience, 29; move to Chicago as Director of Negro Missions for Northern Illinois District, 116, 118, 120–22; opposed to dictatorial approach to church matters, 115; opposition to Vietnam War, 228–29; ordained, 48; overseas trip after retirement, 222–23; paper presented on church and race issue (1938), 80; participant in National Conference on Religion and Race, 189–93; pastoral nature of, 72–73; plans for ministry in Chicago, 122; positive memories of black Americans from childhood, 24–25; preaching in Chicago, 121; presence of, causing controversy in the South, 170–71; primary focus on improving race relations within the church, 160–63; publishing in *American Lutheran*, 95–97; publishing in *The Walther League Messenger*, 95; recipient of Mind of Christ award, 197; recognizing changes in *Lutheran Witness*, 164; response in *Vanguard* to Fackler incident, 173; response to Missionary Board's guidelines for integration, 139–40; retired from LHRAA, 221; siblings of, 12–13; siding with moderates in synod controversy of 1970s, 231–32; speaking to summer institutes at Valparaiso, 133–34; stance on communism, 175, 176–77; statement of views on race relations (1938), 79–80; transfer to St. Louis, reasons for, 64; transferred to St. Philip's Lutheran Church (St. Louis), 56–57; tributes to, 237–38; unique role in American Lutheranism, 3;

unofficial advisor for racial concerns among Lutherans, 127; unsupported during work in Chicago, 124; visit to New York with Sabourin, 108–109; in World War I, 21; writing about race to influential people in Missouri Synod, 83–84; writing for *Vanguard* in retirement, 228; writings on Missouri Synod's 1956 resolutions on race, 153–54

Schulze, Henrietta, 12
Schulze, Henry, 12
Schulze, Herbert, 69, 83n84, 223, 228
Schulze, John, 9, 12, 15
Schulze, Katie, 9, 12, 15
Schulze, Margaret, 21, 48–49; in Chicago, 118, 125, 130; death of, 236; decisions regarding children's education, 83; help in writing *My Neighbor of Another Color*, 80–81; after husband's retirement, 222–23, 225; interest in charismatic movement, 226; on Interracial Good Will Tour to Europe, 197; on raising children in black neighborhoods, 69; recipient of Mind of Christ award, 197
Schulze, Paul, 49, 69, 74, 83, 223, 232
Schulze, Raymond, 69, 72, 83n84, 223, 232
segregation; as legal issue, 82; perception of, 9n1; in St. Louis, early twentieth century, 63
Selma-Montgomery march, 213
The Seminarian (Concordia Seminary), 106
Senechal, Roberta, 35
Sernett, Milton, 23–24, 137
Seuel, Edmund, 76
Simon, Arthur, 214
Simon, Martin, 69

Simon, Paul, 141, 157, 171, 214
Social Gospel Movement, 92
social gospel, 90
social service agencies, Lutheran network of, 93
The Souls of Black Folk (DuBois), 9
Southern Christian Leadership Conference (SCLC), 102, 169–70, 179
Spear, Allen, 119
Springfield (IL); demographics, nineteenth-century, 34; race riots (1906), 35; seminary in, 32–34, 36
Stephan, Martin, 58, 59
St. James African Methodist Episcopal Church (St. Louis), 67–68
St. Louis; makeup of, early twentieth-century, 62–64; Mayor's Commission on Race Relations, 100–101, 104; mission efforts among blacks in, 64
The St. Louis Lutheran, 103
St. Louis Lutheran Society for Better Race Relations, 84, 101–103, 104
St. Louis Society for Better Race Relations, 133
St. Louis University Divinity School, 230
St. Matthew Lutheran Church (New York City), 109
St. Michael (St. Louis), 66
St. Paul Lutheran Church (Westlake OH), 47
St. Philip's Lutheran Church (Chicago), 72, 75, 122
St. Philip's Lutheran Church (St. Louis), 56–57; financially self-sufficient, 72, 75; linked with Holy Trinity Lutheran Church, 64; origins of, 64–65; success of, 65–67
storefront churches, 67, 126
Stowe, Harriet Beecher, 22

Strietelmeier, John, 81, 163, 197
Stringfellow, William, 190
Student Nonviolent Coordinating Committee (SNCC), 102, 169–70, 178, 210, 216
Stukenbroeker, Fern C., 175
Sumner High School (St. Louis), 68
Synodical Conference; Board for Colored Missions, 54–55; differing pay scales for white and black pastors, 77–78; formation of, 37–39; mission work of, 39–41; Missionary Board, 56–57, 64, 88–90, 138–39; no attempt to change race relations in South, 42; race concerns under Behnken, 75; supporting administrative integration of black congregations, 113–14

Taylor, Henry Lewis, Jr., 22
Temme, Norman, 196
Theiss, Otto H., 86, 103–104, 130
Tietjen, John, 229
Till, Emmett, 154
Trinity Lutheran Church (Cincinnati), 13n17, 14, 15–16, 17, 19–20, 26
Trinity Lutheran Church (Montgomery AL), 155, 156
Trinity Lutheran Church (Springfield IL), 47–48
Trotter, Joe William, Jr., 22
Trout, Nelson, 155–56
Turner movement, 19

Ubom, E. A., 177
Unaltered Augsburg Confession, 15
Uncle Tom's Cabin (Stowe), 22
unionism, 16, 135–36, 187
United Lutheran Church in America (ULCA), 136, 138. *See also* Lutheran Church in America
Universal Negro Improvement Association (UNIA), 54

Up from Slavery (Washington), 76

Valparaiso University, 1, 51;
  awarding Schulze honorary
  doctorate, 141; home to LHRAA,
  141; involvement in improving
  race relations (1950s–1970s), 133;
  Lutheran University Association's
  purchase of (1925), 146–47;
  summer institutes, 156–57,
  159–60, 175–76, 177–78,
  201n175, 208, 214, 216, 221;
  unique status among Missouri
  Synod institutions, 147
The Vanguard, 85, 141, 150, 153–54,
  161–62, 170, 173, 192–93, 204,
  220, 237
The Ville (St. Louis), 67–69
Voting Rights Act of 1965, 214–15

Wallace, George, 211
Walther, Carl F. W., 16, 24, 37,
  59–60, 90
Walther League, 75, 86–87
The Walther League Messenger, 95
Washington, Booker T., 41, 53, 76
Webster, Ronald, 98
Wells, Ida B., 125–26
Wells (Ida B.) Lutheran Mission,
  125–26, 131
Wesley, Cynthia, 200
White, Joseph Michael, 14–15, 17
Why We Can't Wait (King), 199
Wichmann, Theodore, 15
Williams, Hosea, 211
Wind, Henry F., 152
Wisconsin Evangelical Lutheran
  Synod (WELS), 37n18
Wisconsin Synod, 37n19
Wisler, Louis A., 79, 99, 128
Wolbrecht, Walter F., 196
women's ordination, 234
Wyneken, Friedrich C. D., 32, 36,
  50n61
Wyneken, Henry, 36

X, Malcolm, 124

Young, Andrew, 179
Young, Rosa J., 41, 69–70, 162–64,
  168

Zion Evangelical Church
  (Cincinnati), 15